# Children's Literature
## Volume 21

Volume 21

*Annual of*
*The Modern Language Association*
*Division on Children's Literature*
*and The Children's Literature*
*Association*

Yale University Press

New Haven and London

1993

*Children's Literature*

*Editor-in-chief:* Francelia Butler
*Coeditors, Volume 21:* Christine Doyle Francis, Anne K. Phillips, Julie K. Pfeiffer
*Editorial Associate:* Michael W. Menard
*Intern:* Samantha Jane Wilcox
*Book Review Editor:* John Cech
*Advisory Board:* Jan Alberghene (representing the ChLA), Margaret Higonnet, U. C. Knoepflmacher, Alison Lurie, Sam Pickering, Jr., Albert J. Solnit, M.D.
*Consultants for Volume 21:* Gillian Adams, Gillian Avery, Bob Bator, Ben Brockman, Mary Carpenter, Margaret Doody, Marie-France Doray, Angela M. Estes, James Farnham, Richard Gillin, Bob Hasenfratz, Patrick Hogan, Elizabeth Keyser, Ruth Kluger, U. C. Knoepflmacher, Lois Kuznets, Claire Malarte-Feldman, Jean I. Marsden, Mitzi Myers, Karen Michaelson, Ed O'Connor, Lissa Paul, Judith Plotz, Donald Rayfield, Tom Roberts, Barbara Rosen, Mary Shaner, Louisa Smith, J. D. Stahl, Nancy Veglahn, Tony Watkins, Ian Wojcik-Andrews, Virginia Wolf, Ning Yu, Jack Zipes

The editors gratefully acknowledge support from the University of Connecticut.

*Editorial correspondence should be addressed to:*
Professor Elizabeth Keyser, Editor
*Children's Literature*
Department of English
Hollins College
Roanoke, Virginia 24020

PN
1009
.A1
C514
v.21

Manuscripts submitted should conform to the new MLA style. An original on non-erasable bond with two copies, a self-addressed envelope, and return postage are requested. Name should appear only on the original. Yale University Press does not accept dot-matrix printouts, and it requires double-spacing throughout text and notes. Unjustified margins are preferred.

Volumes 1–7 of *Children's Literature* can be obtained directly from John C. Wandell, The Children's Literature Foundation, Box 370, Windham Center, Connecticut 06280. Volumes 8–20 can be obtained from Yale University Press, 92A Yale Station, New Haven, Connecticut 06520, or from Yale University Press, 23 Pond Street, Hampstead, London NW3 2PN, England.

Library of Congress catalog card number: 79-66588
ISBN: 0-300-05423-8 (cloth); 0-300-05424-6 (paper)

A catalogue record for this book is available from the British Library.

Set in Baskerville type by Tseng Information Systems, Inc., Durham, N.C. Printed in the United States of America by Vail-Ballou Press, Binghamton, N.Y.

10    9    8    7    6    5    4    3    2    1

# Contents

# From the Editors

This volume of *Children's Literature* encompasses an entire cycle of beginning, ending, and new beginning: the first non-theme issue in three years, it is also the last to be edited at the University of Connecticut before moving to its new home at Hollins College in Roanoke, Virginia. Although the essays in volume 21 were not chosen to fit a predesignated theme, several share common concerns. Yet the volume as a whole is one of our most culturally diverse issues to date, drawing on a broad, international selection of writers and literature.

Innovative approaches to issues of gender connect the first three essays, even though they deal with such varieties of children's literature and culture as those of Victorian England, nineteenth-century France, and contemporary America. In "Reluctant Lords and Lame Princes," Alan Richardson applies feminist revisions of Freudian developmental theory to the depiction of young male protagonists in Victorian literature. As these characters move from childhood—characterized as a feminine period when they associate closely with their mothers—into adolescence, they must assume a more masculine identity. Some characters, such as Hughes's Tom Brown, can make this transition only by becoming part of a violent "cult of masculinity"; others, including Craik's Little Lame Prince and Burnett's Little Lord Fauntleroy, maintain a more feminine identity. These latter books provide young male readers with an example of how to grow up without abandoning identification with the mother. According to Richardson, such texts "function . . . not to subvert the masculine role within patriarchy but to soften it, encouraging 'little' boy readers to identify imaginatively with a patriarchal position made . . . to *seem* more motherly and subject to qualification and deferral."

Examining the question of gender roles from the feminine perspective in "Of Dolls and Girls in Nineteenth-Century France," Valérie Lastinger asserts that in nineteenth-century French literature, a little girl's doll is neither stereotype nor archetype but a device that allows authors to subvert a patriarchal culture without invoking its wrath. Lastinger's background in French children's literature allows her to discuss materials that may be unfamiliar to our readers, but her argument provides us with a widely applicable approach to reading the complexity of the doll-child relationship. Len Hatfield examines masculine and feminine roles throughout the vision of a single author in "From Master to Brother," wherein he articulates a major shift in emphasis between Ursula K. Le Guin's *Farthest Shore* and *Tehanu*. Whereas the first three books of the Earthsea series present authority in patriarchal terms, with women and children depicted as oppositional forces, the view of authority in the fourth volume, *Tehanu*, disrupts this representation. This "last book of Earthsea" does not replace male authority with female authority; rather, it explicitly delineates the limitations of male authority and the increased possibilities that unfold through recognition of the previously marginalized viewpoints of women and children. Hatfield argues that Le Guin uses both narrative technique and thematic developments to propose the efficacy of a new balance of power.

Whereas gender conflicts typically result in one type of alienation and conflict, several authors explore alienation in other forms. Martha Bremser's essay, "The Voice of Solitude: The Children's Verse of Walter de la Mare," encompasses both a generally familiar and a generally unobserved characteristic of de la Mare's poetry. Bremser analyzes de la Mare's familiar romantic lineage in a way that reveals the hyper-literariness of Edwardian children's literature while she demonstrates de la Mare's preoccupation with what is fearful and disquieting in the Romantic concept of childhood solitude.

Allusions to existential philosophy and to modern writing, and the use of narrative repetition, have alienated many readers of Russell Hoban's *Mouse and His Child*. Valerie Krips's Lacanian reading of the novel in "Mistaken Identity: Russell Hoban's *Mouse and His Child*" suggests that these textual difficulties are in fact conscious reworkings of childhood innocence and wholeness designed to produce an alternative view that emphasizes struggle and empowerment. In Krips's view, Hoban's technique disrupts a too-simple reading of this text; in fact, it ultimately places the reader, as well as its mouse protagonists, in the position of trying to create meaning in story, including the story we tell about ourselves. Krips's approach—applying post-structuralist theory to explicate Hoban's text—parallels John Stephens's application of postmodern linguistics to William Mayne's narrative technique and exhibits yet another tendency to distance readers from his texts by requiring that they analyze rather than empathize with the characters and situations. In "Metafiction and Interpretation," Stephens identifies scenes within Mayne's novels *Salt River Times, Winter Quarters,* and *Drift* that both advance the stories and act as models for interpreting the narrative techniques that inform them. Stephens's exposure of Mayne's narrative frames provides evidence that "neither historical experiences nor literary fictions are unmediated or unprocessed."

Sylvia Patterson Iskander's discussion in "Arabic Adventurers and American Investigators: Cultural Values in Adolescent Detective Fiction" counteracts trends of alienation, bringing cultures together by comparing Arabic detective fiction for adolescents to its American counterpart. Although her comparison highlights some underlying cultural differences, the Arabic and American series books she examines exhibit surprising similarities on several counts. Besides introducing readers to stories that have not appeared in English and drawing attention to a surprisingly neglected genre, Iskander's essay forms a transition into the Varia section of this volume, which focuses on children's literature from around the world. Wang Lin's translation of a contemporary Chinese children's story, Sheryl Spitz's provocative observations on the parallels between East Slavic lullabies and hunting songs, and Feenie Ziner's analysis of pagan influences present in contemporary illustrations of a Lithuanian folk tale all provide insights into a variety of literatures and cultures.

As *Children's Literature* moves to Hollins College, we know that editors R. H. W. Dillard and Elizabeth Keyser will continue to rely on readers and authors throughout the United States and the world. We are proud to have shared in the journal's tradition of commitment to excellence, and confidently anticipate the successful continuation of its high standards. From its founding in 1972 through Francelia Butler's faith, hope, and inspiration, *Children's Literature* has been a cooperative venture. In closing, therefore, we should like to thank the many members of the University of Connecticut English Department who have served as editorial staff, contributing their time and talents to the growth and development of this journal, and whose help has been essential to maintaining its high level of scholarship over the past twenty-one years.

# Articles

# Reluctant Lords and Lame Princes: Engendering the Male Child in Nineteenth-Century Juvenile Fiction

Alan Richardson

Wordsworth's phrase "The Child is Father of the Man," from his self-authorizing epigraph to the "Immortality" ode, could equally well introduce any number of nineteenth-century representations of childhood. What in Wordsworth's time are still relatively new-fangled notions—that childhood is a period of crucial psychic and moral development, and that adult life is largely shaped, if not quite determined, by childhood experience—grow increasingly self-evident as the nineteenth century progresses, eventually to become codified in the work of Freud. This genetic, developmental approach to childhood is as central to texts representing the child to itself as to those representing the child to adults. Nineteenth-century British children's fiction, whether didactic, fantastic, or "realistic" in character, almost invariably portrays childhood as a period of psychological and moral growth; indeed, what most differentiates Victorian literary fairy tales and fantasies from traditional fairy tales is this very insistence on development as opposed to the static, "flat" characterizations of the folktale (Luthi 37–65).

It is no accident, then, that works as otherwise disparate as Charles Kingsley's *Water Babies* (1863) and Thomas Hughes's *Tom Brown's Schooldays* (1857) both place their hero's "schooling" at the center of their narratives and draw authority for their fictional projects by reference to Wordsworth, "that venerable and learned poet," as Hughes writes, who "most truly says, 'the child is father to the man'; *a fortiriori,* therefore, he must be father to the boy" (33).[1] And yet, as Geoffrey Hartman has remarked, if Wordsworth's phrase eventually "becomes an axiom for modern developmental psychology," it nevertheless "remains as scandalous a paradox as ever founded a poetry of experience" (183), disordering as it does the expected temporal, genealogical, and disciplinary relations of

*Children's Literature* 21, ed. Francelia Butler, Christine Doyle Francis, Anne K. Phillips, and Julie K. Pfeiffer (Yale University Press, © 1993 The Children's Literature Foundation, Inc.).

parent and child. Taking Hughes's seemingly vague but in fact critical distinction between "child" and "boy" as a starting point, we
can locate yet another scandal within Wordsworth's proposition,
which oddly defers assigning gender to the child, who, in the subject, is neuter and who is sex-typed as male retroactively in the
predicate. Only from the standpoint of the "man" it will become
can the "child" be differentiated as a potential "father." This retrospective or backwards process of gendering also anticipates Freud,
for whom the "pregenital erotic stages" of the pre-Oedipal period
are "sexually undifferentiated" yet reconfigured in terms of male
(or female) development from the later perspective of the Oedipus complex, which "casts its mark back over their whole meaning" (Mitchell 53). It simultaneously imposes an imagined family
romance on the young boy's memories or fantasies of an earlier, "bisexual" psychic era. The child who suffers the father's prohibition
knows itself in retrospect as man.

This disjunction—however temporary or however obscured by
"infantile amnesia"—between the "child" and the male child brings
out a crucial problem for any developmental portrayal of childhood
in juvenile fiction. That boys will be boys we know from Kingsley,
Hughes, and many other Victorian writers for children; but how
do they *become* boys? What, to resort again to the suggestive difficulties of Freud's developmental paradigm, facilitates the (male)
child's abandonment of the mother's warm, affectionate sphere for
the harsh world of the father; what motivates (his) exchange of
"polymorphously perverse" bisexuality for an exclusive, prohibited
romance with the mother—the mother with whom (he) so recently
and intimately identified?

From the perspective of Freud's writings, even as reread by a
Lacanian feminist like Juliet Mitchell, the answer is fairly direct: the
boy assumes his "phallic heritage" because the "male position" is the
only place where "anyone really wants to be . . . within the patriarchal order" (51). But other, more frankly revisionist psychoanalytic
approaches, such as that of Nancy Chodorow, describe taking the
male position as an ambivalent, even somewhat dubious act. Departing explicitly from the traditional Freudian assumption that the
boy child "instantly knows that a penis is better," Chodorow emphasizes instead the "conflictual" aspect of assuming a male identity, a
process that for her is not less but more problematic than the girl
child's accession to femininity. Underlying the child's male iden-

tity, Chodorow argues, is the "early, nonverbal, unconscious, almost somatic sense of primary oneness with the mother"—arising from the indistinct boundaries between mother and child characteristic of the pre-oedipal stage—which persists in an "underlying sense of femaleness that continually, usually unnoticeably, but sometimes insistently, challenges and undermines the sense of maleness" ("Gender" 13). What Chodorow terms the boy's "primary femaleness" entails that the production and maintenance of a male identity is and remains problematic, difficult, and in an important sense negative: "learning what it is to be masculine means learning to be not-feminine, or not-womanly." The boy's ongoing repression of his pre-oedipal femininity can entail, in turn, an aggressive, self-conscious maleness, a valorization of sexual difference *as* difference, a denial of feelings experienced as (because culturally encoded as) feminine: "feelings of dependence, relational needs, emotions generally" ("Gender" 13).

The advantage of Chodorow's theory of gendering for studies of nineteenth-century juvenile fiction is that it brings to the fore two distinct and apparently contradictory modes of representing the development of masculinity to the child—and more particularly, to the boy—reader. Her description of the boy's "negative definition" of masculine identity, and its "assumption by denial" of his primary femininity, helps account for the aggressive masculinity of a boy's book like *Tom Brown's Schooldays,* in which the worst insult is to be called "Molly, or Jenny, or some derogatory feminine nickname" (181). It helps explain the gusto and desperate haste with which Tom leaves the maternal sphere to plunge into a man's world of boxing and bird-nesting, cricket and beer-drinking, and a particularly violent form of football—a world in which desire takes almost exclusively that direction which Eve Sedgwick identifies as "homosocial."[2] We can discuss more critically the virtual cult of masculinity developed not only throughout boys' school stories but also in adventure novels (which almost invariably displace the boy hero into a world no less masculine and aggressive than that of the public school) and even in such fantasies as *The Water Babies,* which teaches its addressee, Grenville Arthur Kingsley (and "all other good little boys" with him), how to take a beating like a "little man" (19:28).

We can, at the same time, begin to account for children's books that portray instead a distinctly feminized boy hero and undercut the development of masculinity in ways that seem to register the power of what Robert Stoller (in an essay cited by Chodorow) calls the "tidal pull" of the "original, primal symbiosis" experienced by the male infant and his mother (353, 355). The problematic status of the feminized boy hero in nineteenth-century British children's fiction has been noted by U. C. Knoepflmacher, who identifies John Ruskin's Gluck, in *The King of the Golden River*, as a "boy-Cinderella" whose very appearance is "decidedly girlish" and curiously antici-pates Sir John Tenniel's drawings of Alice (4, 11). For Knoepfl-macher, Ruskin's "feminized" hero (14) embodies Ruskin's own "regressive" fantasy of childhood innocence, his "defense" against confronting "potentially disabling childhood conflicts he had never fully resolved in the process of growing up" (23). But it is possible to see the program of psychic defense associated with the "feminized boy" (15) hero of Victorian juvenile fiction as expressing a cultural rather than a personal fantasy, as the imaginative resolution of a widely experienced social conflict not limited to the biographies of a few children's authors. If there was a Victorian cult of sorts built around the "manly" public school experience as defined by Hughes and his imitators, there was also a cult—one marked by an inten-sity and extent that may seem bewildering today—centered on the figure of Frances Hodgson Burnett's Little Lord Fauntleroy, that veritable icon of boyish effeminacy, the definitive mama's boy. Nor were such feminized boy heroes limited to the fictions of Ruskin and Burnett: they can be found as well, to cite a few instances, in George MacDonald's *Back of the North Wind* (1871), in Jean Inge-low's *Mopsa the Fairy* (1869), in Mark Lemon's *Tinykin's Transforma-tions* (1869), and in Dinah Maria Craik's *Little Lame Prince and His Travelling-Cloak* (1875).

Jacqueline Rose has argued persuasively that the repression of sexuality characteristic of almost all children's fiction, and the "re-fusal of sexual difference" that marks some children's books (25), reflect adult fantasies of a pristine, innocent, asexual past rather than the rich and fluid sexual life of the child—again, "bisexual, polymorphous, perverse" (5). Yet we should keep in mind that chil-dren's books, although written and selected by adults, are neverthe-less frequently (if not exclusively or ever solely) aimed at children. And the developmental narratives they unfold not only speak to the needs of the adult reading, as it were, over the child's head but also embody the adult's wish to shape the child reader in certain modes, directing its growth in the very act of representing it. These nar-

ratives may not simply prescribe one-dimensional patterns of feminine or masculine behavior and identity—as *Tom Brown's Schooldays*
so transparently offers its boy reader a boisterously "manly" ideal—
but may, more subtly, attempt to guide the child reader through
the dilemmas implicit in the maturational paradigm they encode.
If the transition from child to boy involves a critical moment when
the (male) child hesitates to abandon his feminine identity and side
instead with the father, if the "pull toward merging again into the
mother's femaleness" persists in the psychic life of the young boy
(Stoller 360), we might well expect to find fictional representations
and imaginary resolutions of this ambivalence in the developmental
tales written for children. It is from this perspective that I propose reading *The Little Lame Prince* and *Little Lord Fauntleroy*, both
immensely popular works that feature a "little" boy hero who temporarily rejects his "patriarchal heritage," who continues to identify
with his mother and is portrayed in decidedly effeminate terms, and
who in the end takes on a significantly qualified masculine identity
and a social role at once paternal and maternal.

Craik's *Little Lame Prince* was one of the best-selling children's
fantasies of the later nineteenth century. Set in the kingdom of "No-
mansland," it features a child hero, Prince Dolor, who would not be
king: when placed (still an infant) on his deceased father's throne
and invested with his crown, Prince Dolor "shook it off again, it was
so heavy and uncomfortable" (141). Refusing to take on his father's
identity, Dolor instead takes after his mother, Queen Dolorez, who
dies when Dolor is only six weeks but leaves him, in addition to
her name, her looks (in both senses): Dolor grows into a "pretty
little boy" with "just·his mother's face" (140) and "his mother's
eyes" (142; fig. 1). When Dolor meets his fairy godmother, a "dear
friend" of Queen Dolorez and her effective substitute, she finds
him altogether "as like [his mother] as ever" he could be (148). If
he is like his mother, however, Dolor is "not like other little boys"
(153). Thanks to a "slight disaster" (135) on the day of his christen-
ing (a lady in waiting drops him on the marble stairs), Dolor's body
remains undeveloped from the waist down: "his limbs were useless
appendages to his body" (140), decidedly "not like those of other
little boys" (153). Effectively castrated, Dolor is no more wanted
for the throne than he himself wishes it, and his uncle, Claudius to
Dolor's Hamlet, has no trouble spiriting the prince off to exile and
announcing his death.

Figure 1. "Yes, he was the most beautiful Prince that ever was born." Illustration by J. McL. Ralston for *The Little Lame Prince* (London, 1886).

Dolor's exile takes place in a "round tower," which, for all its phallic prominence on the desert plain from which it rises, is curiously womblike and domestic—a "perfect little house"—within (144). Tended only by a woman servant (and, on occasion, the fairy godmother), Dolor is afforded an extended period in which to remain like his mother and as unlike his uncle, archetype of the "great, strong, wicked man," as possible (177). His life in the tower, though ostensibly one of deprivation, affords the boy-child reader a fantasy not so much of eternal childhood (never growing up like Peter Pan) as of growing older without having to give up his identification with the mother. Even Dolor's magic carpet rides, which seem fantasies of power, are enabled by a decidedly maternal cloak (a "circular" poncho with a "split cut to the center" where there is an accommodating "round hole" for his head [150]), and introduce him to a feminized nature: "There was the glorious arch of the sky, with a little young moon sitting in the west like a baby queen. And the evening breeze was so sweet and fresh—it kissed him like his godmother's kisses" (157–58).

As Dolor grows into a kind of maturity, he takes on a complicated, ambivalent gender identity; his sexuality is at once dysfunctional and overdetermined.

> Prince Dolor was now quite a big boy. Not tall—alas! he never could be that, with his poor little shrunken legs, which were of no use . . . . But he was stout and strong, with great sturdy shoulders, and muscular arms . . . . As if in compensation for his useless lower limbs, Nature had given to these extra strength and activity. His face, too, was very handsome. It was thinner, firmer, more manly; but still the sweet face of his childhood—his mother's face. [171]

Below the waist Dolor remains neuter, while above the waist he seems to have become hyper-masculine, until the femininity of "his mother's face" reasserts itself. His gender identity is not so much androgynous (although it could be easily mistaken for such) as fragmented, his masculine and feminine aspects disjointed and ill-fitting rather than harmoniously blended. Neither quite manly nor altogether womanly, and no longer childlike, Dolor inhabits a "no-mansland" of his own in which gender remains in flux, chaotic and indefinite.

At last Dolor elects to assume the throne after all, in order to pre-

vent a political anarchy ("no government at all!" [178]) that seems
to mirror the anarchic identity of the reluctant prince. But the fantasy's closure is tentative at best. The narrator asks, "Was he . . . 'the
father of his people,' as all kings ought to be?" (186), and refuses
to answer the question. Instead we learn that Dolor's lameness was
"never cured" (187), that, a favorite of his people in other ways, he
"never gave them a queen" (188), and that he eventually abdicates
in favor of a "tall and straight" cousin (189–90). Dolor, that is, may
take on a version of the patriarchal role, but he never becomes a
father, or even a husband, and he passes on the phallic heritage
as early as possible to a successor as "erect" as a king should be
(172). In Dolor's story, the young boy reader can imagine a version of growing up without ever growing into a "great, bad, clever
man" like the more conventionally masculine uncle (176), without
ever growing away from the mother within (and without ever entirely giving up the mother without, as the ageless fairy godmother
remains Dolor's confidant throughout his reign [188]). Dolor is a
curious figure of wishful projection, suggesting at once omnipo-
tence (the flying cloak) and impotence, appealing to readers for
whom potency—the male power and privilege that come only at
the expense of repressing the feminine—remains a dubious inheritance.

Although formally a realistic children's novel, Burnett's *Little Lord
Fauntleroy* is no less concerned than Craik's fantasy to provide wishful resolutions to the dilemma of the growing boy. Published seri-
ally (in *St Nicholas*) in 1885 and in book form in 1886, the novel
sold quickly and extremely well, and the Fauntleroy "craze" (which
swept through Britain as well as America) followed the successful production of stage versions in London and New York a few
years later. Irving Cobb, who published a fictionalized account of
his childhood in 1924, described the Fauntleroy cult in a chapter
called "Little Short Pantsleroy": "A mania was laying hold on the
mothers of the nation. . . . *Little Lord Fauntleroy* infected thousands
of worthy matrons of America with a catching lunacy, which raged
like sedge fire and left enduring scars upon the seared memories
of its chief sufferers—their sons, notably between the ages of seven
and eleven." Compton Mackenzie was one of many British victims
of what he recalled as "that confounded Little Lord Fauntleroy
craze"; he was forced to wear a Fauntleroy costume (black velvet
suit, lacy Vandyke collar) to dancing class while the other boys

wore sailor suits (Thwaite 117–18). These accounts, and others like them (the story, for example, of the eight-year-old boy in Iowa who burned down the family barn when forced to wear the Fauntleroy regalia; ibid.) suggest that the Fauntleroy ideal appealed to parents (particularly mothers) more than children and aggravated rather than allayed boys' anxieties about gender identity. And yet the novel itself, which regularly applies the reassuring adjective "manly" to its little hero, seems to have aimed at a quite different effect.

Cedric Errol, the future Lord Fauntleroy, is initially presented as being "like both [his mother] and his father"—a puerile androgyne. But, as his notoriously feminized appearance ("gold-colored hair" in "loose rings," "big brown eyes and long eyelashes and a darling little face" [5]) suggests, his feminine aspect is dominant (fig. 2). In fact, Ceddie's father is himself described in androgynous terms: "He had a beautiful face and a fine, strong, graceful figure; he had a bright smile and a sweet, gay voice; he was brave and generous, and had the kindest heart in the world, and seemed to have the power to make everyone love him" (3). With his beautiful face, graceful figure, sweet voice, kind heart, and loveable demeanor, Errol *père* recalls not so much the Romantic androgyne as the feminine conduct book ideal of the same period—Fanny Price with a moustache. He turns out to have been, like Ruskin's Gluck, a boy-Cinderella: the youngest and gentlest of three, suppressed in favor of his older, duller, brutes of brothers.

Cedric junior thus doubly inherits, not only a girlish demeanor, but a feminized character as well, replete with what Chodorow calls "relational" qualities: "quick to understand the feelings of those about him," with a "kind little heart that sympathized with everyone" and a "childish soul . . . full of kindness and innocent warm feeling" (6). He calls his mother "Dearest" and when his father dies becomes her all but constant companion (a young democrat, he saves some time for the neighborhood grocer and a friendly bootblack). At age seven, he still appears girlish (strikingly so in the book's original illustrations); he grows out of his "short white kilt skirt" and into a "black velvet skirt"—cut from the material of his mother's gown (5, 8). When it develops that his two boorish uncles have, like his father, died young, and Ceddie has, suddenly, become Lord Fauntleroy, his response is couched in democratic tones: "I should rather not be an earl. None of the boys are earls. Can't I *not* be one?" (12). But, according to the book's representational logic,

Figure 2. Illustration by Reginald Birch for *Little Lord Fauntleroy* (New York, 1886).

refusing to accept the patriarchal inheritance also means (as in *The Little Lame Prince*) refusing to give up what are coded as feminine qualities for those presented as exclusively masculine.

The masculine/feminine oppositions that seem reconciled in the characters of both Cedric and his father become separate and discordant on Ceddie's arrival in England. From the start, Cedric must endure having his mother, "Dearest," banished to an outhouse on the paternal estate, while he is assigned to the great house or "Castle," securely within the masculine orbit of the misogynistic old Earl. The Earl is portrayed as entirely bereft of the relational qualities exemplified by Cedric and his parents. Vicious, savage, ill-tempered, and violent (92), he has neglected his wife as well as his

children; the deaths of all of them are more or less directly attrib-
uted to his self-enclosed sterility. A tacit contest takes place over
the course of the novel, as Ceddie seeks (quite disingenuously) to
humanize, or rather, feminize the old man through his "kindly"
and "affectionate" approaches (138), while the Earl struggles unsuccessfully to detach the boy from Dearest: "Do you *never* forget
about your mother?" (146). Eventually, Ceddie wins: the old heart
thaws, Dearest moves into the Castle, and a new model of nobility—
"simple and loving," "kind and gentle"—is asserted (205).

With his "strong . . . back" and "splendid sturdy legs" (5) Cedric is
no lame prince. And yet his effeminate hair and clothing, his refusal
to give up Dearest, and his distinctly feminized character ally him
much more nearly to Craik's hero than to the rowdy Tom Brown
set, for whom to be called "mammy-sick" is almost as damning as to
be given a feminine nickname (66). Both Cedric and Dolor are separated from their mothers only to discover maternal qualities within
themselves; both insist on redefining the patriarchal role in relational terms. Burnett's fiction, like Craik's, seems addressed to the
younger boy reader who is not ready to enter into the homosocial
world of the public school or adventure story, whose resistance is
disarmed by tales that valorize the boy's feminine characteristics
and promise—however fraudulently—an androgynous adult role.
These stories engender the fantasy that the child is mother to the
man, that to become manly can mean remaining womanly, and that
the patriarch may be mother as well as father to his people.

If the ideal of the womanly boy indeed embodies a cultural as
well as a personal fantasy—as the transatlantic Fauntleroy cult suggests—it remains to be asked why this fantasy would find expression in the later nineteenth century, a period widely perceived as
marked by an intensification, rather than qualifying, of gender differences. Chodorow has suggested that the development of modern "capitalist relations of production" entails both the progressive
isolation of the nuclear family and the exaggeration and rigidifi-
cation of masculine gender roles (*Reproduction* 180–90). Just such
a firming of the prescribed masculine character is delineated by
Claudia Nelson in her study of ideals of manliness in Victorian
boys' fiction and treatises on "sexology" alike, both genres demonstrating a "gradual reclassification of the attitudes and behavioral
patterns considered appropriate to men, often combined with a rejection of qualities associated with femininity" over the second half

of the nineteenth century (545). In an essay on the socializing function of nineteenth-century school stories, Dieter Petzold relates the
growing emphasis on an aggressive, even pugnacious masculinity
over the same period to the human requirements of both industrial capitalism and British imperialism: "The new age of economic
and imperialistic expansion demanded new virtues, such as ambition and initiative, discipline and team spirit, readiness to take
up responsibility, and a talent for leadership" (17). Hughes suggests the association between the playing fields of Rugby and the
needs of a military-industrial empire in envisioning the schoolboys
buried in "many a grave in the Crimea or distant India" or surviv-
ing to manage, as Tom Brown more crudely puts it, "Cherokees or
Patagonians, or some such wild niggers" (279, 253).

What role does the feminized boy of Victorian children's fiction
play in an increasingly masculinized culture? Why do books like *The
Little Lame Prince* and *Little Lord Fauntleroy* find such wide popularity
during a period that witnesses the hardening of male roles in boys'
books generally? It would be tempting to argue that, as women
authors, Craik and Burnett are consciously writing against the grain
of Victorian conceptions of gender, drawing on the conventions of
Romantic "androgyny" in a manner that critically challenges Victorian patriarchy and enjoins a counter-ideal: the "Governor" who
(to quote Wordsworth again) "must be wise and good, / And tem-
per with the sternness of the brain / Thoughts motherly, and meek
as womanhood" (1:559).[3] The conclusions of both stories gesture
toward a feminized vision of society, marked by consensual rather
than coercive modes of governing a kingdom or estate, by a progressive concern with the condition of the poor and dispossessed,
and by relational rather than authoritative methods of social discipline—the power of love displacing the love of power.

It would be naive, however, to overemphasize the feminist, subversive aspect of children's books that, ultimately, redefine the patriarchal role only to reassert it; Dolor assumes the throne, after all,
to quell a popular rebellion evocative of the revolutions of 1848.
Nor does Cedric, in spite of his democratic fervor, finally refuse to
accept his preferred role as future lord of his uncle's quasi-feudal
estate. Rather, the effeminate boy hero of Victorian children's fiction can be viewed as a strategic concession to the male child who,
in response to the very intensification of aggressive masculinity and
the concurrent devaluation of feminine characteristics in the cul-

ture around him, resists taking on his prescribed role. Temporarily releasing him from this cultural pressure, disingenuously promising him an androgynous future, such fictions allay the younger boy reader's resistance in order to coax him into accepting the phallic heritage he may prove otherwise unwilling to assume. Fantasies like *The Little Lame Prince* and *Little Lord Fauntleroy* function, that is, not to subvert the masculine role within patriarchy but to soften it, encouraging "little" boy readers to identify imaginatively with a patriarchal position made (in response to the ambivalence of a critical developmental stage) to *seem* more motherly and subject to qualification and deferral.

Burnett's account of "How Fauntleroy Occurred," subtitled "And a Very Real Little Boy Became an Ideal One," suggests that her fiction is indeed both modeled on and addressed to a younger boy whose eventual assumption of a masculine identity is in no way threatened or undermined by his temporary loitering in the precincts of the maternal sphere. Burnett's son, Vivian, is seven years old when he "becomes" Fauntleroy (160; fig. 3). Burnett's retrospective essay seems at first to cry out for a psychobiographical reading. She confesses that until his birth Vivian "had always been thought of as a little girl" (to be named Vivien): "It was the old story of 'Your sister, Betsey Trotwood'; and when he presented himself, with an unflinching firmness, in the unexpected character of a little boy, serious remonstrance was addressed to him" (161). But Burnett's very openness and self-irony on this point disarms analysis (or at least renders it superfluous). Although she gives her son an effeminate appearance (we learn a great deal about hair-brushing in the essay) up to, and perhaps a little beyond, the age of seven, she stresses that now, at sixteen, Vivian "plays foot-ball and tennis, and battles sternly with Greek. He is anxious not to 'flunk' in geometry, and his hair is exceedingly short and brown" (219). That is, he now conforms to another ideal: Tom Brown at school.

For Burnett, then, the adjective "little" is key. Only as a "little boy" is Vivian feminized, only at a young age does he suggest —in a double sense—the effeminate Fauntleroy, both as model for its hero and as the story's original addressee (according to Vivian's own retrospective account): "Why don't you write some books that *little* boys would like to read?" (142; my italics). That Burnett did see Fauntleroy as effeminate is readily apparent, both from the notorious illustrations by Reginald Birch, which she ap-

Figure 3. "The real Fauntleroy listening to the story of the ideal Fauntleroy." Illustration by Birch for "How Fauntleroy Occurred," *Piccino* (New York, 1897).

proved, and from the casting, in the London and New York stage versions of Fauntleroy, which she supervised, of girls (one aged nine, one "about" seven) in the title role (Thwaite 111; V. Burnett 179). (A film version, produced by Mary Pickford, emphasizes both Fauntleroy's femininity and his identification with Dearest: Pickford herself played both roles [Thwaite 246].) But it is equally clear that for Burnett the effeminate phase had its period and facilitated (rather than simply delayed) the boy's later assumption of a thoroughly masculine character. In the photograph Burnett sent to Birch as a model for the illustrations to *Little Lord Fauntleroy*, Vivian's lace and flowing locks are coyly offset by a small decorative sword (V. Burnett 136), an earnest of his eventual masculinity (fig. 4).

The children's text has sometimes been seen as uniquely tinged by its historical matrix, a "kind of cultural barometer" in its ideological transparency (MacDonald 1). Even if we were to accept the view of juvenile fiction as merely reflecting a preexistent social reality, the

Figure 4. Photograph of Vivian Burnett taken in 1885 and sent to Birch as a model to use in illustrating *Little Lord Fauntleroy*.

inadequacies of such a position should seem clear. But children's books are concerned not only with reproducing ideology but with producing certain kinds of subjects as well; the "ideal" children they represent are intended to help shape the characters of "real" boys and girls. Chodorow's revision of Freudian psychoanalytic theory—which remains one of the most compelling accounts we have of the development of modern subjectivity—suggests that, if ultimately geared toward the functioning of male-dominated industrial capitalism, the boy's maturation within an isolated nuclear family and with the mother as primary socializer entails detours, disruptions, or gaps in the production of masculine subjects. In their recognition of such developmental crises and the ingenuity of their fictional strategies for meeting them, *The Little Lame Prince* and *Little Lord Fauntleroy* attest to the flexibility, the sophistication, and the cultural power of nineteenth-century fiction for children.

## Notes

1. Compare the epigraphs by Wordsworth at the heads of chapters 1, 4, 5, and 6 and the quotation of the "Immortality" ode early in chapter 3 (19:50), all in Kingsley's *Water Babies*.

2. Claudia Nelson argues that the conception of manliness in *Tom Brown's School-days* is only apparently biased toward an extreme masculinity and can ultimately be seen as an "androgynous" one (530), as Tom, toward the end of the novel, must learn to integrate certain relational qualities into his personality. There is much to be said for this view, particularly in accounting for the increasingly important role of the effeminate Arthur in the second half of the book. But Nelson's "androgynous" reading cannot explain why Tom (and the other Rugby boys) should grow up segregated in a nearly exclusively male world or why so much of their "education" (particularly in the novel's first half) involves such hyper-masculine activities as rugby games in which the smaller boys are knocked unconscious or break their limbs.

3. The quotation is from Wordsworth's sonnet "1801." I do not mean to suggest here that Romantic androgyny should be considered an uncomplicated ideal or a feminist gesture in any meaningful sense: see Richardson for a discussion and critique of Romantic androgyny that also draws on the work of Chodorow.

## Works Cited

Burnett, Frances Hodgson. "How Fauntleroy Occurred, And a Very Real Little Boy Became an Ideal One." *Piccino and Other Child Stories*. New York: Scribner's, 1987. 157–219.

———. *Little Lord Fauntleroy*. New York: Scribner's, 1886.

Burnett, Vivian. *The Romantick Lady (Frances Hodgson Burnett): The Life Story of an Imagination*. New York: Scribner's, 1927.

Chodorow, Nancy. "Gender, Relation, and Difference in Psychoanalytic Perspective." *The Future of Difference*, ed. Hester Eisenstein and Alice Jardine. Boston: G. K. Hall, 1980. 3–19.

————. *The Reproduction of Mothering: Psychoanalysis and the Sociology of Gender.* Berkeley: University of California Press, 1978.

Craik, Dinah Maria Mulock. "The Little Lame Prince and His Travelling-Cloak." *The Victorian Fairy Tale Book,* ed. Michael Patrick Hearn. New York: Pantheon, 1988. 133–91.

Hartman, Geoffrey H. "Words, Wish, Worth: Wordsworth." *Deconstruction and Criticism,* ed. Harold Bloom et al. New York: Continuum, 1979. 177–216.

Hughes, Thomas. *Tom Brown's School Days.* New York: New American Library, 1986.

Kingsley, Charles. *The Water-Babies: A Fairy Tale for a Land-Baby. The Life and Works of Charles Kingsley.* 19 vols. London: MacMillan, 1901–3. 19:1–202.

Knoepflmacher, U. C. "Resisting Growth through Fairy Tale in Ruskin's *The King of the Golden River." Children's Literature* 13 (1985): 3–30.

Luthi, Max. *The European Folktale: Form and Nature.* Philadelphia: Institute for the Study of Human Issues, 1982.

MacDonald, Ruth K. *Literature for Children in England and America from 1646 to 1774.* Troy: Whitston, 1982.

Mitchell, Juliet. *Psychoanalysis and Feminism: Freud, Reich, Laing and Women.* New York: Vintage, 1975.

Nelson, Claudia. "Sex and the Single Boy: Ideals of Manliness and Sexuality in Victorian Literature for Boys." *Victorian Studies* 32 (1989): 525–50.

Petzold, Dieter. "Breaking in the Colt: Socialization in Nineteenth-Century School Stories." *Children's Literature Association Quarterly* 15 (1990): 17–21.

Richardson, Alan. "Romanticism and the Colonization of the Feminine." *Romanticism and Feminism,* ed. Anne K. Mellor. Bloomington: Indiana University Press, 1988. 13–25.

Rose, Jacqueline. *The Case of Peter Pan, or The Impossibility of Children's Fiction.* London: MacMillan, 1984.

Sedgwick, Eve Kosofsky. *Between Men: English Literature and Male Homosocial Desire.* New York: Columbia University Press, 1985.

Stoller, Robert J. "Facts and Fancies: An Examination of Freud's Concept of Bisexuality." *Women and Analysis: Dialogues on Psychoanalytic Views of Femininity,* ed. Jean Strouse. New York: Grossman, 1974. 343–64.

Thwaite, Ann. *Waiting for the Party: The Life of Frances Hodgson Burnett, 1849–1924.* London: Secker and Warburg, 1974.

# Of Dolls and Girls in Nineteenth-Century France

Valérie C. Lastinger

Most French children become acquainted with the nineteenth-century poet Victor Hugo through excerpts from his novel *Les Misérables,* a book filled with lively and memorable children. The three main female children characters—Cosette, Ponine, and Zelma—are introduced after the following passage:

> A doll is one of the most imperious needs, and at the same time one of the most charming instincts, of female childhood. . . . To care for, to clothe, to adorn, to dress, to undress, to dress over, to teach, to scold a little, to rock, to cuddle, to put to sleep, to imagine that something is somebody—all the future of woman is there. . . . The first baby takes the place of the last doll.
>
> A little girl without a doll is almost as unfortunate and quite as impossible as a woman without children. [343]

Reading this passage, Laura Kreyder comments that "these famous pages . . . continue to represent the model of the play-relation of the 'child-woman' in yesterday and today's textbooks" (90).[1] Certainly, Victor Hugo remains a dominant patriarchal authority figure in France; within the narrow limits of these few lines, feminists can recognize a deterministic summary of maternity as the only possible female destiny.

Hugo's responsibility is great; his impress on French literature and politics and his influence in the domain of French children's literature are undeniable. French children today commonly read abridged versions of *Les Misérables* (1862) and *Notre-Dame de Paris* (1831). Excerpts from *Les Misérables,* as Kreyder notes, are usually part of grade school curricula, and the favorite passages—those that deal with Cosette as a child—are the passages I consider here.

It is tempting for feminists to portray Hugo as perpetuating a conditioning of female childhood into the maternal role. At the center of this conditioning rests the doll, this reified child—usually, this reified female child. But Hugo deserves a fair hearing; an analysis

*Children's Literature* 21, ed. Francelia Butler, Christine Doyle Francis, Anne K. Phillips, and Julie K. Pfeiffer (Yale University Press, © 1993 The Children's Literature Foundation, Inc.).

of gender role models should not rest on a few lines. These few lines, moreover, should be read with great care, for they are rich and controversial. Indeed, Hugo's text contains a number of "windows" through which readers may glimpse a world not quite so rigid as the one first readily perceived. Typically Hugolian, typically romantic, the rhetoric of the passage is based on a series of binary oppositions or equivalences: imperious/charming; something/somebody; doll-less girl/childless woman; first baby/last doll.

These rhetorical pairs, so familiar to Hugo's landscape and so forcibly penetrating the reader's mind, prove here, however, to be just as many sophisms for the contemporary reader.[2] Where, we may ask, is the rational impossibility in the sentence "as impossible as a woman without children"? The word *impossible* works on at least two levels, implying both biological impossibility and an incompatibility of characters (that is, a woman without children is impossible to live with). Of course, infertility is hardly rare and barren women are not necessarily high-strung and inflexible. Thus taken apart, Hugo's deceptive aphorism implies another: "a little girl without a doll is as possible as a woman without children." Take another of Hugo's assertions: "to imagine that something is somebody, all the future of woman is there." The cleanness of such a phrasing at first seduces, but again one is tempted to reverse the sentence to make sense of it. Under patriarchy, a woman's future is not to imagine that something is somebody but rather to understand that she, some*body*, is some*thing*. The temptation to reverse the axiom is all the stronger since historians have shown that by the late seventeenth century, contrary to earlier practice, babies were certainly considered as some*body* rather than some*thing* (Ariès 53–73).[3]

With such examples of the slyness of apparently clear-cut sentences, one suspects that when it comes to the portrayal of gender, Hugo may also distort stereotypes. In this context, a *stereotype* is defined as an idea that on a superficial level can pass as being expected, predictable, unimaginative. In the opening passage, for example, Hugo appears to reinforce such precepts as "a doll is essential to a little girl," or "women's future lies in maternal fulfillment." But as we have just shown, his approach is nonsensical. His portrayal of a little girl playing house comprises the notions that all girls will not be mothers and that doll play can be unrelated to a little girl's adult role in society.[4]

In her discussion of mothers in children's literature, Lois Rauch

Gibson distinguishes between stereotype and archetype. Using
Jung's definitions, she argues that "an archetype is a 'primordial
image,'" one that "exists in all human minds" (177). Gibson further
implies that an image is either an archetype (a "good" image) or
a stereotype (a "bad" image). But the reading I propose disagrees
with Gibson: a little girl with a doll is neither a stereotype (a mechanism meant to push young females into motherhood) nor an archetype (that is, a primordial idea of motherhood). In the examples
presented here, the little-girl-and-doll teams work on one level
as stereotypes—inconspicuous, bland, maternal. But when studied
closely, these images prove to be a reflection of the author's interpretation of life rather than a stereotype. This interpretation is far
from being common to all human minds; thus, these images are not
archetypes either. Not all dolls are a metaphor for motherhood—
their meaning derives from the outlook of the author rather than
from a general idea.

The reader may thus deconstruct the stereotyped symbols in the
works of a writer such as Hugo in order to detect nonconformist
ideas or at least to question conformist ideas. Would it not then be
appropriate to study such images in children's literature at large?
Gender stereotyping in children's books has been scrutinized in
recent years.[5] But if we distance ourselves from the dichotomy of
stereotype and archetype, we may see how authors have manipulated the image of a little girl and her doll to create some of the
most memorable characters of children's literature.

The publication of Hugo's *Les Misérables* in 1862 coincided with
the decision by French industrialist Monsieur Jumeau to create
a truly French doll, one that would by virtue of the new technology surpass in beauty, color, and luxury anything ever before
seen (Kreyder 94). The industrial revolution had reinforced the
role of toys: more and more little girls received more and more
sophisticated dolls. If the two main examples I develop here come
from French children's literature, the implications of my remarks
go beyond nineteenth-century France.

### Cosette

If Jean Valjean gives Cosette a most famous doll, the introduction
of her first toy in *Les Misérables* comes immediately after the opening passage: "A little girl without a doll is almost as unfortunate
and quite as impossible as a woman without children. Cosette had

therefore made a doll of her sword" (343). The sword held in lieu of a doll is indeed a double-edged one: Cosette, an oppressed and defenseless child, uses her doll-sword as a means of domination as well as submissive nurturing; in this doll-knife, which keeps its cutting quality, there is a projection of power. Cosette mentions the sword during her first encounter with Jean Valjean:

—"How do you amuse yourself?"
—"The best I can. They let me alone. But I have not many playthings. Ponine and Zelma are not willing for me to play with their doll. I have only a little lead sword, not longer than that."
The child showed her little finger.
—"And which does not cut?"
—"Yes, monsieur," said the child, "it cuts lettuce and flies' heads." [336–37]

Cosette speaks about the sword nowhere else. She presents the "toy," moreover, as an object able to bring her the two things she most lacks at the house of the Thénardiers, her hateful, exploitative, and criminal guardians: food ("it cuts lettuce") and power over those who torment her ("it cuts . . . flies' heads"). Later, the narrator describes Cosette with her sword: "Cosette, for her part, had dressed up the sword. That done, she had laid it upon her arm, and was singing it softly to sleep" (343). The narrator "normalizes" the scene, giving it a maternal twist, since it is hardly usual to see a little child rock a sword. But if one can rationalize and present the sword as a pretend doll, then everything is normal. Cosette, however, does not call her sword a doll; she merely says that she plays with it. Cosette's remarks about the cutting power of the sword are framed, as it were, between the narrator's aphorisms ("The doll is one of the most imperious needs . . . of female childhood") and the narrator's uses of the maternal lexicon for Cosette's behavior to the sword (dressed up, laid it upon her arm, singing it softly to sleep). It then becomes difficult to know whether Cosette's described behavior is more important than her speech. She mentions the sword only in connection with power, danger, and death, but the narrator translates her actions toward it as stereotypically maternal. Even though Cosette is the one who has dressed the sword as if it were a doll, it is nonetheless difficult to know how much maternal value Cosette invests in the sword; she talks only of power, danger, and death.[6]

This ambiguity exists until the last mention of the sword, which occurs in a most heartrending scene. Cosette, playing with the sword-baby under the table, has just overheard snatches of conversation between Jean Valjean and Madame Thénardier about the death of Fantine, Cosette's mother: "Cosette, under the table, was looking into the fire, which was reflected from her fixed eye; she was again rocking the sort of rag baby that she had made, and as she rocked it, she sang in a low voice; 'My mother is dead! my mother is dead! my mother is dead!'" (344). Again, it is chiefly through the narrator's intervention that the scene takes on a maternal coloring. One can, of course, read this tableau of Cosette and the sword differently. Is this little girl, hypnotized by the fire, swaying rhythmically, chanting, "My mother is dead," while holding a sword in her hands, rocking a baby to sleep? Or is she executing a rite of exorcism, rocking a highly symbolical sword-baby, which has a much more powerful potential referent than a mere doll?[7] It is, of course, for the reader to decide. But we should at least notice what an ambiguous role Cosette's first doll plays in the narrative.

Once Jean Valjean enters Cosette's life, once the little girl's oppression is alleviated, the sword is never again mentioned. Another "toy," however, takes its place, in the form of a dream-doll. Jean Valjean brings her the most expensive doll available in the village, the one each little girl in town covets. Cosette herself has stopped in front of the merchant's window to admire the doll, which she calls "the lady" (326). Placed in the window as Snow White in a glass coffin, this doll is the woman-object, one all the villagers admire and would like to possess. The doll has arrived at the toy-shop the very morning Jean Valjean arrived in town, and the narrator remarks: "The whole day, this marvel had been displayed to the bewilderment of the passers under ten years of age, but there had not been found in Montfermeil a mother rich enough, or prodigal enough to give it to her child" (327). Jean Valjean, both rich enough and prodigal, buys the object of collective desire and gives it to Cosette, the woman-child he will raise protectively, guarding her from outside influences. Cosette is in many ways a doll he thinks he can shape. In time, however, she will rebel against her "father's" authority, by refusing to give up her unsuitable lover.[8]

With a doll, Jean Valjean gives Cosette a first cue of his aspirations for her. Traditionally, the father-figure gives his daughter an image of femininity in order to subdue her into her patriarchal role, mainly that of a beautiful object. To use Sandra Gilbert's and

Susan Gubar's words about Snow White, the doll is "the eternally beautiful, inanimate *objet d'art* patriarchal aesthetics want a girl to be" (40). Indeed, the narrator alludes to a reified feminine destiny for Cosette on several occasions, in particular when Cosette watches the doll in the window: "Cosette was measuring with the sad and simple sagacity of childhood the abyss which separated her from that doll. She was saying to herself that one must be a queen, or at least a princess, to have a *thing* like that. . . . She gazed upon this beautiful pink dress, this beautiful smooth hair, and she was thinking, 'How happy must be that doll!'" (326, emphasis added). If maternity plays any part in this new relationship, however, it does so in a most original manner: *the lady* is not to be a child substitute for Cosette. On the contrary, *the lady* is the benevolent mother the little girl never knew. The doll is "a great doll nearly two feet high dressed in a robe of pink-crape with golden wheat-ears on its head, and which had real hair and enamel eyes" (326). Because adult-replica dolls were common during the nineteenth century (as are our Barbies and G.I. Joes), Victor Hugo's choice of a doll is not remarkable.[9] Such dolls existed simultaneously with the more traditional baby-dolls or child-dolls. It is of course easy to explain different intentionalities: the adult-doll plays the role of an image after which the child can model herself (or, in the case of G.I. Joes, himself), whereas the baby-doll is designed to provide the little girl with practice for a future maternal role.[10]

Hence, when Jean Valjean gives Cosette a doll, he does not put a baby in her arms. Rather, he puts "the hand of the *lady* in her little hand" (347). Cosette is truly the daughter of the *lady* since it is her hand and not the doll's that is described as small. For the little girl, to play with the doll is not to nurse her but rather to put herself under her protection:

> Cosette placed Catherine on a chair, then sat down on the floor before her, and remained motionless, without saying a word, in the attitude of contemplation.
> —"Why don't you play, Cosette?" said the stranger.
> —"Oh! I am playing," answered the child. [347]

From the onset, Cosette poses her doll as a powerful mother figure.

The doll's very name, Catherine, alludes to Catherine the Great, a figure not normally associated with maternal devotion. To nineteenth-century readers, Catherine II was a potent feminine reference: an intellectual, a reformer, Catherine symbolized the encroachment by a woman on masculine power. Indeed, the text certainly supports such an identification. *Les Misérables* is set during the Napoleonic Wars, which include the infamous campaign against Russia. Furthermore, a few paragraphs before Catherine the doll is named, the narrator makes a rather odd comparison between Mme. Thénardier and a political force. As Ponine and Zelma Thénardier point out Cosette's boldness for playing with their doll, the narrator observes: "The face of the Thénardiess assumed the peculiar expression which is composed of the terrible mingled with the commonplace and which has given this class of women the name of *furies*. . . . A *czarina* who had seen a moujik trying on the grand cordon of her imperial son would have had the same expression" (345, emphasis added).[11]

The czarina metaphor here counterbalances the epithet "fury." Here again, the negative fury and the legitimate, although violent, mother-czarina are opposed. Madame Thénardier is a typical angel-witch combination. But the czarina image becomes central only when Cosette names her mother-doll Catherine.

In order to gain access to the throne, Catherine the Great had to plot against her husband, Peter III, czar of Russia. She infiltrated the imperial family, did away with the man in power, and usurped the throne. Similarly, in the novel, Cosette props her doll on a chair and adopts a subordinate position by sitting at the doll's feet. The little girl, upon accepting the objet d'art proposed as a model by the father, transforms this subordinate female figure by naming it Catherine: Catherine the Great is the one who collects art objects, who orders and buys them, rather than the one who is collected, ordered, and bought. For Cosette, the doll is a means to transform or reject others' expectations of her; the sword of power lies within any doll, however disguised.

If Hugo does indeed portray a little girl with a doll, the special twists of the narrative make it difficult to view the image as stereotypical. The intricate game played between the narrator—the traditional romantic figure of male authority—and the characters makes possible such a subversion of roles. Thus, between a sword and an empress, Victor Hugo, a well-known medium, masterfully turned the tables on traditional views of female behavior and destiny.

*Sophie*

Another nineteenth-century doll can be found not in the works of a revolutionary political persona but in those of a woman who wrote exclusively for children, the comtesse de Ségur (1799–1874). Ségur is hardly less well known in France than Victor Hugo, but she wrote for a different audience, and the substance of her ideas is therefore all the more subversive and productive. From the perspective of French nineteenth-century literature, combining Victor Hugo's and Sophie de Ségur's dolls in one essay is compelling; all stand out as unforgettable features of childhood readings. With the help of a doll, Sophie de Ségur, mother of eight, discusses post-partum depression, infanticide, female rebellion, and destiny in books for eight-year-old children.

In one of her best-known works, *Les Malheurs de Sophie* [Sophie's misfortunes], written in 1859, Ségur presents a bold use of "subversive stereotyping." Some critics have felt that this book lacks a linear structure and is no more than a narrated version of playlets reminiscent of the eighteenth-century writer Arnaud Berquin (Soriano 478). Yet, although the opening story about Sophie's doll is told in just two chapters, it actually continues through three volumes. A careful reading of this story leads to a drastically different view of Ségur as well as of her use of so-called stereotyped images.

"A white wooden box sat on a chair; the nurse opened it. Sophie caught a glimpse of the blond and curly head of a pretty wax doll; she cried with joy and tried to seize the doll, which was still covered with wrapping paper. . . . The nurse . . . took her scissors, cut the cords, took off the papers, and Sophie was able to hold the most beautiful doll she had ever seen" (1:273). Chapter 1 of *Les Malheurs* begins with a parody of childbirth when Sophie receives a package from her father. She opens it with the help of her maid, turned midwife for the occasion. The maid opens the box-uterus and extricates the doll-child's head. The impatient Sophie-mother cries with joy and anticipation. The midwife cuts the cord and clears the baby's body of the wrapping tissues reminiscent of a newborn's coat of vernix. The mother at last holds the baby, relishing each of its features: "Sophie was able to hold the most beautiful doll she had ever seen. The cheeks were rosy with little dimples; the eyes, blue and sparkling; the waxen neck, chest and arms, charming and plump" (1:273).

It would be hard to imagine an opening that would more strongly and accurately reinforce a little girl's future in happy maternity. The only cries here are cries of joy and not pain. As one critic explains, "Sophie must exert her femininity by assuming the role of a mother for her doll. . . . Sophie must learn that she is a woman, and therefore a mother" (Kreyder 91). This conventional opening, however, holds for no more than two pages, as Sophie readily starts what soon becomes a pattern of abuse and mutilation that culminates in the "death" of her "daughter."

Before seeing how Sophie treats her doll, however, let us examine the detailed scene of its arrival. The doll, which oddly enough has no name, is, like all Sophie's presents, a gift from her father.[12] We learn first of the doll's origin: "Come and help me open a box Father sent me from Paris; I believe it is a wax-doll, because he promised me one" (1:273). Given this incestuous origin (the "father" of Sophie's doll is her father), is it so odd after all that the doll should have no name? She is the unspeakable, the fruit of the greatest taboo of all.

The doll is clearly a model of femininity sent by a father to his daughter; the doll, after all, comes from Paris, a center of nineteenth-century male genius and expansionism. This idea of the doll-model establishes a theme of competition between Sophie and her new image of femininity. The only physical descriptions in *Les Malheurs* are that of the doll, quoted above, and the one of Sophie: "She liked to be well dressed and to be found pretty. However, she was not pretty; she had a good round face with a fresh complexion, with a lively expression, beautiful gray eyes, a turned up nose, somewhat strong, a large mouth always ready to smile, straight blond hair, cut short like a boy's" (1:289).[13] These descriptions become all the more fascinating when one realizes that the doll is an improved, idealized version of Sophie. We have to ponder with Isabelle Nières, "What if the doll were the ideal double, the inaccessible model? What if Sophie's pranks were but a repetition of the kill[ing] of her beloved doll?" ("Adaptations" 58). The little girl just cannot win out over the doll: Sophie has a fresh complexion, but the doll has rosy cheeks. Sophie has very pretty gray eyes, but its eyes are bright blue. Sophie has a good round face, but the doll is charming and plump. Sophie has a large mouth, always ready to laugh, but its gracious smile puts becoming dimples on its rosy cheeks. Sophie's hair is blond and straight, cut like a boy's;

the doll's blond hair is curly. A similar parallel can be established with their clothes. Sophie is dressed plainly, in Rousseauistic fashion (1:289). The doll, in contrast, though dressed almost identically to Sophie, achieves an elegance through details of a finery that must exacerbate Sophie's aspirations (1:273). Clearly, as was the case with Cosette's Catherine, the doll, beautiful and pictorial, represents the femininity Sophie is to strive to achieve.

How can anything other than a rebellious reaction be expected from a rambunctious child like Sophie? In spite of her mother's warnings, the little girl leaves her wax doll in the sun, thus blinding it (1:274–76). She scalds its feet while bathing it (1:276). She disfigures it as she washes its face, burns its locks in an attempt to curl them, breaks its arms while teaching it tricks (1:276). Finally, Sophie tries to teach the doll how to climb trees, and breaks it (1:276). The mutilations she inflicts on her doll are invariably directed toward its "feminine" attributes: the curly hair, the rosy colors, the body, and the proverbial feminine grace. The patriarchal figure of femininity cannot resist such harassment and breaks into a hundred pieces. Sophie's human nature has given battle to patriarchal idealism, and the little girl has won the first round.

Such compulsive behavior can scarcely escape the reader's notice, and critics have explained it as part of Sophie's learning experience: "Barbarity comes from the fact that she treats her doll as if it resembled her; all of her loving attentions turn into mutilations. . . . Sophie must therefore experience the varied nature of the artifact a doll is" (Kreyder 97). It is difficult, however, to dismiss Sophie's behavior as so many "mistakes" and to hold that she cannot differentiate between herself and an object. Throughout the rest of the book, in fact, a mock parallel between the doll's mutilations and Sophie's experiences is maintained. Sophie burns her feet in a footbath (1:278–79), attempts to curl her hair (1:289–91), and almost breaks her neck doing trick riding exercises on her donkey (1:338–56). But although Sophie eventually breaks (kills) her doll, her own experiences are less lethal: she burns her doll's hair, but to curl her own, she merely puts her head under a gutter on a rainy day.

Sophie's actions, then, are so many voluntary mutilations of her baby. If Ségur's point were to show how little girls learn unconditional maternal love through doll-play, as some critics say she does (Kreyder 91; Mathé 122), how can we account for the ending of chapter 1, in which Sophie's lack of sorrow is forcibly spelled out?

After all these misfortunes, *Sophie did not love her doll, which had become ugly* and of which her friends made fun; at last, one last day, Sophie wanted to teach it to climb trees; she had it climb on a branch and sit; but the doll, which wasn't very stable, fell. Its head struck against some rocks and broke into a hundred pieces. *Sophie did not cry, but she invited her friends to come* and bury her doll. [1:276, emphasis added]

As far as Sophie's maternal feelings are concerned, the closing sentence, "Sophie did not cry," is at best an understatement. Chapter 2 opens with a festive tone: "Camille and Madeleine arrived one morning for the doll's funeral; they were delighted; Sophie and Paul were no less elated" (1:277). The jollity is maintained throughout the short ceremony, which ends in a gay wrestling match among the "mourning" company:

To end the party, they ran to the garden pond and filled their watering cans to water the lilacs; this was the opportunity to start new games and to laugh as they watered each other's legs and ran laughing and shouting. One had never seen a merrier funeral. It is true that the deceased was an old doll without colors or hair, without legs or head, and that nobody loved her or missed her. The day ended gaily and when Camille and Madeleine left, they asked Paul and Sophie to break another doll so as to have another such amusing funeral. [1:277]

After such an illustration of doll play, one ponders how Ségur's text can be read as a mothering lesson for apprentice-mothers. Kreyder's interpretation is all the more surprising because it is based on this very episode—there are no other broken dolls in Ségur's works. Such a misreading can only be explained in terms of the reader's expectations of Ségur. The model of the "good" mother, Ségur is often quickly explained as having been a devoted mother whose late writings were merely a substitution for a progeny "lost" to adult life (Kreyder 127). This merely reiterates the legend established by Ségur's family in an attempt to soften and justify the existence in a respectable aristocratic family of the monstrous woman writer. If the reader is conditioned to see Ségur as a woman playing on the side of patriarchy (accepting without questioning her maternal destiny), then it becomes impossible to read Ségur's texts on maternity as anything but an illustration of a patriarchal order. As I have argued elsewhere, however, such an interpretation of Ségur's life is undercut by numerous anecdotes, and certainly, textual evidence does not sustain such a reading of her writings.[14]

From our perspective, then, if these two chapters have anything to do with a mothering experience, it is with infanticide. But one may also wonder if what Sophie kills and buries is not the patriarchal interpretation of what femininity should be rather than maternity itself. If we examine the description of the funeral, we notice the particular care with which Ségur describes the coffin, made out of an old box: "The children entered Mme. de Réan's room, where the nurse was just finishing the pillow and mattress for the box; the children admired this charming coffin; they placed the doll in it and they covered it with a coverlet of pink silk so that its crushed head, melted feet and broken arm would be concealed" (1:277). This highly ornate passage, detailed almost to an extreme, strikingly opposes the crushed body with the pink silk. The prominence of the motif of the coffin is reminiscent of the tale of Snow White. Nowhere can we find a stronger reverse rendering of the glass coffin: "Snow White lay in her coffin for years and years. She didn't rot, but continued to look as if she were asleep, for she was still as white as snow, as red as blood, and as black as ebony" (Grimm 190). In Grimm's tale, the desire for a beautiful daughter springs in the heart of the queen mother as she is working on her needlework: sewing at her window, she pricks her finger, and the drops of blood on the white snow account for the specificity of Snow White's physical appearance.[15] If we are to take sewing as an acceptable manifestation of female activity in patriarchy, it is telling that the very stitches that bring Snow White to this world are instrumental to the burying of Sophie's doll. Whereas Snow White in her coffin remains forever beautiful and desirable, the doll is ugly—unlike Snow White, she has lived a life other than contemplative. Snow White is consumed by the prince; Sophie has consumed her doll.

The children rejoice at the doll's funeral not because the doll deserved to die for departing from a patriarchal model but because Sophie has subverted the patriarchal model of femininity for an instant. Snow White is saved from her death by a man because she had a valid patriarchal life of domesticity. The doll, mutilated and dismantled, remains buried, since "nobody love[s] her or misse[s] her." There is no place in patriarchy for the girl who leads an adventurous life, but Sophie does not yet comprehend the relation between her own mischievous behavior and the doll's death—the direct result of Sophie's desire for freedom, projected onto her doll.

In Sophie's treatment of her doll, we find the clues of the tension experienced by the little girl. On the one hand, she destroys all the features that make her doll a perfect objet d'art, even though she heartily covets for her own enjoyment some of the attributes she massacres in her doll (curly hair, for example). But at the same time, Sophie projects on the doll some of her desire for freedom (climbing trees); if Sophie presently enjoys this liberty, it is threatened outside Mme. de Réan's matriarchal house. The doll is broken both because Sophie rejects and desires its pictorial character and because she has pushed the limits of sexual equality too far.[16]

Tension does exist within Sophie's family over what constitutes a desirable female model. Recall that it is the remote father who sends the doll from the higher headquarters of patriarchy. But as readers, we can infer that Mme. de Réan has a different plan in mind for her daughter. In fact, we know that it is Sophie's mother who has chosen the unbecoming apparel (1:289). We are also led to understand that, like the author, Mme. de Réan supports Rousseau's theories on education as presented in his *Emile, ou de l'éducation* (1762). Just as Mme. de Réan wants Sophie to become used to "sun, rain and cold" (1:289) with a light dress, Rousseau demanded that children be accustomed to weather and other hardships, such as a cold bath (*Emile* 66–67). Of course, Rousseau made a large distinction between the education Emile and his companion—also named Sophie—were to receive. In *Emile*, Sophie's upbringing, geared toward domesticity, was to make her a model of patriarchal repression: the purpose of a young girl's education is to tame her: "Girls . . . must be inhibited early. This misfortune . . . is indistinguishable from their sex. . . . All of their life, they will be enslaved to the most continuous and severe constraint, that of propriety" (481). By implementing Emile's regimen in a female nursery, Mme. de Réan is already subverting a patriarchal model.

In contrast, M. de Réan, though very much physically absent from Sophie's life, makes it clear that Sophie is to be a well-tamed female. His gifts, a sewing box and a doll, are gender-specific. And Sophie's parents differ when she disastrously attempts to improve her physical appearance. After the episode of the dowsed hair, for example, Mme. de Réan is rather upset and promptly unveils Sophie's intention: "'What a beautiful idea must have struck you, young lady!' she said. 'If you could see your face, you would laugh at yourself as I am doing now. . . . For your punishment, you will stay at dinner the way you are, your hair in a spike, your dress drenched, so that your Papa and your cousin Paul can see your beautiful inventions'" (1:290). In contrast, M. de Réan, at first condemning Sophie's vanity ("Wishing to become pretty, one can only become ugly" [1:290]), cannot stand the sight of his ridiculous daughter and pleads with his wife: "My dear, I ask for your mercy this time. If she does it again, it will be different" (1:290). However, can he ignore that with Sophie there is always a next time? But although Mme. de Réan is always harsher on Sophie than her husband, she does not punish her daughter for mistreating the doll. When Sophie rejects her father's patriarchal image of femininity, therefore, she is siding with her mother. The burial of the doll marks Sophie's short-term victory, but it even more strongly suggests the long-term victory of patriarchy. Although Sophie dances at her doll's funeral, the more important issue is whether she will be able to dance when the patriarchy buries her for leading a life similar to the doll's, full of acrobatics and antics.

The remainder of *Les Malheurs* presents the logical continuation of the conflict of nature versus society. Little by little, Sophie attempts to transform herself into a feminine object—one similar to the doll she has destroyed. But Sophie's transformation into an objet d'art will require changes that will come at a far greater price than a dowsing of her stubbornly straight hair. This mutation will spread over the length of two other novels, *Les Petites Filles modèles* [The exemplary little girls] and *Les Vacances* [Summer vacation].[17] Sophie will undergo such torments as amnesia, loss of name and identity, and child abuse.

At the end of *Les Malheurs*, Sophie and her cousin Paul embark for America, where M. de Réan is to inherit the considerable fortune of a friend. At the beginning of *Les Petites Filles modèles*, Sophie has become Sophie Fichini, with a horrible stepmother who beats her relentlessly and deprives her of food and clothing. Madame Fichini eventually abandons Sophie to Mme. de Fleurville, the mother of Sophie's friends Camille and Madeleine. At the chateau de Fleurville, broken by her harsh experiences, Sophie is finally reborn among a community of women who, to ensure their social acceptance, appear to submit to the patriarchal order. In the third volume, *Les Vacances*, Sophie remembers how she came to be the charge of Mme. Fichini: her mother died in a shipwreck from which her father and she were saved, and they proceeded to go to America; there, in exchange for the friend's fortune, M. de Réan had to adopt the common name of Fichini. Thus, the mother who subverted patriarchal education dies, and her rebellious daughter spends years in Purgatory under a new "lesser" common identity and with a new mother. In Purgatory, she endures sufferings as harsh as the doll once had.

The chateau de Fleurville, where Sophie spends the rest of her childhood after being abandoned by her stepmother, is female territory. Even though fathers and male cousins eventually make their appearance, the chateau is the property of the widow Mme. de Fleurville, who is less overt in her departure from patriarchy than Mme. de Réan. A fervent advocate of physical exercise for young girls, Mme. de Fleurville is much closer to the "good" mother, with a temperance that Mme. de Réan sometimes lacked. She never grows impatient, always welcomes the disturbance of her children, and is a model of domestic economy. Accordingly, Mme. de Fleurville, more than Mme. de Réan, encourages her daughters to improve their physical appearance. By contrast with Sophie's, Camille's and Madeleine's hair are the objects of tender care: "Camille's pretty fine blond hair and Madeleine's brown silky hair were divided in two parts, well smoothed, well braided and attached above the ear with small combs; whenever there was company for dinner, a black velvet bow was added" (1:154). In *Les Malheurs*, we learned indirectly that Camille's hair does not owe all its beauty to nature, since, finding Sophie drenched, Mme. de Réan is quick to guess that Sophie "absolutely wants [her hair] to curl like Camille's, who wets hers to curl it" (1:290). Similarly, Camille's and Madeleine's outfits closely resemble the one Mme. de Réan dressed Sophie in, but the Rousseauistic tendencies are toned down at Fleurville. Rather than wearing a short-sleeved, low-necked dress in winter as well as in summer, as Sophie once did, Camille and Madeleine sport light dresses only "when the weather is hot" (*PFM* 1:154).

Yet, Mme. de Fleurville lives somewhat at the margins of patriarchy. An excellent administrator, she engineers and supervises the industrialization of the machinery on her property: "'I propose a great walk to the mill through the woods,' said M. de Rugès. 'We will go look at the new mechanic established by my sister de Fleurville, and while we examine the machinery, you children will play'" (*Vac*

1:390). Since the adult group invited for the walk comprises two men and four women, we are to understand that the industrialization is a social phenomenon of concern to both men and women, because women can also adequately ensure the prosperity of a patrimony. Finally, Mme. de Fleurville's behavior condones patriarchal order, since in the end, her daughters and her charge, Sophie, all enter into the most traditional of endogamous marriages. Under Mme. de Fleurville's benevolent influence Sophie is at last tamed, something Mme. de Réan had failed to achieve, or even, one may suspect, had failed to desire for her daughter.

In her first three novels, Ségur did more than revive her version of the playlet genre of the eighteenth century. She wrote the adventure of a young girl from nature to civilization. Like the doll, like Sophie, and, one might add, like Ségur herself, the tale is nonlinear and fragmented: structure, characters, stereotypes reflect like so many mirrors the central theme of Sophie's journey toward womanhood in a patriarchal world. At the closing of *Les Vacances,* Sophie is transformed into a well-adjusted social being, ready to take her place in the patriarchal order: the predominant character of the three books, she becomes in the last chapter one in the crowd, one of the crowd. Her fate is mentioned in one sentence, along with one about all the other characters who have appeared in the trilogy. She is from now on identical to any other young lady in her circle: "Sophie became more and more like her friends, whom she left only at the age of twenty, when she married Jean de Rugès" (1:520). Sophie has destroyed the doll given to her as a model of femininity, but in the end, some nine hundred pages later, she, too, joins the ranks of the "petites filles modèles" (exemplary little girls).

How then should Ségur's tale of a little girl with a doll induce us to rethink the gender role models? First, as we have seen, one should not necessarily equate the stereotypes of doll play with stereotypes of the maternal role: Ségur's books are rich in nuances, complexities, and insights on maternal feelings. In *Les Petites Filles modèles,* Ségur also expresses with Marguerite's doll the anxiety of the loss of freedom that is the price of motherhood. At first overjoyed because she won a magnificent doll, Marguerite is soon torn between her desires and the responsibility she has toward her "child." As Camille, Madeleine, and Marguerite are taking a long walk in the woods, Marguerite carrying her doll, the three little girls want to eat wild strawberries. The cumbersome doll stands between

Marguerite and her desires (one might even say between Marguerite and her primary needs of nourishment and free motion), and she soon decides to abandon her "maternal" responsibilities:

> Marguerite hastily joined her friends, who were putting their strawberries onto large chestnut tree leaves. She also started picking some up; but, hampered by her doll, she could not at the same time pick them up and hold them in her hand, where they were crushed as soon as they were picked up. "Goodness, what am I to do with this boring doll? She is a bother to me when I want to run, to pick up and keep my strawberries. What if I were to put her at the foot of this big oak tree? . . . There is moss there; she will be very comfortable." [PFM 1:163–64]

Of course, when a storm comes, Marguerite runs away with her friends and her strawberries, forgetting all about her doll, choosing her social life and her physical desires over her "child." Marguerite is devastated at first by the loss of her doll; after the doll is found, however, we readers never see Marguerite play house again. Like a mother suffering from post-partum depression, Marguerite wishes to be disencumbered of a "child" she loves but is nonetheless unable to accept.[18]

On a more pragmatic level, Ségur anticipates current psychological practices, showing the value of puppet therapy by having a little girl relive a traumatic experience through doll play. Marguerite has been involved in a frightening horse-drawn carriage accident in which her mother is seriously injured. By reenacting the scene with Camille and Madeleine's dolls she is able to overcome the trauma of this accident. Marguerite identifies the dolls with her mother and herself: "Oh, the beautiful dolls! Here is one as big as myself. . . . Ah! This big one lying in a beautiful little bed! She is sick just like poor mama" (PFM 1:127). Playing with a doll-size carriage, Marguerite repeats the details of the accident and is reassured by her friends that everything will be all right:

> "Goodness!" cried Marguerite in tears, "I broke your carriage, Camille. I am very sorry; for sure, I will not do it again."
> Camille: "Don't cry, my little Marguerite, this will be nothing. We are going to open the door, re-seat the voyagers in their places, and I will ask mama to replace the window."

Marguerite: "But if the passengers have a headache, like mama?"

Madeleine: "No, no, they have hard heads. Look, they are all back in place and they are in marvelous health."

[1:128]

Ségur's literary dolls, far from being stereotyped and unidimensional, express an array of emotions and exemplify a number of situations. Although we have to admit that in Ségur's literary world, as anywhere else, dolls are used as means of reinforcing a sexist patriarchal order since they are given only to little girls, we have to acknowledge Ségur's talent to express the ambiguities, tragedies, and adventures of females as they explore the boundaries of that order.

Victor Hugo's and Sophie de Ségur's dolls are unusual for having survived their historical periods. Cast as instruments of patriarchy, these dolls are nonetheless fully developed, sophisticated narrative devices. What makes Hugo's and Ségur's dolls worthy of critical attention is not necessarily the uses of their sometimes rebellious natures. On the contrary, what is important, particularly in Ségur's writing, is the detailed analysis of patriarchal oppression through "innocuous" toys. Sophie de Réan's tale, certainly, is in part one of oppression: critics have sometimes pondered the exact nature of the miseries of the title *Les Malheurs de Sophie*. *Les Malheurs* is mainly the book of many deaths—that of the doll, that of Sophie's numerous pets, that of Sophie herself. But if Sophie, rebellious like her doll, dies in the hands of her stepmother, she is also reborn in a space that we can hope is not patriarchy as the doll knew it.

It is true that we know nothing of Sophie de Réan after her marriage to Jean de Rugès (an anagram of Ségur). But we cannot assume that it will be a marriage in which maternity will dominate; in short, we cannot assume that it will be a "traditional" marriage, blessed by many children of which Sophie's doll was a precursor. In truth, if Ségur's endings often consist of a list of the fates of each character we have encountered in her books, and if marriage is almost always the outcome of a young woman's life, mention of progeny is never made. It is up to Ségur's reader to imagine Sophie de Rugès's married life: the author leaves her heroine married in a society where single women had neither power nor recognition.[19] However, Sophie, if she marries, is childless. Will Sophie de Rugès opt for maternity?[20] Will she become involved in engineering like her adoptive mother Mme. de Fleurville? Will she, like Mina in *La Fortune de Gaspard* (1866) and so many women in the nineteenth and twentieth centuries, find a career in philanthropy? Will she write like her creator and namesake? Sophie de Ségur, although she has let the young Sophie de Réan be domesticated, has contrived a space in which her heroine will have some choice about her future. We cannot assume that Sophie de Rugès is trapped in an oppressive marriage. In the end, Ségur's use of dolls remains ambiguous; or rather, Ségur cleverly avoids an open break from patriarchal order—a move her censors would have been quick to suppress. We can truly say that Ségur makes her dolls a means through which her heroines can challenge patriarchy and find their place in a new social order.

In Hugo's *Les Misérables*, Cosette's dolls, although well developed, do not reach the level of complexity seen in Ségur's writings. The endless possibilities of doll play for a child are well portrayed by Hugo, a male author who was able to show an acute awareness of the possibilities of a traditionally feminine toy. For in *Les Misérables*, Hugo subverts the maternal patriarchal intent of the doll. Cosette is not kept in line with a baby doll she is supposed to mother; rather, she nurses a knife, a source of masculine power disguised in acceptable feminine, maternal clothes—swaddling clothes. Cosette's other doll, the *lady*, is also an opportunity for the reader to challenge the patriarchal norm of the "naturally" nurturing female child: for Cosette, in refusing to nurture her doll, shows her own need to be nurtured. Here again is an unstereotypical use of a gender-specific toy; through dolls, Hugo can implicate many feelings in his heroine, who would otherwise remain rather unidimensional. Cosette is not a passive female child oppressed by patriarchy; rather, through sophisticated doll play, she can escape passivity.

Although there are many other dolls in nineteenth-century literature for children, none have made a more lasting impression on French children's imaginations than those of Hugo and Ségur. For generations yet to come, Cosette's and Sophie's dolls will remain objects of desire and sources of delight. Although dolls were specifically feminine toys in the 1850s as they can be today, we should not dismiss authors like Ségur and Hugo as sexists. For, like a prisoner who would ornament her cell with the means available to her, Ségur and Hugo transcend patriarchy by reimagining the roles of dolls and girls.

### Notes

I wish to thank West Virginia University's College of Arts and Sciences, the West Virginia University Faculty Senate, for their financial support during the preparation of this chapter. I would also like to thank Cheryl B. Torsney and Michael D. Lastinger for their constructive suggestions.

1. The translations from French are mine, except for those from Victor Hugo.

2. For the nineteenth-century reader, the maternal destiny of women was certainly under much less scrutiny than today and thus Hugo and his contemporaries were less likely to detect the subversiveness of these aphorisms. But they were subversive nonetheless at the time they were written. The refusal of the maternal route by French and English women has been solidly established as a strong trend since the eighteenth century. We know, for example, that contraception has been used since the beginning of time (see, for example, Greer 155). Referring to the pervasive eighteenth-century practice of abandoning children as a form of "contraception" as it were, Abbott Seagraves has remarked that "'disguised infanticide' was a further [population] limiting device throughout Western Europe in the late eighteenth and early nineteenth centuries. . . . [And the work of Darwin, von Öttingen, and Langer] provides vivid documentation of this practice as it was systematically carried out in England and France" (quoted in Greer 226). Even though we can guess that it was the mother who abandoned the child, thus refusing her maternal role for whatever reason, it makes no difference who the abandoner was. The truth is, the acceptance of maternity as the only possible female destiny was not universal. Therefore, there is ground here to propose that Hugo's words may hide a double meaning. Furthermore, I do not attempt to treat questions of intentionality for Hugo or Ségur here, which would necessitate a different type of approach.

3. "Thus, even though demographic conditions had not changed much from the thirteenth to the eighteenth century, even though infant mortality had subsisted at a very high rate, a new sensibility conferred these fragile, threatened beings a particularity which had been denied to them before: just as if common conscience had only then discovered that a child's soul was immortal" (Ariès 66). One can also think of Jean-Jacques Rousseau's demands that from infancy a child be treated as a human being with needs of her or his own. For Rousseau, who condemned the practice of swaddling, for example, an infant was indubitably some*body* rather than some*thing* (for details on Rousseau and the newborn child, see *Emile* 65–68).

4. That is not to say that I contest the weight of motherhood on female destiny in the nineteenth century. On the contrary, I merely suggest here that all of Hugo's contemporaries were aware of the sophism of such affirmation. We can argue, along with John Stuart Mill, that in order to impose such a rigid destiny onto females, patriarchy must be aware of the weakness of the argument of nature in defining gender roles: "If women have a greater natural inclination for some things than for others, there is no need of laws or social inculcation to make the majority of them do the former in preference of the latter" (203). In challenging the argument of nature, Mill has motherhood in mind: "The general opinion of men is supposed to be, that the natural vocation of a woman is that of a wife and mother. I say, is supposed to be, because, judging from acts—from the whole of the present constitution of society— one might infer that their opinion was the direct contrary" (203).

5. Among the many articles and books on the subject is *What Are Little Girls Made Of? The Roots of Feminine Stereotypes,* in which Belotti studies both real and literary dolls (the latter in very broad, general terms); this study has proven to be very popular, both in French and in its English translation. Also see Lois Rauch Gibson's article quoted above.

6. It could be noted that power, danger, and death are all components of maternity, but there is little textual evidence, other than subliminal, to suggest such a connection in *Les Misérables.* Indeed, the subliminal evidence is very strong: Mme. Thénardier is a powerful mother figure, even though Cosette is aware that she is not her daughter. Thus, in *Les Misérables,* Hugo reiterates the Cinderella plot, the two undeserving stepsisters being preferred to the rightful Cosette by a blind, wicked stepmother.

7. We may notice that the sword in Hugo's text refers to many images invested with issues of power (Napoleonic Wars, phallus, and so on).

8. Again, one may note Hugo's play on words and the reversal of gender roles. The *"mother* rich enough . . . to give [the doll] to her child" (my emphasis) is finally found in the person of Jean Valjean—the *father* figure.

9. Ségur puts adult dolls in the hands of the little heroines of *Les Petites Filles modèles (PFM)* [The exemplary little girls], whereas Sophie, the heroine of *Les Malheurs de Sophie* [Sophie's misfortunes], receives a child doll. In *Les Petites Filles* as in *Les Misérables,* the dolls are referred to as "ladies." But Ségur finds it necessary to specify that she is talking about the dolls: "These ladies (the dolls) had just changed residence" (*PFM* 1:122). We can thus infer that although such dolls were common, their status as "adult" could be ambiguous and necessitated clarification.

10. For the sake of the argument, even though in some cases little boys are also presented with baby dolls, the phenomenon remains largely a motif of female childhood. The baby doll thus usually reinforces mothering rather than parenting.

11. In his translation, Charles E. Wilbour uses the expression "Thenardiess" to refer to Mme. Thénardier in order to render the derogatory French usage "la Thénardier." I have respected the translation but use the more common—albeit weaker—Madame Thénardier in my own prose.

12. On the role of M. de Réan as a remote giftgiver, see Doray (51) and Kreyder (98–100). Kreyder offers a particularly pertinent reading of this characteristic of the father, in the light of Sophie's Oedipus. It would be interesting to know if dolls are usually a present of the father or the mother in children's literature as well as in reality. As for Ségur's works, of the two main dolls that play a significant role in her narratives, one is given by a father (Sophie's) and the other one is won by the little Marguerite in a lottery (*PFM* 1:161). In both cases, the doll is a present that comes from "above." For Sophie, it comes from her distant but all-powerful Parisian father, and anyone familiar with French culture knows how much Paris stands above the rest of France. For Marguerite, the doll comes from chance—or destiny. Even though it is Mme. de Rosbourg, her mother, who purchased the prizes, the mediation of the lottery blurs the origin of the identity of the giver, especially in the mind of a young child such as Marguerite, a little girl of five. In *Les Petites Filles,* Camille and Madeleine also have dolls, but nothing is known of their origin.

13. For a good discussion of the question of the physical beauty of Ségur's heroine, see Doray (125).

14. For an extensive discussion of this problem, see my "Excentricité et conformité: Sophie de Ségur, femme et écrivain." See also Doray (9–15).

15. As Sandra Gilbert and Susan Gubar point out, "The story begins in midwinter, with a Queen sitting and sewing, framed by a window. As in so many fairy tales, she pricks her finger, bleeds, and is thereby assumed into the cycle of sexuality. . . . All the motifs introduced in [the] prefatory paragraph—sewing, snow, blood, enclosure—are associated with key themes in female lives" (37).

16. For an extensive discussion of Ségur's treatment of the equality of the sexes, see Doray's chapter on the problem, "Masculin-Féminin" (115–41).

17. The fictional order of the novels is as follows: *Les Malheurs de Sophie, Les Petites Filles modèles, Les Vacances.* The chronological order of publication has *Les Petites Filles* coming first, then *Les Malheurs,* and *Les Vacances.* As for the creation order, it seems safe to assume that the three books were conceived as a whole, since cross references occur in all three novels. But for more details on a chronology that is not without problems, see Isabelle Nières's "Pour en finir avec le malheur de Sophie."

18. If in Marguerite's case, the ultimate motive of the abandonment is her immaturity (she is five years old), I by no means suggest that immaturity is the cause of post-partum depression. Rather, I wish to emphasize that merely by describing it, Ségur introduces abandonment as a possible outcome of a mother-child relationship that was at first happy.

19. Even though we do not know what type of marriage Sophie enters, Ségur's innovative depiction of the married life of her heroines is well documented (Doray 130–40). Ségur's subsequent novels (and in particular *L'Auberge de l'ange gardien* [1863], *La Fortune de Gaspard* [1866], and *Après la pluie le beau temps* [1871]) are interesting for the treatment of the woman's role in the relationship. *La Fortune de Gaspard* offers a direct discussion of sexuality, which has incomprehensibly escaped the fierce censorship to which her husband, son, and editor subjected all of Ségur's novels (see Marc Soriano's introduction to the novel in the Jean-Jacques Pauvert edition).

20. In fact, in Ségur's writings, the mother of a large family is often ridiculed: the author's ideal seems to be a two-child family. This is a particularly interesting comment on the didacticism of Ségur, whom we know was herself the mother of eight. For more commentary on this subject, see Kreyder (78).

## Works Cited

Ariès, Philippe. *L'Enfant et la vie familiale sous l'Ancien Régime.* Paris: Le Seuil, 1973.

Belotti, Elena Gianini. *What Are Little Girls Made Of? The Roots of Feminine Stereotypes.* New York: Schocken Books, 1976.

Doray, Marie-France. *La Comtesse de Ségur: une étrange paroissienne.* Paris: Rivages, 1990.

Gibson, Lois Rauch. "Beyond the Apron: Archetypes, Stereotypes, and Alternative Portrayals of Mothers in Children's Literature." *Children's Literature Association Quarterly* 13 (Winter 1988): 177–81.

Gilbert, Sandra, and Susan Gubar. *The Madwoman in the Attic: The Woman Writer and the Nineteenth-Century Literary Imagination.* New Haven: Yale University Press, 1979.

Greer, Germaine. *Sex and Destiny: The Politics of Human Fertility.* New York: Harper Colophon Books, 1984.

Grimm, Jacob. *Grimm's Tales for Young and Old.* Trans. Ralph Manheim. New York: Doubleday, 1977.

Hugo, Victor. *Les Misérables.* Trans. Charles E. Wilbour. New York: Random House, 1931.

Kreyder, Laura. *L'Enfance des saints et des autres: essai sur la comtesse de Ségur.* Fasano (Italy): Schena-Nizet, 1987.

Lastinger, Valérie Crêtaux. "Excentricité et conformisme: Sophie de Ségur, femme et écrivain." *Bulletin de la société des professeurs français en Amérique* (1988–89): 49–57.

Mathé, Sylvie. "La Poupée perdue: ordre et désordre dans *Les Petites Filles modèles* de la comtesse de Ségur." In *Theory and Practice of Feminist Literary Criticism,* ed. Gabriela Moora and Karen S. Van Hooft. Ypsilanti: Bilingual Press, 1982. 117–30.

Mill, John Stuart. "The Subjection of Women." In *The Feminist Papers*, ed. Alice S. Rossi. New York: Bantam Books, 1973. 196–238.

Nières, Isabelle. "Pour en finir avec le malheur de Sophie." *La Revue des livres pour enfants* 131 (Spring 1990): 62–73.

———. "Quelques adaptations des *Malheurs de Sophie:* de la métamorphose à l'anamorphose." *La Revue des livres pour enfants* 101 (Spring 1985): 54–60.

Rousseau, Jean-Jacques. *Emile, ou de l'éducation.* Paris: Garnier-Flammarion, 1966.

Ségur, Sophie de. *La Fortune de Gaspard.* In *Oeuvres.* 3 vols. Paris: Bouquins, Robert Laffont, 1990. Vol. 3.

———. *Les Malheurs de Sophie.* In *Oeuvres.* 3 vols. Paris: Bouquins, Robert Laffont, 1990. Vol. 1.

———. *Les Petites Filles modèles.* In *Oeuvres.* 3 vols. Paris: Bouquins, Robert Laffont, 1990. Vol. 1.

———. *Les Vacances.* In *Oeuvres.* 3 vols. Paris: Bouquins, Robert Laffont, 1990. Vol. 1.

Soriano, Marc. *Guide littérature pour la jeunesse: courants, problèmes, choix d'auteurs.* Paris: Flammarion, 1975.

Soriano, Marc. "Bibliothèque rose ou série noire?" Introduction to Sophie de Ségur, *La Fortune de Gaspard.* Paris: Jean-Jacques Pauvert, 1972. ix–lx.

# From Master to Brother:
## Shifting the Balance of Authority in
## *Ursula K. Le Guin's* Farthest Shore
## *and* Tehanu

### Len Hatfield

In literature as in "real life," women, children, and animals are the obscure matter upon which Civilization erects itself, phallologically. That they are Other is (*vide* Lacan *et al.*) the foundation of language, the Father Tongue. . . .

By climbing up into his head and shutting out every voice but his own, "Civilized Man" has gone deaf. He can't hear the wolf calling him brother—not Master, but brother. He can't hear the earth calling him child—not Father, but son. He hears only his own words making up the world. He can't hear the animals, they have nothing to say. Children babble, and have to be taught how to climb up into their heads and shut the doors of perception. No use teaching woman at all, they talk all the time, of course, but never say anything. This is the myth of Civilization, embodied in monotheisms which assign soul to Man alone. [Le Guin, *Buffalo Gals* 9–10]

In recent years Ursula K. Le Guin has taken up an explicitly feminist position in a passionately energetic critique of patriarchal culture.[1] But these lines also show her understanding of the structural parallels between patriarchy's marginalization of children and its repression of women (as well as "unruly men" and the other "animal presences" of her *Buffalo Gals* collection). In many ways, the transition from the third and once last book in the Earthsea series,[2] *The Farthest Shore,* to the fourth book, *Tehanu,* marks a similar move from a representation of patriarchal structures of authority to a critique and displacement of them by means of a "mother tongue," a phrase Le Guin has usefully borrowed and developed from feminist theory.[3] This form of language has long been both hidden and neglected in Western culture, and Le Guin represents it thus in the fictive world of Earthsea.

*Children's Literature* 21, ed. Francelia Butler, Christine Doyle Francis, Anne K. Phillips, and Julie K. Pfeiffer (Yale University Press, © 1993 The Children's Literature Foundation, Inc.).

But to think about authority in literary works solely in representational terms may obscure the ways that texts also use rhetorical structures either to legitimate or to undercut their representations of authority. Le Guin explores the problems of legitimacy with particular clarity in *The Farthest Shore* and *Tehanu*. In structural terms, the new volume creates a fresh transition between the ending (third and fourth) volumes of the series. These new transitional structures provide readers an excellent arena for observing patterns of narrative authority at work.

The Earthsea novels use a sophisticated narrative technique—shifting the point of view from the mimetic to the diegetic level—in order to present their thematic representations of social and cultural patterns of authority.[4] *The Farthest Shore* shows the patriarchal world of "old" Earthsea and suggests how authority can be used and abused within a male-dominated cultural system by focusing readers' attention on the dynamics of authority between adults and children in the relationship of Ged and Arren. In contrast, *Tehanu* provides a powerful critique of such repressive social patterns in its representations of the passing of the old order and advent of a new, more genuinely human one, particularly in the web of relations that encompass Tenar and those around her. Yet the narrative structures in each novel reinforce the point of these representations—that identical energies and social patterns account for the parallel repressions of children and women. Readers who attend not only to Le Guin's representations of authority in Earthsea but to the narrative structures of these novels can develop a richer understanding of Le Guin's analyses of cultural and narrative patterns of authority.

To take my responses as indicative of such a readerly evolution, I begin reading *The Farthest Shore*, the third book, already cherishing its fictive world of island and village folk, its magic, and its simple, elegant assertions of the great Taoist principle of Equilibrium. In this world, the "Old Speech"—the "language of true names"—has the power to transform, reveal, and bind; its authority rests on these powers, as well as on its antiquity and its part in the Making, the founding of the world. As a reader, I am easily caught up in the book's descriptions of spaces and characters. By following the series, I have become comfortable with its depictions of village life, its stories of travel, the ancient and dangerous wisdom of its dragons, and the quietly mysterious power of its mages.

But as many readers know, *The Farthest Shore* places these wonders in desperate doubt: magic is leaving the world, and toward the end of the book, even the Old Speech no longer avails. In a painful testing of the mimetic world's constitution, Earthsea begins to look in the penultimate book of the series much like an outward-facing mirror, a picture of our "real" world—too often a hard and gritty place where motives are seldom simple and magic rarely works.

*The Farthest Shore* puts further stress on its presentation of wonder whenever the storyteller takes on the protagonist's point of view: the narrator's sentences often collapse the diegetic and mimetic levels into one. For example, during the journey through the Southern Reaches when Arren begins to manifest the effects of the Dark Mage's influence, the narrator reports the boy's now cynical view of magic virtually from Arren's perspective, lending the authority of the tale's teller to the faulty viewpoint of the young prince: "There was nothing in magery that gave a man true power over men; nor was it any use against death. The mages lived no longer than ordinary men. All their secret words could not put off for one hour the coming of their death" (99). At such moments, the text invites readers (even those rereading the novel) to accept the view that Earthsea is dying. Yet we resist this invitation by reminding ourselves of the bigger picture—the view from that most diegetic level in which the larger order of the volume in hand becomes apparent (we know how it will end). From this vantage, readers can take in the openings and endings of each book and so understand how these structures, too, convey certain kinds of authority. More important, perhaps, readers may find encouragement because the whole created by the series steadily undercuts the immediate claim, at times so convincing in *The Farthest Shore,* that things are falling apart. In spite of such traumas, that is, we keep rereading the book.

This readerly ambivalence arises from the ways that narrative texts in general claim authority for themselves, and these tactics for claiming textual authority recur in Le Guin's other children's books. Le Guin frequently provides her readers with mimetic situations that expose problems with adult authority. In *Catwings,* for example, when Susan and Hank find the winged kittens playing in an empty field, the children keep the secret because they are convinced that people (the adults) will fail to understand and preserve these wonders; Hank says, "You know how people are" (38). In a parallel way, in "Buffalo Gals, Won't You Come Out Tonight," a child who is the sole survivor of a plane crash finds sustenance and heal-

ing among the mythic animals of the wilderness, particularly the
not-so-adult coyote, a trickster-like female character who glories in
freedom, instability, and irregularity. Although the child eventually
returns to the adult world, she does so only after she has come to
perceive the world's great mythic cycles and the spirits of its places
and animals from outside the domain and authority of adults. Social
structures and traditions in Earthsea likewise emphasize the ways
children must negotiate with adult authorities. It is especially easy
to see this pattern if we look closely at the structures of authority in
Earthsea's adult traditions and institutions for magic.[5]

Much like other fantasies that echo the history of medieval
Europe, the Earthsea books represent the adult authority system
of magic in hierarchies reminiscent of monarchic governments,
guilds, and priestly or scholarly orders. Earthsea's magical system
shows authority descending in two ways, from a historical and a
supernatural source, and in this it patterns itself after the ancient
political and religious systems of Taoism. As a number of scholars
have shown, the greatest source of magical power in Earthsea is the
Old Speech;[6] both mages and dragons assert power and authority
by their use of this ancient language, but their power is itself expressed in hierarchies. Among humans, where authority accrues
from the largely historical sources of tradition and discipline, the
guildlike order of the magical system is apparent in rankings according to power and knowledge (from "mere" weather workers
up the ladder to true mages and the Council of the Wise on Roke
Island, where young mages are trained). Echoing its medieval European counterpart, and adapting the principle of noblesse oblige,
this power structure brings responsibility to those privileged by it.
As Ged often demonstrates in *The Farthest Shore*, the Archmage
must both protect and restore those weaker than himself.

The supernatural aspect of authority arises from the magical
power that the language of the Making provides, and the richest
examples of this power are the dangerously wise dragons, creatures that embody both the historical and supernatural elements
of magical power through their inherent antiquity and their use
of the Old Speech. These beings bear great authority, an influence
only increased by their willingness to attack humans and by an alien
mentality that makes their conversation seem both true and untrue
to human listeners. Dragons constitute a dangerous potential for
Earthsea: they threaten the stability of the magical order of the
secondary world, and the mages are their counterbalance.

Authority in Earthsea also derives from achievement and association; early on, Ged speeds his rise in the magical system by becoming a Dragon Lord, a man who can deal on equal terms with
these creatures. Indeed, one way to assess mimetic authority in the
first three Earthsea books is to distinguish the kinds of mastery that
the male characters demonstrate, a distinction pointed up by the
contrasting connotations traditionally assigned to "masterly" and
"masterful." The "masterly" Ogion, for example, acts quietly yet
effectively in the manner of a master whenever we encounter him.
By contrast, we get a full demonstration of the "masterful," with its
suggestions of arrogance and pomposity, when young Ged attempts
to demonstrate his magical superiority over Jasper in an adolescent
contest in *The Wizard of Earthsea.*[7] Thus, it is tempting to align these
senses of "mastery" with what might be called the adult and child
views of authority—so that "masterly," the quiet one, would be considered the "adult" view, while "masterful," the arrogant one, would
become the child's view of this quality.

Nevertheless, and despite the temptation, the novels resist our
impulse to reduce these complex dynamics to an either-or division:
even in the patriarchal sections of the series, a successful Dragon
Lord is not simply masterful (and childish) or masterly (and adult).
Ged cannot be just masterly in his handling of the great dragons
of Earthsea—he must be masterful. His authority rests not only on
the quiet, somewhat retiring manner of "masterliness," which we
associate with his mentor, Ogion the Silent, but as much upon the
balance of such restraint with the more aggressive, display-oriented
manner of the "masterful." Were he unable to show himself full of
mastery, he could not face the dragons—a fact underscored whenever Ged speaks to these wonders. Not only must he cry fiercely to
them in the Old Speech because he is, relatively, so small, but he
must also demonstrate by his posture that he deserves their respect.
As he comments hoarsely after an interview with Orm Embar in *The
Farthest Shore,* "It is not easy—talking with dragons" (153).[8] Most of
Ged's dragon visits should remind readers of our images of circus
lion-tamers: in both cases, the spectacle is nearly as important as the
relationship, and the tamer in these threatening situations adopts
the role of the authoritative master but balances this posture with a
keen awareness of the animals' power.

Such a comforting view of balanced mastery in the old Earthsea, however, obscures an important detail: in the first three Earthsea books, the relationships of power are represented as occurring

solely between dominant males and some form of the alien Other
(dragons, dark powers, children, or adolescents). In fact, this feature of Le Guin's secondary world is echoed in her more recent
comments, in "The Fisherwoman's Daughter," about her earlier
strategies for narratives about male heroes:

> Even when subverting the conventions, I disguised my subver-
> sions from myself. It took me years to realize that I chose to
> work in such despised, marginal genres as science fiction, fan-
> tasy, young adult, precisely because they were excluded from
> critical, academic, canonical supervision, leaving the artist free;
> it took ten more years before I had the wits and guts to see
> and say that the exclusion of these genres from "literature"
> is unjustified, unjustifiable, and a matter not of quality but of
> politics. So too in my choice of subjects: until the mid-seventies,
> I wrote my fiction about heroic adventures, high-tech futures,
> men in halls of power, men—men were the central characters,
> the women were peripheral, secondary. [*Dancing at the Edge of
> the World* 233–34]

So where is the peripheral woman in the first three Earthsea
books? To the degree that the dragons represent a wild, powerful
Other, they may also suggest a view of woman from the perspective
of the patriarchy. The female is the source of inspiration (the muse)
but is also often an incomprehensible force of power, seductive and
dangerous. The male must approach the Other cautiously, and in
Earthsea as elsewhere, he must never look "It" in the eyes. Only
the exceptional male can be called a Dragon Lord—a label applied
from within the male-dominated, hierarchical system of authority.
To be able to communicate with the dangerous Other and survive
becomes a sign of "mastery."

This is not to say that Earthsea's dragons are female, even if their
gender is often not specified. Rather, they fulfill the role of symbolic
Otherness that patriarchy usually assigns to the female. Women, in
fact, are remarkably absent in both *Wizard* and *The Farthest Shore*,
whereas in *The Tombs of Atuan* (volume two) Le Guin presents an
almost exclusively female community and dragons do not appear.
On reflection, then, it is not surprising to find parallels between the
women and dragons of Earthsea, provided we recall that women
constitute a hidden, neglected Other within the patriarchal order:
throughout the first three volumes, women's magic is denigrated by

the mage-hierarchy but remains functional. It is also *subterranean*, dark, groping, and sometimes associated with the dark Powers of the Earth.[9]

In *Tehanu,* for the first time in the series, the text explicitly connects the dragons and patriarchy's hidden Other, first in the old Dragon Woman whom Tenar recalls (144) and most powerfully in the child Tehanu at the novel's end. In this one character, Le Guin unifies patriarchy's external Other (the symbolic Woman) with its internal Other (those characters she had made secondary and peripheral in the first three books).[10] Indeed, all the female characters in *Tehanu* serve the still larger goal of helping to write a new fictive era in which such ancient oppositions as self-other and male-female can merge into a powerful and widely inclusive web of relations.

But patriarchal Earthsea's magical system also highlights its opposite, the potential danger against which it is designed as a ward or boundary. Indeed, both *Wizard* and *The Farthest Shore* pose their moral (and cosmic) dilemmas largely in terms of the hierarchy of this magic system, where a figure of great natural power attempts to use his ability either without proper training (as in Ged's case) or from outside the boundaries of established values (in Cob's). These figures threaten the limits that allow the world to exist— boundaries echoed in the systematic ranking of magicians and the restraint of their powers for good. More simply, this mimetic system of authority restrains chaos, a common-enough goal of adult authority.

Young Ged and, later, Cob question the magical system in ways reminiscent of the challenges children make to adult authority. Both wish to circumvent the slow and limited ways of adults in favor of immediate rewards and fulfillments of desire. Ged's adolescent assault on adult authority in Roke erupts as an attempt to break through the discipline of the system in order to claim what he sees as his proper status. Cob similarly despises limits—in particular, the one imposed by death—and (like Ged), convinced of his power, he pursues and appears to achieve eternal life whatever the cost.

Indeed, the final confrontation between these two mages further maps their conflicts with authority onto the relationships among children and adults. Finally unmasked and powerless in the land of death, Cob reveals his fear at not being able to close or even escape the hole he has made in the world, a breach associated with immortality throughout the novel. In his attempt to master the world and retain his self forever, Cob has created a cosmic imbalance, rejecting the natural cycle of life and death. Reiterating his obsession with his deeds, he moans in a "mixture of despair and vindictiveness, terror and vanity" that he can neither control nor escape his destructive creation (181). Yet, like a father setting to rights the misdeeds of a child, Ged relentlessly but gently brings Cob to realize his errors before sealing the hole and releasing into death this figure who never really grew up (184–85).

The traditional alignments of selfishness, shortsightedness, and impatience with the "childish" and innocence, joyfulness, and vulnerability with the "childlike" seem to fit this resolution well. The similar challenges Ged and Cob make against adult authority arise because of their refusal or inability to understand the necessity of limitation in the great balance of Earthsea: in the secondary world of Earthsea, real power requires limitation; life balances with death. Ged makes the point explicitly in explaining Cob's confusions to the Dark Mage:

> Did you not understand? Did you never understand, you who called up so many shadows from the dead, . . . even . . . Erreth-Akbe, wisest of us all? Did you not understand that he, even he, is but a shadow and a name? His death did not diminish life. Nor did it diminish him. He is there—*there*, not here! Here is nothing, dust and shadows. There, he is the earth and sunlight, the leaves of trees, the eagle's flight. He is alive. And all who ever died, live; they are reborn and have no end, nor will there ever be an end. All, save you. For you would not have death. You lost death, you lost life, in order to save yourself. [180]

Denying Cob's attempts to arrest change and create a self-centered immortality, Ged shows that the only eternal life possible in Earthsea is the unending life of the system. In that web of life and death, "A living body suffers pain, . . . a living body grows old; it dies. Death is the price we pay for our life and for all life" (180). In effect, the adolescent Ged and the adult Cob pit their considerable child-talents and, later, their magical skills against that system and lose.

Of course, the differing qualities of these losses demonstrate alternate strategies for resolving conflicts of desire with authority: in refusing to mature, Cob resists and enlarges the reach of his challenge until he is finally forced to accept his limits in death.[11] By contrast, in "growing up," Ged submits to and internalizes the structure of authority, transforming lawless into lawful desire and later reaching the pinnacle of the magical system of authority as the Archmage. This adult retains childlike delight in playful art magic and manages some of his greatest accomplishments by following the innocence of children like Prince Arren. Such a pattern suggests an important underlying theme in all of the first three Earthsea books: after coming to awareness, children discover that adult systems of authority exist and must soon negotiate a relationship with them. Maturing, or the "fruitful resolution" of this conflict, leads to wisdom, authority, and a certain freedom; refusing such resolution may provide short-term rewards but ultimately leads to a necessarily destructive imposition of limits.

As a reader thinking about Earthsea, I envisage mostly this secondary world and its characters, the ones who live within the magical hierarchy. But I enrich my perceptions of this representation when I begin to notice the behavior of the storytellers, those detached yet intimate viewers constantly floating behind and sometimes seeming to see through the eyes of each protagonist. In this intermediate zone the diegetic and mimetic levels interact most clearly in establishing the authority of the larger whole of each novel and, larger still, of the series itself.

In general, in each book the narrator adopts the limited omniscient perspective, ranging relatively closer or farther from the protagonists and other characters. From a distance, the tale teller reveals the characters' errors and joins the reader in mocking characters' foibles. The narrator's nearness promotes authenticity of feeling, so that we read not only a description of inner attitudes but also an enactment of their effects on the character's perceptions. The narrator's varying stance also gives us an anchor for the range of other adult perspectives in the mimetic world, one possible "normal" or "adult" view among many. The varying adult authorities differentiate themselves by their relationship to the child protagonist, from those adults who are supportive and helpful to those who are hostile and dangerous. This pattern of child-adult relationships occurs throughout the series, for example, in the contrast between Duny's abusive and neglectful father (the village smith) and Ogion, his name-giver and true father in *Wizard*. Readers similarly follow Tenar as she transforms into Arha, and the narrator helps us assess the subtle differences among her harsh and demanding false mothers in *Tombs*. The design concludes in Arren's evolving relationship with Sparrowhawk in *The Farthest Shore*. In each case, the narrator adopts sufficient distance to show us the variety of adult figures of authority, inviting us to be aware of their strengths and limitations, and encouraging us to assess their role in hindering or helping the young protagonist's development.[12]

Perhaps the best moments to watch the narrator's moves to reinforce mimetic authority come when the child protagonist is deeply confused, so that readers must try to decide which view (the child's or the adult-narrator's) is authoritative after all. For example, in *The Farthest Shore*, Arren's resentment of Ged's highly un-mage-like behavior seems to color everything he sees. Sailing with the older man far from charted waters, the boy increasingly suffers the creeping doubt that spreads under the Dark Mage's influence. But what is intriguing is how the narrator quietly embraces this viewpoint. Speaking of Ged, she begins from outside Arren: "Arren saw now what a fool he had been to entrust himself body and soul to this restless and secretive man" (99). But almost at once the teller slightly shifts her relation with Arren, so that the spoken view seems almost indistinguishable from the boy's. Now Sparrowhawk's problem isn't only his own, but something that troubles the whole world, a general "failure of wizardry . . . among men" (99). Worse, Arren knows more than this old coot about the "real" situation in the world. Adopting a tone of finality, the narrator subtly shifts the claim of authority from a personal observation to one that encompasses all Earthsea: "It was clear now that to those who knew the secrets, there were not many secrets to [the] art magic. . . . Reality was not changed" (99). Here the narrator seems to sit within Arren and speak his confusion, irritation, and resentment. Naturally, this partially reliable narration increases Arren's credibility by making us feel as he does from within. But paradoxically, by placing his disaffection in the foreground, the narrator's collusion with the child's view causes readers to contrast Arren's assessment with the Ged-characters of the previous volumes. As a result of this momentary switch to the diegetic level, the boy's view becomes less credible, so that even as we feel the mimetic authority of his perceptions and responses, we also discount them.

Such back-and-forth movement between these levels accounts for much of the rich ambivalence of the reading experience. It suggests that, when deep in the mimetic moment and "identifying" with Arren, the reader may not be thinking about the larger pattern of things. Thus, when Arren repeatedly questions Ged's real powers and motives, because of the narrator's shifting so closely to the prince's point of view, we see two things at once, listen to two contending claims of authority. On the diegetic level, Arren simply falls more and more under Cob's spell. Yet on the mimetic level, his questioning happens often and compellingly enough that it seems to rise to a nearly diegetic authority, so that the whole narrative fabric starts to look flimsy—as if all Earthsea (its wonders, magic, dragons, and mages) were nothing but a lovely child's story, not now credible. As a result, before the end I feel uncomfortably close to Arren who sees "nothing with the clear eyes of despair" (106).

When Ged eventually reseals the doorway between nothing (the external world's wretchedness) and this fictive (childlike) world of magic and dragons, most readers rejoice. That we do arises from the nearly diegetic authority the narrator has lent to the child's mimetic viewpoint. Like Arren, we learn from the inside that what he thought was the "adult" view of the world (that of Cob and the various bereft ones we meet along the way) is after all but a child-ish confusion.

This is compelling artistry: Le Guin balances us between thinking Ged *is* fooling himself and thinking he isn't. When Le Guin's narrator colludes with the text's fictive systems of authority, she reinforces our experience of characters' negotiating their relationships with various adult authorities, a feature of the mimetic level. But these collusions also serve the authorial purpose of teaching by showing instead of by telling. It is through this switching between narrative levels of authority, moreover, that the text creates the situational ironies that in turn encourage readers to identify with one view and not another, helping us to assign an effectively balanced mixture of mimetic and diegetic authority to characters' perceptions and feelings.

Another compelling example of this narratorial play with the protagonist presents itself in what the series calls the "last book of Earthsea," *Tehanu.* It is manifest that every central character in the foregoing books undergoes a process of development or growth and that in each book Le Guin enriches the reader's experience by frequently realigning the relationship between protagonist and narrator. But in *Tehanu* this realignment takes on a considerably larger range of reference, not least because of the book's claim to be the last in the series.

In addition to this enhanced sense of closure, readers face several other important shifts in the final book. The structures of authority are no longer presented largely in terms of the conflicts of the child and adult views of this social power. In fact, because Tenar, the girl we met in *Tombs of Atuan,* is the protagonist, now an older woman, it might be argued for a moment that this last book is not part of the series in the same way that the earlier tales are: this seems hardly to be a children's story at all.

But this is precisely how Le Guin makes the point that patriarchal adult males ignore or repress children in virtually the same ways they do women. Mimetically speaking, *Tehanu* still explores the lack of authority experienced by figures on the "edges" of power, but this time it is not only children but also women and powerless men who provide the text's sharp critique of existing types of authority. In this regard, the last book of Earthsea evokes the spirit of Le Guin's commencement address at Bryn Mawr College in 1986. Challenging the graduates to deny the oppressions of "our schools and colleges, institutions of the patriarchy," Le Guin observes that such training teaches us all "not to listen to the mother tongue, to what the powerless say, poor men, women, children: not to hear that as valid discourse" (*Dancing at the Edge of the World* 151). *Tehanu* demonstrates how the mimetic world of Earthsea has also taught such inattention and silencing, not only to the perverse, such as the revolting child- and woman-abuser Handy and the misogynistic dark mage Aspen, but even to the respectable men of power. This last becomes clearest when we see the various male characters respond to Tenar's attempts to point the way to the new archmage.

*Tehanu* opens just after Cob's defeat, with Earthsea suffering a crisis of authority provoked by Ged's disappearance. His later reappearance turns out to be precisely opposite of what we might have hoped: as the postscript of *The Farthest Shore* foretells, Ged is a man returned powerless, less Dragon-Lord than Dragon-Baggage. Ged's inability to resume control at the center of patriarchal power on Roke creates a vacuum at the top of the hierarchy: though a king has been placed on the long vacant throne, there is now no one to take up the symmetrically male position of power as leader of the mages. Worse, the normal processes for discovering a successor archmage have produced little more than an ambiguously mysterious clue, so far as the Council of the Wise can understand:

the Master Namer's trance vision allows him to say only "a woman on Gont" (142). The Master Windkey delivers this news, yet in spite of his sensitivity and genuine commitment to goodness and knowledge, the mage cannot even grasp Tenar's suggestion that the new figure of power might actually be a woman, as he demonstrates by observing, "'A woman'—not much to go on! Evidently this woman is to guide us, show us the way, somehow, to our archmage" (144). Tenar remembers the old fisherwoman's claim that she had once lived with dragons themselves, that most transcendentally authoritative group in Earthsea. But she cannot tell the Windkey this truth, largely because he simply cannot hear it. Even though she likes him, she knows he will not hear her marginal mother language: "His deafness silenced her. She could not even tell him he was deaf" (144).

Indeed, readers encounter here one of the mimetic world's most radical shifts in key, as Tenar tries to break through the mage's patriarchal deafness in order to suggest a completely other form of magic in Earthsea. After he has agreed that the Roke masters will be many years at work to restore the old magical order, Tenar tries to make her point: "I wonder if there might be more to be done than repairing and healing. . . . Could it be that one such as Cob could have such power because things were already altering . . . that a change, a great change, has been taking place, has taken place?" (144). Again the mage mistakes her concern for fear about her own safety, but Tenar argues that the great change in Earthsea may well have created the conditions for the arrival of the new king, Lebennen, a young man who has escaped the institutional deafness of his elders and who listens carefully to her. It is to Lebennen, finally, that she can present her suspicion: "Couldn't it be that there's a woman on Gont, I don't know who, . . . but it could be that there is, or will be, or may be, a woman, and that they seek—that they need—her. Is it impossible?" (146). Even with Lebennen, Tenar must speak tentatively, proceeding by questions and self-qualifications rather than by strong assertions. The narrator observes dryly that Lebennen "listened. He was not deaf. But he frowned, intent, as if trying to understand a foreign language" (146). Though still learning this "foreign language," the young man we saw growing up in *The Farthest Shore* as Arren continues to grow as the new king Lebennen. In this he offers hope that some of the powerful males in Earthsea may change.

Although formerly one of the most powerful males, Ged has

saved the world but returned as one of those "powerless men" to whom the great (males) do not listen. Ged's only hope of recovery comes from retreating to simple life as a goatherd. Lacking the power of magic, the exhausted Sparrowhawk must relearn how to live in the world—including how to cope with fear, pain, and violence but also love, sexual desire, and family life. Just as Ged taught Tenar to pursue her identity and name in *Tombs*, so she now teaches Sparrowhawk the ways of the ordinary world. In this, she quietly enacts her own matriarchal tongue, demonstrating a fresh way to authorize and legitimize behavior by connecting it to the average lives of the human community.

Le Guin here parallels Tenar's newly emerging authority with Carol Gilligan's recent work on the psychological and ethical development of women.[13] In discussing how women artists have often worked in the very midst of their family lives, Le Guin paraphrases Gilligan's theory of a male "ethics of rights," which contrasts sharply with a female "ethics of responsibility": "A man finds it (relatively) easy to assert his 'right' to be free of relationships and dependents . . . while women are not granted and do not grant one another any such right, preferring to live as part of an intense and complex network in which freedom is arrived at, if at all, mutually" ("Fisherwoman's Daughter" 231n). This captures effectively the emphasis in an ethics of responsibility upon the web of relationships in a social community: Tenar brings the "fallen" Ged back into the lives of her people, introduces him to the web, as it were. This system of ethics tends not to produce heroes, the hierarchically elevated mages or lords, but instead to promote the connections among "ordinary" people.

The ending of *Tehanu* demonstrates the correctness of Tenar's uncertain and "ordinary" magic—first in the glorious return of the great dragon, which happily ends the reign of Aspen's misogynistic reign of hatred and brutality, replete with enslavement, violence, torture, and threatened death—both for Tenar and the powerless Ged. But more important, this ending also seems to "repay" Therru, the abused girl, for her suffering, because she is revealed to be the Tehanu, or summer star, a dragon-child. She is the "long looked-for" of the Segoy, in the earlier books identified as the one who had founded the world and here called Kalessin, the eldest dragon; she embodies the reunion of human and dragons that promises a return to the golden age of Earthsea. All this comes through the child-victim, a physical embodiment of the excluded speakers who have been largely silenced in the patriarchal order of Earthsea.

These revisions in the mimetic structures of authority in Earthsea signal a powerful expression of diegetic feminist concern. But the newly explicit feminist ideology is, again, effectively underscored by Le Guin's manipulation of the narrator's stance and relation with the protagonist. Throughout *Tehanu,* the narrator has moved in to focus on events through Tenar's viewpoint, giving readers an interior perspective on her fears, anxieties, anger, and hope. As in *Tombs,* Ged is observed only from the outside, which has the effect, in the "new world" of *Tehanu,* of empowering the female (once ignored) viewpoint. Because the female perspective has become central, the narrator can legitimize the evocative but non-linear thinking of Aunty Moss, the old witch woman: "Nobody had ever taught her to think consecutively. Nobody had ever listened to what she said. All that was expected, all that was wanted of her was muddle, mystery, mumbling. She was a witchwoman. She had nothing to do with clear meaning" (50). From the newly centralized women's view readers also gain a terrifying clear perception of the effects of Aspen's misogynistic hatred during his final assault on Tenar and Ged.

What happens in *Tehanu* is finally more than simple narratorial collusion with the book's main themes. Because of Le Guin's adroit movement forth and back across the text's mimetic-diegetic boundaries, readers can experience the book's expression of the mother tongue even in the order of the plot. In this insistence on our awareness of these interpenetrating domains of narrative, she echoes the textual moves of *Always Coming Home,* in which the mother tongue has destructured traditional narrative order far more radically than in *Tehanu.* There the text has become fragmented, delinearized, and restructured in a "messy" way that forces readers to rethink the very process of learning the outlines of a secondary world in the first place—and all this in concert with the text's repeated self-reflexive allusions to its fictionality.

In contrast, *Tehanu* largely retains the traditional order of a folk narrative: beginning, middle, and end appear in their expected places, and plot sequence is nicely linear. Only at the level of the relation between this "last" and the three earlier books of Earthsea is the reader invited to see the intervention of the mother tongue

for what it is: a re-vision and restructuring of both the mimetic
and diegetic orders of authority in the series, precisely by means of
the travail and magical victory promised in the burned girl who is
revealed as the harbinger of a new world.

Language is the key to this transformation, and as we have seen,
Le Guin leads us to the alternative world through Earthsea's most
authoritative creatures. The dragons, guesses Ged, have a unique
relationship with the Old Speech of power and authority. As he
tells Therru, "Dragon and the speech of the dragon are one. One
being. . . . They do not learn, . . . They are" (196). To conceive
the dragons in this way is to see them as being free from a number
of patriarchal dilemmas—especially the binary oppositions of the
subject/object and the mind/body. In effect, Le Guin argues that
men's use of the Old Speech in the art magic of the old Earthsea
did not reach far enough in its understanding. The mother tongue
functions as a counterpoint to the traditional human (male) usage
of the Language of the Making, a critical heuristic, which points
toward a domain of experience and knowledge hitherto ignored.
Aunty Moss summarizes the difference between Father and mother
tongue earlier in the novel when thinking about the differences
in Earthsea between men and women. When Tenar asks, "What's
wrong with men?" the old woman suggests that men are bound up
inside their bodies in ways women are not: "A man's in his skin, see,
like a nut in its shell, and it's full of him. Full of grand man-meat,
manself. And that's all. That's all there is. It's all him and nothing else, inside" (51–52). By contrast, a woman has none of these
boundaries, nor their incipient oppositions: "Who knows where a
woman begins and ends?" asks Aunty Moss. For once clearly as-
serting her alternative and womanly form of authority in Earthsea, the old woman goes on: "I have roots, I have roots deeper
than this island. Deeper than the sea, older than the raising of the
lands. I go back into the dark. . . . Before the moon I was. No one
knows, . . . no one can say what I am, what a woman is, a woman
of power, a woman's power, deeper than the roots of islands . . .
older than the Making" (52). These are strong and expansive assertions of authority, yet they parallel the ways the mimetic world
has previously authorized the dragons themselves—women are em-
powered through their association with the language and time of
the world's creation, an association that suggests their power to do
and to endure quite beyond the limits of the patriarchal order that

has dominated Earthsea until now.[14] By linking the Language of the Making with the values associated with the mother tongue, Le Guin has revised the Old Speech from its previous role as a tool of the patriarchal order to a language of Being and Naming which focuses upon the ancestral and hitherto hidden realm of the female Other. The mother tongue works here much as it does in the Bryn Mawr Commencement Address as a parallel critical language pointing toward a world and a language that include the experiences and perceptions of males and females.[15]

Near its ending, the text further reinforces such a vision by a carefully calculated and dramatic shift in the narrator's point of view: for the first time in the book, we see events through Therru's perspective. The nearly silent and once dreadfully scarred child has had time to heal and discover something resembling family life with Ged and Tenar. Yet now she has the magical and, importantly, entirely untrained capacity to use the language of true names and to see through Aspen's binding/blinding spells, which hold her mother and father; she even knows the evil mage's true name: "The one called Aspen, whose name was Erisen, and whom she saw as a forked and writhing darkness" (219). With these abilities, she calls the eldest dragon and releases Aunty Moss from more of Aspen's death-dealing. As a result, readers quickly see that this is not exclusively a child: she speaks to the old witch woman "in the voice she had for these people" (220), and upon Kalessin's arrival she speaks with the Eldest in the Language of the Making (223). Tehanu-Therru becomes the future of magic in Earthsea, and the narrative diegetically reinforces this eruption of the marvelous by shifting between this "child's" viewpoint and that of the "ordinary" adults. To this degree, the last book of Earthsea becomes a beginning and, in keeping with Le Guin's pragmatic-romantic view of the child, embodies that beginning in a return to ordinary life and death at Ogion's rural retreat with the death of the peach tree that Tenar and the child have been growing throughout the narrative. This new family decides to stay in Ogion's old house, simply, as Tenar tells herself, because "I think we can live there" (225).

The thematic parallels between the dragons' unity of being and the hitherto hidden power of woman blend mimetically and diegetically in the book's ending and in the transformation of little burned Therru into the dragon-child, Tehanu. To human perception in Earthsea so far, dragons have been wild, fearsome, wonderful—

dangerously Other. Yet just as they need not learn the Language of the Making, so Tehanu demonstrates at the novel's climax a similarly immediate oneness of mind and language.

Tehanu's Otherness has been prepared throughout the book in references to the human-dragon relationship. This first occurs in the story that the old dragon-woman of Kemay sang to Ogion of the golden age when dragon and human were one species (9–13). Tenar's retelling of this to the still largely silent Therru prepares readers for her later discovery of the hitherto hidden side of weaver Fan's painted fan, which depicts great humans on one side and dragons grouped similarly on the reverse. When held to the light, however, the two representations meld, revealing that "the men and women were winged, and the dragons looked with human eyes" (105).

Thus, though to most of the characters Therru-Tehanu is an unlooked-for wonder, to readers she appears as the culmination of this series of hints and foreshadowings. Like the dragons, she sees the truth and acts as needed, unshackled by the habits of perception and language that constrain most of the adults in her world, shackles that provide Aspen a means of controlling Tenar, Aunty Moss, and Ged near the novel's end. Tehanu's liberation of all these adults, like her untutored calling of the eldest dragon, signals the reinstatement of women's language. For attentive readers, this becomes mother tongue speaking through a powerful melding of the mimetic and diegetic domains.

The Earthsea novels allow us to watch Le Guin rethink the ways adult males marginalize children and women, and these fictive reflections parallel sharply her nonfiction reactions to the same thing that is sometimes done to children's literature by a so-called adult viewpoint. As she put it in 1986, "We kiddilitters remain outsiders."[16] It is precisely this move to *silence* the child's or other peripheral voices speaking the "irrelevant" detail that provides such "adults" with the ability to do and to act decisively, but sometimes also insensitively or even wrongly. As Le Guin suggested about the Earthsea series in a recent interview, "Power is the central theme of all the books; what is power and who has it?" (Loer).

As a result of Le Guin's shift from implicit to explicit feminist critique of patriarchy between *The Farthest Shore* and *Tehanu*, the series offers a rebalancing of both its mimetic and diegetic patterns of authority. In the old Earthsea trilogy readers encounter representations (in Ged and Arren) of a hierarchical, male-dominated power structure that presents as its ideal the master, a man who enacts an authoritative mix of knowledge and power. This figure embodies the best aspects of male mastery, including a holistic adult view that succeeds because of its openness to and appropriations of childlike desires and motives and its retention of child delight but equally because of its (often compelled) rejection of the limitations of the Father Language.

In the new Earthsea that emerges from the advent of the star-child Tehanu, these implicit subversions of patriarchy become explicit as we watch Tenar move from unspoken and half-realized internal criticisms of the male order into the light of day and full expressions of the mother tongue. Here, the force of Le Guin's narrative technique also comes sharply into focus, as readers find themselves enacting narrative patterns of inclusion and connection rather than exclusion and hierarchy. In this both the representations and their structures move from an ethics of rights to an ethics of responsibility. Finally, in Earthsea, the marginalized speak, and men can become brothers (not masters) by learning to listen to and participate in the "ordinary" community with their mothers and sisters.

*Notes*

1. In recent years, Le Guin has signaled a change from what might be called an implicit to an explicit form of feminist discourse in many of her writings. That she feels this change to have been necessary and deep-delving appears, for example, in her reflections on being a "housewife-artist" in "The Fisherwoman's Daughter": "I was free—born free, lived free. And for years that personal freedom allowed me to ignore the degree to which my writing was controlled and constrained by judgments and assumptions which I thought were my own, but which were the internalized ideology of a male supremacist society" (*Dancing at the Edge of the World*, 233–34). Le Guin has discussed her self-redefinition as a feminist writer in interviews with Greenland, Neal, and (in relation to *Always Coming Home*) in a panel discussion at the Nineteenth Mythopoeic Conference in 1988, transcribed by David Bratman. Ann Whelton has also briefly discussed *Tehanu* and feminism.

2. The Earthsea series began with *A Wizard of Earthsea* (1968) and *The Tomb of Atuan* (1971). The first chronicles the development and early maturity of Ged, or Sparrowhawk, from his boyhood on Gont through his formal education and "mastery" of art magic. *Tombs of Atuan* focuses primarily upon Tenar's early life as Arha, the servant of dark powers; Ged eventually rescues Tenar and takes her with him to Earthsea.

3. See Garner, Kahane, and Sprengnether; Le Guin, "Bryn Mawr Commencement Address" and "Fisherwoman's Daughter," 149, 151–53, and 224n, respectively,

in *Dancing at the Edge of the World;* and Le Guin, "Introduction," *Buffalo Gals and Other Animal Presences.*

4. Genette divides a narrative's inner and outer domains into the mimetic and diegetic levels of textual authority; this differentiation helps refine our awareness of the many ways narratives make claims for authority in terms of their fictive as opposed to their "real world" referents. That is, mimetic authority is represented in the fictional world, while diegetic authority refers to the world encompassing the fictive one, starting with the operations of the narrator but moving quickly out to such matters as the text's style and organization, its relations with other texts, and finally its place in the "real" world. Mimetic authority is fictive; diegetic connects to us "out here" (see Genette 128–37). Dividing a text's claims to authority into mimetic and diegetic levels helps account for the reader's responses to the shifting codes of authority in each book and helps us understand the Earthsea series better as a whole.

5. These qualities, in turn, help create the books' diegetic authority—the legitimacy of the mimetic realm as a whole (the credibility of the "secondary world," in Tolkien's terms), by reinforcing our sense of the books' larger coherence and consistency. This holistic consistency is often cited as a means for evaluating the quality of fantasy fiction in general; see Tolkien or Rabkin for examples.

6. Le Guin's language of true names has been widely discussed; see, for example, Bittner, Bucknall, Crow and Erlich, Crowe, Esmonde, Gunew, Selinger, and Spivack.

7. See Fowler, who argues for just this kind of distinction. But in spite of these nuances of usage, *masterful* does underscore the power and even, to some degree, the bravado of the male master—that confidence which allows the bearer to outface opposition of all sorts, even the most awe-inspiring kind. It is important to note as well that these masterful types are almost exclusively male in Le Guin's Earthsea books.

8. Note the other dragon conversations in *Wizard* and *The Farthest Shore.* The sense of exhaustion he experiences before the grand and the magical finds an interesting echo in C. S. Lewis's *That Hideous Strength* whenever Ransom must talk with the planetary angels: both instances argue for human humility in the face of greater age, knowledge, wisdom, power, and authority—in effect, serving as a restatement of the Romantic theory of the sublime and its peculiar power to overwhelm the human observer.

9. A full development of this line of argument should also prove a fruitful way to approach *The Tombs of Atuan,* in which the dark Earth powers of the womblike death religion are served by a women's community. In Earthsea generally Le Guin represents such powers as ancient and inimical to "man" (witness the Stone that threatens to turn Ged into a Gibbeth in *Wizard,* as well as the ongoing danger these powers pose to him in his journeys in the labyrinth of *Tombs*). Because of this, Ged's rescuing Tenar from Atuan must be seen as a liberation from an evil oppression at the hands of a male "master."

At the same time, the women's community at Atuan is very much in the service of a larger male-directed exploitation of these ancient magical forces (as develops in the political struggle between Kossil, the priestess of the Godking, "the Man Immortal," and Arha, the "Eaten One" of the Nameless powers). In effect, a more balanced male master frees her from the oppressions of women serving less balanced ones.

The relations of light with dark forces associated with the Earth in *Tombs* repeats a pattern established in *Wizard* with the evil Terrenon Stone, owned by Benderesk, who claims to be Lord of the Terrenon even as he serves it. In both cases, these dark Earthly powers, although linked with women (Serret in *Wizard,* and the women's community in *Tombs*), principally serve the purposes of the male hierarchy, lending an ironic cast to the wisdom of the Roke Mages that "the Old Powers of the earth are not for men to use. They were never given into our hands, and in our hands they will work only ruin" (*Wizard*, 118). See Craig and Diana Barrow for an important parallel discussion of *Tombs* and *The Farthest Shore* (as well as *Tehanu* in a brief note, p. 41, n. 1), feminism, and anthropology.

10. A parallel description of women as patriarchy's hidden Other turns up earlier in *The Dispossessed*, when Shevek ponders the misogyny of Urrasti male scientists and suggests that deep within and unconsciously "they contained . . . a woman, a repressed, silenced, bestialized woman, a fury in a cage. He had no right to tease them. They knew no relation but possession. They were possessed" (60).

11. Cob amounts to the second alter-ego or shadow self (the first being his own raw desire for power, which Ged unleashed in *Wizard*), another vision of what Ged might have become had he not resolved his conflict with the adult system more fruitfully.

12. Consider Selinger's assessment of Duny's aunt, who first provides Duny the seeds of his future magical identity (26–28). The initiatory or developmental aspects of the first three books in the series have also generated much critical comment: see especially Crowe, Esmonde, and Selinger.

13. See, for example, Gilligan's *In a Different Voice* and "Woman's Place in a Man's Life," as well as Le Guin's "Fisherwoman's Daughter" and the "Bryn Mawr Commencement Address."

14. Aunty Moss's description of the reach of a woman's mind is a mythicized evocation of the fundamental differences between men and women, and it parallels recent feminist psychology's rethinking of women's development, particularly in the area of ego-boundaries. As Chodorow argues, from their earliest relationships, girls develop differently from boys: "Mothers tend to experience their daughters as more like, and continuous with, themselves. Correspondingly, girls tend to remain part of the dyadic primary mother-child relationship itself. This means that a girl continues to experience herself as involved in issues of merging and separation, and in an attachment characterized by primary identification and the fusion of identification and object choice." Mothers tend to regard their boy children in a contrasting way, as a "male opposite," so that "boys are more likely to have been pushed out of the preoedipal relationship and to have had to curtail their primary love and sense of empathic tie with their mother." This has the result of a "more emphatic individuation and a more defensive firming of ego boundaries" among boys and men (*Reproduction of Mothering*, 166, 167). These views provide effective support for Silverman's arguments in *The Subject of Semiotics* that theories of the psychological (and social) "subject" have been radically revised in the twentieth century, with increased emphasis placed on cultural mediation (especially in the processes of development) and less acceptance given to arguments based on spiritual or even biological (as Chodorow has it, "anatomical") foundations (see, for example, Silverman, chaps. 4, 5).

15. Le Guin argues in the Bryn Mawr Commencement Address that the mother tongue must erupt, volcano-like, to correct and coexist with the legitimate functions of the Father tongue. But her challenge to the graduating women in her audience is to have a clear understanding of the limitations of the male perspective: "I don't want what men have. I'm glad to let them do their work and talk their talk. But I do not want and will not have them saying or thinking or telling us that theirs is the only fit work or speech for human beings. Let them not take our work, our words, from us. If they can, they will, let them work with us and talk with us. We can all talk mother tongue, we can all talk father tongue, and together we can try to hear and speak that language which may be our truest way of being in the world, we who speak for a world which has no words but ours" (159).

16. In her review of Molly Gloss's *Outside the Gates* (New York: Atheneum, 1986) (*Dancing at the Edge of the World*, 297). But also see, for example, Le Guin's comments on "kiddilit" and the responses to children's literature by certain publishers and critics in such essays as "Dreams Must Explain Themselves" (in *The Language of the Night*), the Introduction to *Buffalo Gals and Other Animal Presences*, and "The Fisherwoman's Daughter" (*Dancing at the Edge of the World*).

## Works Cited

Barrow, Craig and Diana. "Le Guin's Earthsea: Voyages in Consciousness." *Extrapolation* 32 (Spring 1991): 20–44.

Bittner, James W. *Approaches to the Fiction of Ursula K. Le Guin.* Ann Arbor: UMI Research Press, 1979.

Bratman, David. "The Making of *Always Coming Home:* A Panel at Mythopoeic Conference XIX, Berkeley, California, July 31, 1988. Ursula K. Le Guin, Todd Barton, Margaret Chodos-Irvine, George Hersh, Panelists." *Mytholore* 65 (Spring 1991): 56–63.

Bucknall, Barbara J. *Ursula K. Le Guin.* New York: Ungar, 1981.

Chodorow, Nancy. *The Reproduction of Mothering.* Berkeley: University of California Press, 1978.

Crow, John H., and Richard D. Erlich. "Words of Binding: Patterns of Integration in the Earthsea Trilogy." Olander and Greenberg 200–239.

Crowe, Edith L. "Integration in Earthsea and Middle Earth." *San Jose Studies* 14 (1988): 63–80.

Esmonde, Margaret P. "The Master Pattern: The Psychological Journey in the Earthsea Trilogy." Olander and Greenberg 15–35.

Fowler, H. W. *A Dictionary of Modern English Usage.* Rev. Ernest Gowers. 2d ed. London: Clarendon, 1965.

Garner, Shirley Nelson, Claire Kahane, and Madelon Sprengnether, eds. *The (M)other Tongue: Essays in Feminist Psychoanalytic Interpretation.* Ithaca: Cornell University Press, 1985.

Genette, Gerard. *Figures of Literary Discourse.* New York: Columbia University Press, 1980.

Gilligan, Carol. *In a Different Voice: Psychological Theory and Women's Development.* Cambridge: Harvard University Press, 1982.

———. "Woman's Place in a Man's Life." In *Feminist Frontiers II: Rethinking Sex, Gender, and Society,* ed. Laurel Richardson and Verta Taylor. 2d ed. New York: McGraw-Hill, 1989.

Greenland, Colin. "Doing Two Things in Opposite Directions." *Interzone* (March 1991): 58–61.

Gunew, Sneja. "Mythic Reversals: The Evolution of the Shadow Motif." Olander and Greenberg 178–99.

Lassiter, Rollin A. "Four Letters about Le Guin." In *Ursula K. Le Guin: Voyager to Inner Lands and to Outer Space,* ed. Joe De Bolt. Port Washington, N.Y.: Kennikat Press, 1979. 89–114.

Le Guin, Ursula K. *Buffalo Gals and Other Animal Presences.* New York: Penguin, 1990.

———. *Catwings.* Illustrations by S. D. Schindler. New York: Orchard Books, 1988.

———. *Dancing at the Edge of the World.* New York: Grove Press, 1989.

———. *The Dispossessed.* New York: Avon, 1974.

———. *The Farthest Shore.* New York: Bantam, 1975.

———. *The Language of the Night.* New York: Putnam, 1979.

———. *Tehanu.* New York: Atheneum, 1990.

————. *The Tombs of Atuan.* New York: Bantam, 1975 [orig. publ. 1971].

————. *A Wizard of Earthsea.* New York: Bantam, 1975 [orig. publ. 1968].

Lewis, C. S. *That Hideous Strength.* New York: Macmillan, 1965.

Loer, Stephanie. "'Earthsea' Story Focuses on the Power of Women." Review of *Tehanu. Boston Globe,* May 21, 1990, 38.

Neill, Heather. "Strong as Woman's Magic." *Times Educational Supplement,* November 9, 1990, R9.

Olander, Joseph D., and Martin H. Greenberg, eds. *Ursula K. Le Guin.* New York: Taplinger, 1979.

Rabkin, Eric S. *The Fantastic in Literature.* Princeton: Princeton University Press, 1976.

Selinger, Bernard. *Le Guin and Identity in Contemporary Fiction.* Ann Arbor: UMI Research Press, 1988.

Silverman, Kaja. *The Subject of Semiotics.* New York: Oxford University Press, 1983.

Spivack, Charlotte. *Ursula K. Le Guin.* Boston: Twayne, 1984.

Tolkien, J. R. R. "On Fairy Stories." In *The Tolkien Reader.* New York: Ballantine, 1966.

Welton, Anne. "Earthsea Revisited: *Tehanu* and Feminism." *VOYA* 14 (April 1991): 14–17.

# The Voice of Solitude:
# The Children's Verse of Walter de la Mare

Martha Bremser

One of the most widely held assumptions about children's literature is that if it is not overtly didactic or moralistic, it is in some way Utopian. Written by adults for a class of readers that (theoretically) does not include adults, children's literature must somehow be serving the escapist needs of its writers. In many cases the *guise* of children's literature appears to provide the writer with the freedom to express what he or she otherwise might not—either because the writer feels a special affinity with the child as distinct from an insensitive society (Edward Lear is a good example) or, more commonly, because childhood is seen as a safe haven in which to indulge fantasy urges, an amoral love for adventure, or even, in the case of someone like Lewis Carroll, slightly dangerous or subversive ideas. At the furthest extreme there is even literature that so exploits the world childhood is thought to represent that it loses sight of its supposed audience and distorts the original nature of the subject that inspired it: J. M. Barrie's *Peter Pan* is the most obvious example. The critic Jacqueline Rose, pointing to the blatant expression of adult longing behind both Barrie's creation of a boy who would "never grow up" and the huge commercial success of subsequent editions and imitations (eagerly purchased, of course, by adults), makes the powerful statement that "children are not the cause of this literature. They are not the group for which it was created" (102).

But even that literature which is considered nonexploitative is nonetheless regarded as embracing, in some way, an adult ideal—because the author is reaching out to a world that no longer exists for him or her. The writers who first responded to a blossoming market in (nondidactic) children's literature in the mid- to late nineteenth century were, overtly or not, celebrating the notion of a child's uninhibited imagination by borrowing it for inspiration and so were elevating what was considered to be the child's uncorrupted nature and capacity for pure happiness. Of course, such ideas about

*Children's Literature* 21, ed. Francelia Butler, Christine Doyle Francis, Anne K. Phillips, and Julie K. Pfeiffer (Yale University Press, © 1993 The Children's Literature Foundation, Inc.).

the child's enviable qualities go further back in English literary history than the Victorian period and concern more than just works written *for* children. But without a doubt, the accepted norm has come to be that children's books represent the "Arcadia" of literature. As Humphrey Carpenter, defending this notion, claims, "All children's books are about ideals. Adult fiction sets out to portray and explain the world as it really is; books for children present it as it should be" (1).

Walter de la Mare, perhaps the most underrated children's poet of the twentieth century, departs from this Arcadian view in a radical way. He is a poet who uses highly conventional verse forms and whose work is full of literary echoes, and thus he may seem the last person imaginable to challenge accepted ideas. In many ways a misplaced Romantic, de la Mare wholeheartedly embraces Romantic critical philosophies and approaches the child with the idealism of early nineteenth-century celebrations of childhood's nature. Equally, his inheritance of Victorian values is far from critical. But in eerie, almost undetectable ways, a darker vision asserts itself in de la Mare's poetry both for and about children and suggests a view of the child that is the complete antithesis to the notion of blissful ignorance. It is to that side of de la Mare's work that I turn here, considering de la Mare's relation to certain important predecessors and defining his ultimate departure from their influence to a world disturbingly unlike Arcadia.

Of course, the question of "poetic influence" is difficult, even controversial; in thus considering the idea of an altered or revised tradition, it may seem inevitable to apply a particular theory of influence, such as Harold Bloom's. Certainly it is helpful to keep in mind the idea, as Bloom puts it, that "poetic influence . . . always proceeds by a misreading of the prior poet, an act of creative correction that is actually and necessarily a misinterpretation" (30). But Walter de la Mare's forefathers are many; and because de la Mare, if anything a cripplingly modest writer, does not fit into Bloom's model of a self-assertively "strong" poet, such an approach can only be limiting here. More important, as a close look at de la Mare reveals, the modifier in his altered vision is not the self-obsessed writer but the actual child himself, an image and symbol that the poet, rather like Keats inhabiting other modes of being in pursuit of "negative capability," *becomes*. And the key to the child's transforming qualities for the poet as creator is the condition of solitude— both wonderful and terrible—which de la Mare sees as the true life of the child and which therefore can be recognized as the most vital impulse behind his pursuit of a child's vision.

De la Mare's first and most notable inheritance of the image of the solitary child is from the Romantic poets and springs from the association between child and artist. In de la Mare's first poetry collection, *Songs of Childhood* (1902), a poem that became a classic (and perhaps over-quoted) piece of delaMarean fancy suggests that the poet's earliest affinities were with Coleridge: the child who announces, "If I were Lord of Tartary" not only brings to mind the Coleridgean ideal of childlike spontaneity, joy, and creative energy but actually ends up echoing some of Coleridge's most famous lines.[1]

> If I were Lord of Tartary,
>     Myself, and me alone,
> My bed should be of ivory,
>     Of beaten gold my throne;
>
> And in my court should peacocks flaunt,
> And in my forests tigers haunt,
> And in my pool great fishes slant
>     Their fins athwart the sun.

A subtle humor can be detected in these lines, for they capture the confident, bragging tone of the child carried away by imagination. But the deliberate focus on exultant solitude—"Myself and me alone"—reflects a more general emphasis on the creative properties of the inner self, thus leading to the poem's final rhapsodic celebration of the vision (which no longer needs the qualifying "If"), at once the voice of the boastful child and the very prototype of high Romantic style:

> Lord of the fruits of Tartary!
>     Her rivers silver-pale!
> Lord of the hills of Tartary,
>     Glen, thicket, wood and dale!
> Her flashing stars, her scented breeze,
> Her trembling lakes, like foamless seas,
> Her bird-delighting citron-trees
>     In every purple dale!                    [5–6]

The influence of Coleridge is obvious in the stanza's imagery and language; and the words "Her flashing stars, her scented breeze," bring to mind the unforgettable cry from "Kubla Khan"—"His flashing eyes! His floating hair!"—as if to bring the child's vision of that legendary kingdom into the realm of poet and mystic. A pedantic reviewer in 1902 quipped, "A little exalted for the child" (*The Bookman* 217)—perhaps missing the possibility of furtive wit in the young poet's juxtaposition of a child's boast with the language of Romantic grandeur. But more important, there lies behind this unabashed delight in childish "make-believe" a serious philosophy, which essentially locates the very source of human creativity in a child's first imaginative ventures. And the child's abandon to the creative inner self, of such great symbolic value for the Romantic poets, is here carried through and enacted in verse—through the voice and spirit of the child alone. As de la Mare puts it in a later essay, subconsciously or not excluding the artist from this privileged perspective, "There is no solitude more secluded than a child's, no absorption more complete, no perception more exquisite and, one might add, more comprehensive" (*Early One Morning* 176). For de la Mare, the child of quiet and "wonderment" is above all else the ideal towards which the poet strives; the child's special world is not merely a symbol to enlighten and inspire, but a "truth," his existence one of profound "inward reverie," a waking vision (*Pleasures* 177).

In thus pairing the child's instinctive solitude with a capacity for "reverie"—that state suggesting a closeness to further forms of knowledge, and not just happy impulsive fantasy—de la Mare shows perhaps a deeper affinity with Wordsworth. Throughout all of de la Mare's poetry, and not just his children's verse, there is a pervading sense of a lost spirituality on earth that might be connected with the "childhood" of the race, thus prompting the regret summed up in Wordsworth's words, "But yet I know, where'er I go, / That there hath passed away a glory from the earth." Wordworth's search backward into an earlier self was in many ways suggestive of a more universal search for humankind's previous lost existence, and in his poetry we see an underside to the traditional view of childhood innocence—a sense for childhood's mystery, which is what de la Mare then takes up and brings to his own version of pre-adult life. Out of his unconstrained, "unconscious intercourse" with the sug-

gestive mystery of his environment, de la Mare's child, like Wordsworth's, shows his access to the special kind of intuitive insight, or
"vision," which touches upon the deepest and most hidden forms of
human knowledge. Wordsworth's description of his childhood self
"commun[ing] with all that I saw as something not apart from, but
inherent in, my own immaterial nature" (*Poems and Prefaces* 537) is
reflected in de la Mare's prose writings about the "profound self-
communion" (*Pleasures* 177) of the child within his environment
and is echoed in countless poems that portray an outer world of
shadows and silences felt deeply by the child. Indeed, in a rare example of personal reflection upon his own childhood (in the late
long poem *Winged Chariot*, 1951), de la Mare depicts a very Wordsworthian encounter with a mysterious place, whose mute communication of meaning both frightens and intrigues the solitary child.
A strange door becomes to the imaginative child "the guardian of
an inner solitude"; though he does not grasp it entirely, the subject
here senses that his curiosity in such lonely play is about the self:

> Yet there was mystery too: those steps of stone—
> In the green paddock where I played alone—
>     Cracked, weed-grown,
> Which often lured my hesitant footsteps down
>
> To an old sun-stained key-holed door that stood,
> The guardian of an inner solitude,
> Whereon I longed but dreaded to intrude;
> Peering and listening as quietly as I could.
>
> There, as I knew, in brooding darkness lay
> The waters of a reservoir. But why—
> In deadly earnest, though I feigned, in play—
> Used I to stone those doors; then run away,
> Listening enthralled in the hot sunny day
> To echo and rumour; and that distant sigh,
> As if some friend profaned had made reply,—
> When merely a child was I?                           [558]

Here de la Mare's style of "recollection" shows strong similarities with Wordsworth's depiction of childhood, portraying not just
physical aloneness but a haunting, suggestive inner loneliness as an
essential quality of the child's life, and revealing a Nature that can
be mysterious, frightening, and strangely conscious. Like Words-

worth, de la Mare sees a relationship of spiritual oneness between the child and the living, nonhuman environment, and through their communion he glimpses a further world that hints of the eternal.

Where de la Mare differs, of course, is in the actual "children's verse," in which the speaker is not a poet recollecting previous states of being but is the child himself, standing within the very moment of immediate experience. De la Mare's child carries with him a Wordsworthian combination of deep perceptiveness and imaginative vigor, but more, he is the very one who tells of the continued childhood experience of being "haunted" by what his profound sensibility absorbs from the environment. It is the childlike willingness to wonder about the shadows that can bring beauty, even transcendence; and for de la Mare it unfolds in the telling—as in the experience of the child watching a "haunted" cottage in a wood as it changes in the light of the setting sun:

> From out of the wood I watched them shine,—
>     The windows of the haunted house,
> Now ruddy as enchanted wine,
>     Now dark as flittermouse.
>
> .   .   .   .   .   .   .   .   .   .   .   .   .   .
>
> The twilight rain shone at its gates,
>     Where long-leaved grass in shadow grew;
> And back in silence to her mates
>     A voiceless raven flew.
>
> Lichen and moss the lone stones greened,
>     Green paths led lightly to its door,
> Keen from her lair the spider leaned,
>     And dusk to darkness wore.

De la Mare often begins with a place or a moment, and by entering the childlike state of receptive consciousness he builds an essential nonevent into a weird and rarefied experience, virtually making a story out of the very act of perception. The poet's capacity for weaving magical poetical "mood" recreates the enchanted stillness of a child's perceptive moment, but this is accompanied by a darker, more profound sense of awareness. An effective use of pause at the end of each stanza—"A voiceless raven flew"; "And dusk to darkness wore"—compounds the mystery, to suggest the child's overwhelming sensation of potent atmosphere and untold significance.

The poet now essentially "within" the child's mind, the gulf between actual observation and descriptive fancy disappears, and out of this single image of a lonely house, the enraptured child experiences— and relays—a timeless moment.

> Amidst the sedge a whisper ran,
>    The West shut down a heavy eye,
> And like last tapers, few and wan,
>    The watch-stars kindled in the sky.                [36]

De la Mare makes us feel that the child's sense of lonely wonder, as he peers upon a house in the wood or hides behind a bush to await the appearance of fairies, is the emblem and source of our own most poignant moments of awareness. But unlike a socialized adult, the child effortlessly sees beyond the beauty to the mystery, to the looming shadow of inexplicable meaning in the empty house at twilight. Here, through the child's mind and awareness, is that Keatsian suspension in unknowability, the negative capability of the mind to be "in uncertainties, Mysteries, doubts, without any irritable reaching after fact and reason" (Keats 43).

What we see more and more is de la Mare moving toward a complete embracing of the child's vision and sensibility, to the point of excluding the tempering or balancing influence of the adult poetic mind. His ability to retain the child's voice throughout and his determination to leave the half-knowing, suspended state of childlike vision without the qualifying effect of poetic "meditations" upon it suggest his belief that the reversion to childhood is the *only* way to experience fully the imaginative life. Yet—and this is crucial—for all this investing of childhood with profound levels of thought and being, de la Mare does not lose sight of the real, day-to-day child. The same child who feels eternity in the whisper of a breeze or whose utterance takes on the profundity of his awareness is the one who announces loudly and in a completely different mood:

> I can't abear a butcher,
>    I can't abide his meat.
> The ugliest shop of all is his,
>    The ugliest in the street . . .                    [140]

or who rails against the world's mysteries when in a mood of petulant boredom: "Why does the sun so silent shine?— / And what do I care if it does?" (140). This is not just evidence of de la Mare's continued desire to speak to an audience of real children, or the saving grace of humor, which keeps his verse from too heavy or sentimental a reverence toward the child. It indicates the consistency and seriousness of his first-person voice, which combines so effectively the inner speculations and outward sense of immediacy in a child's life.

De la Mare, then, may have inherited the image of the solitary child from the Romantics and given it life; but his use of the first-person child-speaker comes from a more recent predecessor. Robert Louis Stevenson's *Child's Garden of Verses* (1885) was in many ways the quintessential product of the Victorian Cult of the Child— indeed, the verses at times suggest that feeling of happy escape into the uncomplicated joys of childhood (especially when we remember that they were written when Stevenson was recovering from illness, as if to provide a balm for adult pain).[2] But there is a striking straightforwardness about Stevenson's approach, and he himself wrote of his poems that "they seem to me to smile, to have a kind of childish treble note that sounds in my ears freshly—not song, if you will, but a child's voice" (*Letters* 416). A close look at de la Mare's first venture into children's verse (*Songs*, 1902) in particular suggests that it was to Stevenson that de la Mare owed his original idea of writing from "the child's-eye view" (Townsend 140), and it was in Stevenson's gentle hints about the life of "The Child Alone" (as one section of *A Child's Garden of Verses* is called) that he first saw a way to express his own understanding of childhood solitude in "rhymes" for the young.[3] Where Traherne or Herrick or later, William Blake, explored the potential of a faux naif voice,[4] here now was a convincingly real child speaking, and a poetry that embraced something approximating the reality of a child's existence, as seen from the inside.

Stevenson found a way to duplicate childlike speech in a simple, purified language, and he used it to voice the thoughts and speculations of the solitary child on a voyage of discovery through the games and mysteries of everyday life. A child digs a hole in the sand and watches the sea fill it up or buries in the garden a tin soldier to be secretly dug up later, and he tells of these projects, as though to the self, with a directness and simplicity that deny the adult presence—either as listener (such secrets would never be shared with grown-ups) or as hovering adult author interpreting such moments. The sing-song, self-satisfied confidence of the child-speaker in the verse of the buried soldier—"I shall find him, never fear / I shall find my grenadier"—yet contains the blunt awareness: "But for all that's gone and come, / I shall find my soldier dumb." But Stevenson deliberately leaves it at that: the child proclaims his knowledge of the plain truths he sees, and even acknowledges (in a voice perfectly suggestive of a child's internal conversation) his own creative autonomy in the world of secret and silent toy soldiers:

> Not a word will he disclose,
> Not a word of all he knows.
> I must lay him on the shelf,
> And make up the tale myself.
>
> [*Complete Poems* 48–49]

In Stevenson we find hints that the solitary child's concerns are far from trivial or merely playful; there is an unstated question, behind these unaffected accounts, of where the sea comes from when it fills the sand or about whether a toy soldier has a consciousness. The child who ponders that "I have a little shadow that goes in and out with me" or who perceives the presence of an unseen "playmate" whenever he is playing alone is on the brink of a greater awareness, as if sensing a possible double, or second self, in the solitary world of childhood play. This is the recognition by the child of his own imaginative powers—indeed, of the role of the imagination in the definition of the self: "I must . . . make up the tale myself." So Stevenson, significantly, was the first to combine the ordinary day-to-day details of childhood life with that Romantic notion of pre-adult "vision"—and in this combination of the ordinary and the profound may lie the most important model for de la Mare's approach to children's verse.

But in *A Child's Garden of Verses* the child's perceptions remain incomplete, the state of mind essentially contented: for all their independence, Stevenson's children-speakers, chattering away in their own world of purely childlike games and perceptions, ultimately make us aware of the grown man behind them who is fondly reconstructing a simple "child's garden" of existence through the medium of the imagined childhood self. The final poem of the collection most openly demonstrates this, stepping out of the book's assumed childlike speaking role to suggest to its young listener the process of adult memory that underlies these voices from a child's world. Indeed, by addressing itself "To Any Reader," the verse removes itself from the private, self-communicating world of the solitary child-speaker to hint at the experience of memory and nostalgia that might be part of an *adult* reader's participation in Stevenson's personal tour through a child's world.[5]

> As from the house your mother sees,
> You playing round the garden trees,
> So you may see, if you will look
> Through the windows of this book,
> Another child, far, far away,
> And in another garden, play.
> But do not think that you can at all,
> By knocking on the window call
> That child to hear you. He intent
> Is on all play-business bent.
> He does not hear; he will not look,
> Nor yet be lured out of his book.
> For long ago, the truth to say,
> He has grown up and gone away,
> And it is but a child of air
> That lingers in the garden there.          [*Complete Poems* 59]

That "child of air" who is yet down-to-earth, playing among the trees, is from the beginning the sort of being whom de la Mare, following this example, pursues in his poetry. Like Stevenson, he is attuned to the smaller details and rituals that make up a child's solitary "play-business"; and because of Stevenson's example he is not afraid to make these things the subject of verse. At the same time, he is reaching through that child's silent moments toward a ghost that symbolizes a state of mind both within and beyond the adult self. His identification with the contentedly lonely child inspires a reflective poem that, like Stevenson's of twenty-three years before, subtly blends adult remembrance with a child's heedlessness to create a striking quality of double consciousness:

> There is a garden, grey
>    With mists of autumntide;
> Under the giant boughs
>    Stretched green on every side,
>
> Along the lonely paths,
>    A little child like me,

With face, with hands, like mine,
  Plays ever silently;

On, on, quite silently,
  When I am there alone,
Turns not his head; lifts not his eyes;
  Heeds not as he plays on.

After the birds are flown
  From singing in the trees,
When all is grey, all silent,
  Voices, and winds, and bees;

And I am there alone:
  Forlornly, silently,
Plays in the evening garden
  Myself with me.                                    [96–97]

The similarities with Stevenson's poem are obvious: the reader is invited to look, as through a window of time, into the silent "garden" of childhood that is represented necessarily by a solitary child, at one with himself in a way that the longing adult can be only through looking back. Both Stevenson's child, who "will not look," and de la Mare's child, who "lifts not his eyes," seem in their defiant self-absorption to be denying eye contact with the poet who looks on them, as if to emphasize their distance from him. But in de la Mare's poem, importantly, the speaker remains a child. In its universe we hear no authorial intrusion; we do not encounter the gentle condescension of the Stevenson poem but seem instead to be overhearing the steady, undistracted voice of a child conversing with himself, alone on a dreamlike plane that "heeds not" the outer world. De la Mare's versification furthers the sense of a dimension just beyond the adult's grasp: where Stevenson's precise couplets and steady iambic rhythms suggest a concrete, easily defined situation, de la Mare's broken rhythms and open pauses convey the uncertain nature of his venture into the Unknown. Stevenson's rhymes are confident and employ hard, distinctive consonants ("look/book," "intent/bent"); de la Mare's are softer and less assertive, and he finishes the line more than once with the word "silently"—a word with a dying rhythm that brings the line to a whispered, inconclusive end. Finally, the imagery parallels this: Stevenson's garden, cozily situated behind a house and described no further than to evoke the familiar domestic setting of everyone's childhood, is transformed by de la Mare into an eerie place of mists and mossy giant boughs and "lonely paths," where the silent echoes of "voices and winds" bring to mind a world on the other side of death.

De la Mare thus takes the child's vision of "another child" a step further than Stevenson did, to the point of suggesting that it is actually the child, and not the adult counterpart, who recognizes himself both from the inside and from the outside—thereby reaching, in his unconscious, instinctive way, that level of double awareness that Stevenson's poem reaches only through the processes of adult reflection, or at least through admitting the presence of the grown poet in the poem's own consciousness. (De la Mare makes the astute observation elsewhere that in these earlier verses, "Stevenson plays at being a child" [*Early One Morning* 306].) The delaMarean child is able not only to step out of the self and to observe his double but to step out of time, almost as though seeing the ghost of the child that will remain further on in time, "After the birds are flown." Where Stevenson is unable to resist slipping into a reflective adult's voice, de la Mare has become the child—and in doing so has expanded, not limited, his vision.

Children are, of course, prone to believe in imaginary companions at play, thereby demonstrating an uninhibited license of the imagination that both poets see as indicative of the child's special gift for spiritual self-sufficiency. But de la Mare, by keeping the utterance within the parameters of a childlike consciousness (instead of saying, in an adult voice, "So you may see, if you will look"), hints at the internal processes—half-hidden, like the garden, in "mists"—that define childlike thought and imagination. His capacity to enter, much more than the early poem, the regions beyond objective understanding in the child's mind brings to his verse a sense of "the metaphysical gropings of the young child" (Walsh 181): here the speaker is wondering about nothing less than the definition of being, about the meaning of "self" and "otherness." And more than anything else, the poem's encroaching awareness of inexplicable concepts is a function of the subject's solitude: not only does de la Mare emphasize the child's isolation from the world through the repetition of such words as *alone* and *lonely,* but he makes it a gray, mysterious world of silence—the undisturbed universe of the self.

Two things emerge from this subtle yet powerful revision of the solitary child we see in Stevenson. One is a far more serious investigation of the child's sense of metaphysical complexities. When de la Mare writes that children, because unbound by their senses, can look upon "facts" as "chameleons," he is emphasizing the ability of the child's mind to transcend the usual divisions of deductive thought to grasp universals. "Between their dreams and their actuality looms no impassable abyss," writes de la Mare (*Pleasures* 176). Our assumptions of a knowable physical actuality or state of being are gently undone by the unfettered fancies and speculations of the child's pre-intellectual thought processes; his questions about the self are at the heart of our ultimate ignorance before the mystery of the universe:

> O, whither go the nights and days?
>   And where can to-morrow be?
> Is anyone there when *I*'m not there?
>   And why am I always me?          [*Pleasures* 177]

De la Mare sees the metaphysical riddles "which no philosopher has yet wholly answered" as the day-to-day stuff of the child's "inward reverie" (177)—and he would have been gratified to see modern philosophers reaching similar conclusions, as in a recent study that aims to show how the questions preoccupying the mind of the curious child are, in their essence, comparable to those asked through the centuries in philosophy.[6] But de la Mare can then convey this through humor, as in *Peacock Pie* (1913), his most playful and down-to-earth book of children's verse, wherein children pause amid their daily lives with light-hearted reflections that subtly reveal the unique, and often troubling, insights of their solitary worlds. One child states,

> "It's a very odd thing—
>   As odd as can be—
> That whatever Miss T. eats
> Turns into Miss T."                              [146]

while another remarks:

> "Mrs. Earth and Mr. Sun
>   Can tan my skin and tire my toes,

> But all that I'm thinking of, ever shall think,
> Why, neither knows." [138]

Therefore, the second, and more important, consequence of de la Mare's alteration of Stevenson's "Child Alone" lies in the way that such uncannily accurate observations take us to the border of a darker world of uncertainty. Whereas Stevenson's verses may contain a shiver of darker awareness, they do not stray from their "garden" of peaceful contentment; fear, though hovering behind the perceptions of the solitary child, can always be cured by the "comfortable hand" of Nanny, the "Dear Alice" of the book's dedication. De la Mare, by contrast, chooses to explore the decidedly *un*easy, and he treats it with the solemnity of a child's belief in the further worlds and other realms of being that the overly objective adult chooses to ignore. Perhaps no other poet before or since has so persistently plumbed the depths of a child's penchant for the Unknown—and the unnerving—that lurk within the self. Even Wordsworth, who considers with great sensitivity the distinct nature of childhood fear, ultimately connects it with an overall sense dawning of spiritual understanding in the developing self: for this is the central theme and concern of the poem that considers the darker side of childhood, *The Prelude*. Wordsworth's extremely effective rendering of childlike "awe," as in the famous lake episode of Book 1 (which tells of the boy's fear before the looming presence of a dark mountain against the sky), reveals, as does de la Mare's verse, the child's perception of "unknown modes of being" (l.393). But most important, its lessons play a part in the larger discovery of the "Wisdom and Spirit of the Universe" (l.401)—something fully apprehended only in adulthood.

De la Mare, governed far less by an overriding design or spiritual philosophy, instead states that "when a child imagines, he can not only see and hear horror but can smell and taste it. Its presence surrounds him like the stench of a bog" (*Early One Morning* 196). As the final twist of strangeness, de la Mare then depicts the horror side-by-side with the familiar moments of an ordinary child's life— as when the child looks down the cellar steps and sees a personified mold, "John Mouldy," sitting in the shadows of a normal domestic setting. The utter tangibility of this creature of darkness is yet made convincing by the matter-of-factness of the child's description, and the odd presence of a smile makes the vision both jolly and sinister:

I spied John Mouldy in his cellar,
Deep down twenty steps of stone;
In the dusk he sat a-smiling,
    Smiling there alone.

He read no book, he snuffed no candle;
The rats ran in, the rats ran out;
And far and near, the drip of water
    Went whispering about.

The dusk was still, with dew a-falling,
I saw the Dog-star bleak and grim,
I saw a slim brown rat of Norway
    Creep over him.

I spied John Mouldy in his cellar,
Deep down twenty steps of stone;
In the dusk he sat a-smiling,
    Smiling there alone.                                    [7]

De la Mare does not hide the potential for such sinister understanding in the child but rather suggests that the child is more
honest about accepting its presence in our lives. There are poems
about unexplained disappearances, untimely deaths, and disturbingly peculiar or eccentric characters; fairies, who can be magical
and gossamer in one verse, are "shrill" and "mocking" in the next;
nature, the child's own home, turns gray, eerie, and forbidding.
The sparkling image of snow, which often decorates de la Mare's
lighter verses, quite frequently takes on an all-encompassing blank-
ness, as though the child, in a frozen moment of solipsist awareness,
knew the world as an empty blank apart from the self: "None there
but I: / Snow, snow, and a wintry sky" (97).

But again, the insidious power of this perspective comes from
de la Mare's control of such shadowy worlds within the apparently
light-hearted. The playful context of a "jingle" or a "rhyme" allows
him to exploit the underside of the quaint and the whimsical to
great effect; and an almost obsessive fascination for the unexpected
finds its most successful expression when kept within this small,
seemingly safe, yet infinitely suggestive world. There is a poem in
*Peacock Pie*, for example, about a strange presence in the midst of
childhood quaintness whose persistent knocking from nowhere is

the same sort of tease to the eager imagination as Poe's raven, but here in the land of the "wee" and the "small":

> Some one came knocking
> At my wee, small door;
> Some one came knocking.
> I'm sure—sure—sure;
> I listened, I opened,
> I looked to left and right,
> But nought there was a-stirring
> In the dark still night . . .          [140–41]

Or in "The Little Green Orchard," the happy daintiness of what its title depicts—a diminutive haven for the child's solitary hours—is played against the ghostlike watch of a more tangible "someone" whose looming presence is instinctively felt by the child. Even the quaint words of the title take on a peculiar resonance when repeated as a refrain throughout:

> Someone is always sitting there,
> In the little green orchard;
> Even when the sun is high,
> In noon's unclouded sky,
> And faintly droning goes
> The bee from rose to rose,
> Someone is always sitting there,
> In the little green orchard.

With an air of nonchalance, yet "all a child's certainty of insight" (*Best Stories* 21), the fanciful belief in invisible company turns into the calm assurance that it is Death there, waiting for us all:

> When you are most alone,
> All but the silence gone,
>
> .  .  .  .  .  .  .  .  .  .  .  .
> Someone is waiting and watching there,
> In the little green orchard.          [164]

The subtle equation in de la Mare's world between the child's acknowledged second self and the shadowy character of Death is one of his most compelling and disquieting insights: an underlying image throughout all his work is that of an inner "other," or alternate self—but not surprisingly, only the ego-less child, as here, can really accept its potential identity as a previous or future self and, therefore, as Death.

De la Mare's models—especially the Romantics but even before them the seventeenth-century poets like Vaughan and Traherne who first addressed childhood spirituality—certainly considered the child's strange closeness to death as the eternal other world from which he had so recently departed. Wordsworth in particular credited the child with an *understanding* of—not just implied proximity to—the silent world that made its presence known to him as a boy in rare and profound moments. But for the Romantic poets the child's knowledge of death is forever linked to "intimations of immortality." Traherne's hopeful exclamation that childhood must be "an antepast of Heven sure!" is still heard in Romantic contemplations on childhood, which hope that *through* the child we adults may glimpse the Eternal, and so

> Can in a moment travel hither
> And see the Children sport upon the shore
> And hear the mighty waters rolling evermore.
> ["Ode: Intimations of Immortality" ll.169–71]

Only de la Mare shows us the child's darkness, solitude, and knowledge of death without reaching after a vision of childlike paradise by which to balance such disturbing insights; his child-symbol is not the escape from bald and unsparing truth but the very route to it. One of the most repeated phrases in de la Mare's verse spoken in the child's voice is the calm and simple statement, "I know"—as if to say that only the child can face the final and irreversible aspects of our existence, most of all death:

> A very, very old house I know—
> And ever so many people go,
>
> .    .    .    .    .    .    .    .    .    .    .    .
>
> Comes the blank door, and there's the door.
> Go in they do; come out no more.                    [170]

Part of a child's capacity to embrace reality so calmly lies in that Keatsian acceptance of mystery; rather than analyze, the child happily remains in a suspended, half-knowing state of mind—as in the above poem, which has the quality of an unsolved riddle. But far from escaping into a world of riddles he only half-comprehends, the child acknowledges the horror, too:

> I know where lurk
> The eyes of Fear;
> I, I alone,
> Where, shadowy-clear,
> Watching for me,
> Lurks Fear.                                                        [97]

What the child embraces, therefore, is more than a sense for death—the counterpart to the pre-life existence recently left behind; it is a more disturbing insight into the darkest and most undefinable realism of experience. It is, to put it another way, a sort of unblinking nihilism: only the child can confront head-on the meaning of Nothingness, and only through a child's consciousness can we begin to guess at the reality that lies on the other side of being. The final verse in *Peacock Pie*, entitled "The Song of Finis" (for more than one reason), goes deeper into the world of strange and unsettling possibility to show us this. Seeming at first simply to be a humorous and fanciful exercise in stretching the limits of plausibility, de la Mare's poem pictures horse and rider against a backdrop of suspended Time and Space: "At the end of all the Ages / A knight sate on his steed." The knight in this verse becomes both a child's otherworldly visitor in a land of make-believe and an emblematic figure of Man at the end of his individual quest—or indeed at the end of Time, here depicted surrealistically through the visual image of a precipice. The peculiar, unexpected ending, as the knight charges into Nothingness, may be read as Nonsense; possibly de la Mare is toying with the mundane fact of the book's "finis" into the empty "space" of blank end paper. Yet at the same time, this verse leaves us with a vague image of a solitary encounter with the Beyond—something, we sense, the child reader is far less likely to question than we are. It whispers of a meaning just beyond our grasp, and de la Mare links our ability to guess it with a child's acceptance of possibility beyond reason.

> No bird above that steep of time
>     Sang of a livelong quest;
> No wind breathed,
>     Rest:
> "Lone for an end!" cried Knight to steed,
>     Loosed an eager rein—

Charged with his challenge into Space:
    And Quiet did Quiet remain.                              [188]

Again, de la Mare employs unexpected pauses (as in the single-worded line, "Rest") to bring us closer to the world of silence; and his use of childlike rhythm and repetition leaves us with a lasting refrain that tells hauntingly of infinity: "And Quiet did Quiet remain." Yet if the child takes us to the brink of profound mystery, he also symbolizes in his solitary questionings our own isolation. This is the ultimate confrontation between self and world—and what should be the knight's final cry but "Lone for an end!"? This is the truth only the child can accept: the knight, who belongs to the child's world and not to ours, knows, accepts and faces his end, whatever it may be beyond the silence—and he faces it alone.

Thus, the child remains alone, metaphorically as well as physically isolated in de la Mare's poetic universe, suggesting a distance from our lives and attitudes that can never be recovered. For the modern human, who no longer has the reassurance of traditional Christian faith to promise reunion with childhood's Paradise, this is a source of sadness, an archetypal knowledge of loss that underlies most of de la Mare's writing. For the poet, who yearns for the child's simplicity, purity, and imaginative insight and yet must remain both an adult and a conscious artist, it is devastating, for one must either resort to an utterly childlike vision and form of expression or admit one's failure as a mature artist. This is the feeling we get from reading de la Mare. We have seen how his poetry suggests, subtly but repeatedly, that only through a total reversion to a childlike sensibility may we reach the full insights poetry can offer, and a knowledge of the poet's overall oeuvre only emphasizes this, and suggests his sense of conflict and ultimate lack of resolution about the possible joining of child and poet.

Thinking back to the Romantics, whose influence can be felt so strongly throughout de la Mare's work, we must realize that the crucial aspect of the Romantic philosophy of the child, which de la Mare completely ignores, is the idea of applying childlike qualities to an ideal of human development and growth. For Wordsworth, Coleridge, or Blake, the child's harmonious blend of innocent freedom and intuitive perceptivity could be envisioned as humanity's salvation, brought triumphantly to the efforts of a self-perfecting adulthood to the point at which the child is seen as a virtual savior. This ideal of "transformation," or "the utopian fulfillment of potentialities," could be called the central theme of Romanticism, and its goals were envisioned more often than not through the child as "Perpetual Messiah" (Plotz 63). It follows, therefore, that for the imaginative artist—the Poet, at the center of this Romantic revolution—the importance and greatness of the creative effort was assured (or at least assumed). For de la Mare, in contrast, the opposite is true; this is a poet who, at the height of his career, wrote a poem entitled "The Imagination's Pride," preaching temperance in the (adult) mind's relationship with its impulse toward fantasy and claiming the self's own solitude as "shelter" against the lure of the imagination's "utmost scope":[8]

> Be not too wildly amorous of the far,
> > Nor lure thy fantasy to its utmost scope.
> Read by a taper when the needling star
> > Burns red with menace in heaven's midnight cope.
> Friendly thy body: guard its solitude.          [244]

De la Mare may make rather easy statements like "Childhood is the name of the world's immediate future" for the introduction of a book (*Early One Morning* xx), thereby suggesting a progressive philosophy like the Romantics'—but essentially he looks to the child detached, alone in a symbolic as well as real sense, separated from the rest of humanity by a gap that he cannot or cares not to bridge. His adaptation of Coleridge's critical theories, for example, in an essay that borrows directly from the earlier poet's division of Imagination and Fancy, ultimately rejects the notion of interplay between the visionary and the analytic mind and insists on the value of the pure, intuitive and spiritual, unwilled childlike vision.[9] Further, his focus on the youngest possible asexual child ("childlike" as opposed to the later "boylike") as a model shows his wariness—almost a fear—of child development and certainly does not fit into Romantic ideas of the organic, progressive, forward-looking impulses of the creative mind.

At the same time, the escapism and nostalgia of post-Romantic children's writers is not his either. Although de la Mare once jokingly characterized himself by saying, "Our friend Walter is a Victorian" (Hassal 493), his vision of childhood solitude and isolation goes far beyond the "Arcadia" built out of Romanticism by his

Victorian forebears, the creators of the "golden age" of children's literature. There is no need, having seen de la Mare's poetic depictions of horror, loneliness, and uncanny strangeness in a child's life, to place his poetry in the same escapist vein; if anything, the child's intuitive knowledge, which we glimpse through de la Mare, suggests realms and levels of meaning actually beyond our limited understanding.

It cannot be stressed enough that de la Mare ultimately sees an unbridgeable gap between child and adult and, more than his most important literary role-models, comes to deeply pessimistic conclusions about the human race, which the child's distinctive nature only emphasizes. So in this poet's unique child-voice we may hear apparently innocent—yet therefore more damning—references to human egotism, such as in the selfish domination of the environment:

> Hi! Handsome hunting man.
> Fire your little gun.
> Bang! Now the animal
> Is dead and dumb and done.
> Nevermore to peep again, creep again, leap again,
> Eat or sleep or drink again. Oh, what fun!          [268]

Or we find more tragic derivatives of the child symbol, such as the fool, who chatters nonsensically about the horrors of war with ". . . words/I hardly know the meaning of" (208–9), or Hamlet as the "Mad Prince" who appears in a mock nursery rhyme asking, "Who said 'Peacock Pie'?" and leaves us with the image, both silly and haunting, of "life's troubled bubble broken" (187). In all of these verses, the disturbing blend of nonsense with deeper resonances of meaning seems to communicate (like the Knight of Nothingness) most directly to a child's consciousness. Indeed, the possiblity of a shell-shocked soldier speaking as the fool, or the shattered Prince Hamlet as a mad nursery character speaking in riddles, proposes that each is able to make a profound utterance *only* by reverting to a child's voice—and again, that the child, alone in the dark and mysterious world of the Self, understands more than we ever may do.

De la Mare's voice of childhood solitude, then, does not just indicate a special sensitivity to the child's profound moments of aloneness—those moments of a child's existence that Wordsworth or

Stevenson touched on so effectively, thus setting off the later poet's exploration into the life of the child alone. Rather, de la Mare's poetry suggests an almost desperate quest for states of consciousness and insight discovered in childhood solitude, with a resistance to any progressive views of humanity in which the child's existence might be seen as having only a *symbolic* value—that is, as serving only in a secondary way humanity's higher goals and artistic visions. Most compelling, and most disturbing, of all, therefore, is the dela-Marean child's all-pervading awareness of Nothingness. This suggests that the ultimate reality which the prerational child knows and accepts and which the adult increasingly denies through the processes of maturity, is the emptiness, the blank open space of the knight's "end," the snowy whiteness of "an icy quiet," the all-enveloping silence of the deserted garden or orchard. The child's instinctive habitat is the shadowy, empty place that prefigures the grave, "When you are most alone, / All but the silence gone" (164).

De la Mare's child carries a persistent sense of finality: he has an intimate acquaintance with states of nonbeing; he constantly senses the void on the other side of physical existence. The childlike intuition that exists alongside an innocent contentment is thus a sort of *inborn* nihilism: this is the secret of the child's solitude, a secret he progressively turns from, as from his preference for being alone, as he grows older—for it is the only way to confront and survive the business of life.

De la Mare, as a poet, both expressed his own nihilism through a repeated contemplation of humanity against a "Vast" and uncaring universe and escaped it through a pursuit of artistic beauty, an ideal he attempted to reach through technical perfection and an often decorative style. His apparent solace in a child's world, however, proved to be the closest he could come to an honest expression of his deepest impulses: for a child's simple utterance comes closest to the silence. The child's prelinguistic forms of communication and insight are what the poet seeks in the pauses and silences of verse; and the child's acceptance of solitude and silence around him indicates the facing of a reality that is only complicated and evaded by verbal discourse—for ultimately, "All sounds to silence come" (376). De la Mare's original interest in childhood and children's verse may have been born of a certain idealism and escapism, testimony to his Romantic and Victorian roots; but it was as if the taking on of a true child's voice brought de la Mare beyond words, to the center of the child's vision, which was also his own. The solitariness of the child is the reality of human existence—the isolation of each individual— but it is the condition the socialized adult is most afraid to acknowl- edge, and so it is glimpsed only through these poetic visions of the quiet, self-absorbed child, alone in his garden of life and death, at one with the Silence which is both his beginning and his end.

### Notes

1. All citations of de la Mare's poetry are from *The Complete Poems* (London: Faber, 1969).

2. Stevenson was an invalid for much of his adult life, suffering from a chronic bronchial condition. In the years 1881–84 most of *A Child's Garden of Verses* was writ- ten, and many of the verses were composed while he was in Hyères recovering from a particularly bad period of ill health (Colvin 1:289–93). Eleanor Graham writes that many of the verses were written as Stevenson "lay in the half darkness of a sickroom in Hyères with his right arm tied to his side to lessen the risk of further haemorrhage" (12).

3. Interestingly, both Stevenson and de la Mare modestly insisted on calling their poetry for children "rhymes." Stevenson said of his verses, "These are rhymes, jingles; I don't go in for eternity and the three unities" (Stevenson to Sidney Colvin, October 1883, in Colvin 334). De la Mare's standard subtitle for his children's verse collections, such as *Peacock Pie* (1913) and *Bells and Grass* (1941), was "A Book of Rhymes." His Introduction to *Bells and Grass,* almost an apologia, consistently refers to the book's verses as "rhymes"—even though some were not originally intended for children in their manuscript form. This can be seen in a 1905–6 MS Notebook in the De la Mare Papers (uncataloged), Bodleian Library, Oxford. See also de la Mare's Introduction to *Bells and Grass.*

4. See, for example, Marcus, especially chapter 3, "The Poet as Child: Herbert, Herrick and Crashaw," which explores the highly sophisticated use of "childlike" traits in language for the purposes of religious verse. De la Mare himself certainly read such early poets as Herrick, Herbert, Traherne, and Vaughan; and both his numerous anthologies (especially the much-loved *Come Hither,* 1923) and his poetic writings reveal his liking in particular for the simplified diction and appealing rhythms first of Elizabethan songs and, later, of religious verses like Herrick's. But he was also alert to the distancing effect of verse that combined a childlike voice with an angelic one—and he may have been pointing to this when he commented that Blake's children seem to have attended some "celestial nursery school" (*Early One Morning* 5) to utter the poetry that they do. Though he greatly admired Blake, de la Mare was from the start searching for a much more earthly—literally "down-to- earth"—child.

5. The final section of *A Child's Garden of Verses* is called "Envoys" and consists of addresses to figures from the past (such as "Mother" and "Auntie"), thus alluding to the author's sentimental trip through childhood. "To Any Reader," though obvi- ously addressed on an immediate level to a child audience, refers on a different level to Stevenson's childhood self now "grown up and gone away"—and so includes, like the nods in Mother's and Auntie's direction, other reading adults sympathetic to (and sharing in) Stevenson's nostalgia.

6. Gareth Matthews's *Philosophy and the Young Child* is a short but suggestive study

comparing real conversations with children—with particular emphasis on their inquisitive queries and speculations—to the fundamental questions of philosophy.

7. This quotation is from "The Almond Tree," one of de la Mare's most moving and effective tales, which chronicles the strange events leading to the death of a child's father. The phrase is apt but not fully clear in its meaning until the end of the tale, where we sense that the child has foreseen such events. In this, as in many other de la Mare tales and poems, the child is calm and even nonchalant about accepting death—and his ability to observe it directly and plainly is what lends an eerie suggestion of deeper meaning to his words, as in a wonderfully understated poem, "The Funeral," which contains the verse:

> They took us to the graves,
> Susan and Tom and me,
> Where the long grasses grow
> And the funeral tree:
> We stood and watched; and the wind
> Came softly out of the sky
> And blew in Susan's hair,
> As I stood closely by.

After this delicate and poignant moment, which even hints of a communication from the breeze, the child describes tea in the nursery afterwards and concludes with simple observation: "And, looking out of the window, / I heard the thrushes sing; / But Tom fell asleep in his chair. / He was so tired, poor thing" (44).

8. De la Mare often linked the temptations of the imagination with those of romantic love—as such both were delicious, secret, and ultimately highly dangerous impulses. At his best de la Mare translated intense personal longing into a generalized, archetypal poetic yearning, as in his famous poem "The Ghost" (196), which blames but also glorifies the "sweet cheat" of imagination and human longing. But de la Mare was only capable of this intensified creative power for so long, and as his inspiration faded through the years he became more and more inclined to preach the comforts of "guarded solitude." His identification with the child figure takes on a new dimension when seen in this context—especially when we realize, for example, that some of his earliest, rather awkward love lyrics (MS Notebook, 1905–6) were published only when they had been transformed into children's verse (*Bells and Grass*, 1941), with the child as speaker. A very early lyric that begins with the line (rather derivative of Elizabethan song), "Why do you weep, Lady? / Why do you weep?" becomes, nearly forty years later, the soft cry of the sensitive child: "Why do you weep, Mother? Why do you weep?" (422). Or the burning regret of a remorseful lover—"Weep no more; how dark a face / In thy hair!"—is turned into the guilt of a child who foresees the pain of memory in a poem called "The Playmate," which continues, "Oh, I shall see / How many years, this silent place / Where I was cruel to thee!" (425).

9. In an essay on Rupert Brooke ("Rupert Brooke and the Intellectual Imagination," 1919, reprinted in *Pleasures and Speculations*), de la Mare turns to images of the child to define two types of imagination that are clearly based on the Coleridgean model. His terms are *childlike* and *boylike:* the first, like Coleridge's Imagination, is the truly visionary, perceptive state, while the second, like the Fancy, entails the outward, consciously intellectual activity of the mind. "The one divines, the other discovers. The one is intuitive, inductive, the other logical, deductive. The one is visionary, the other intellectual. The one knows that beauty is truth, the other reveals that truth is beauty" (179). Importantly, one replaces the other in the development

of the child: "life flings open the door of the nursery," the child becomes a boy, and the pre-intellectual, "secret existence of a really childlike child" is lost (177).

## Works Cited

Bloom, Harold. *The Anxiety of Influence: A Theory of Poetry.* New York: Oxford University Press, 1985.

Carpenter, Humphrey. *Secret Gardens: The Golden Age of Children's Literature.* London: George Allen and Unwin, 1985.

Colvin, Sidney, ed. *The Letters of Robert Louis Stevenson.* New York: Charles Scribner's Sons, 1889.

De la Mare, Walter. *The Complete Poems.* London: Faber, 1969. Including poems from:

*Songs of Childhood* (1902)

*Poems* (1906)

*Peacock Pie: A Book of Rhymes* (1913)

*Motley and Other Poems* (1918)

*The Veil and Other Poems* (1921)

*Bells and Grass: A Book of Rhymes* (1941)

*Winged Chariot* (1951)

———. *Early One Morning in the Spring.* Chapters on Children and Childhood as It Is Revealed in Particular in Early Memories and in Early Writings. London: Faber, 1935.

———. "Rupert Brooke and the Intellectual Imagination." Lecture for the School of Rugby, 28 March 1919, reprinted in de la Mare, *Pleasures and Speculations.* London: Faber, 1940.

———. *The Best Stories of Walter de la Mare.* London: Faber, 1942.

———. Unpublished manuscripts and papers, including MS Notebook, 1905–6. In collection (uncataloged) at the Bodleian Library, Oxford.

Graham, Eleanor. Introduction to Robert Louis Stevenson, *A Child's Garden of Verses.* Modern ed. Harmondsworth: Puffin Books, 1952.

Hassal, Christopher. *Edward Marsh: Patron of the Arts.* London: Longmans, 1959.

Keats, John. *The Letters of John Keats.* Ed. Robert Gittings. Oxford: Oxford University Press, 1970.

Marcus, Leah S. *Childhood and Cultural Despair.* Pittsburgh: University of Pittsburgh Press, 1978.

Matthews, Gareth. *Philosophy and the Young Child.* Cambridge: Harvard University Press, 1980.

Plotz, Judith. "The Perpetual Messiah: Romanticism, Childhood, and the Paradoxes of Human Development." In B. Finkelstein, ed., *Regulated Children, Liberated Children.* New York: Psychohistory Press, 1979.

Review of *Songs of Childhood* in *The Bookman* (London), March 1902, 217.

Rose, Jacqueline. *The Case of Peter Pan; or, The Impossibility of Children's Fiction.* London: Macmillan, 1984.

Stevenson, Robert Louis. *A Child's Garden of Verses* (1885). In *The Complete Poems of Robert Louis Stevenson.* New York: Charles Scribner's Sons, 1923.

———. *The Letters of Robert Louis Stevenson,* ed. Sidney Colvin. New York: Charles Scribner's Sons, 1889.

Townsend, John Rowe. *Written for Children.* 2d rev. ed. Harmondsworth: Pelican Books, 1983.

Walsh, William. *The Use of Imagination: Educational Thought and the Literary Mind.* London: Chatto and Windus, 1959.

Wordsworth, William. Notes on the Poems dictated to Isabella Fenwick in 1843. In *Selected Poems and Prefaces by William Wordsworth,* ed. Jack Stillinger. Boston: Houghton Mifflin, 1965.

————. *The Oxford Authors: William Wordsworth,* ed. Stephen Gill. Oxford: Oxford University Press, 1984.

# Mistaken Identity:
## *Russell Hoban's* Mouse and His Child

Valerie Krips

The longing for a past of innocence and wholeness haunts many a narrative, not least those that find themselves, either by design or accident, ranked among books for children. Such a longing often finds expression in an idealization of the child and of childhood itself. This idealization, which reaches back at least as far as Rousseau, still animates certain contemporary ideas of the child and provides a subtext both for fiction written for children and for criticism of that fiction. When criticism finds child protagonists to be the site of "hope" or "deep feelings," or when an interpretation credits a child with the ability to reshape or revitalize his or her world simply because he or she is a child, then we are almost certainly in the presence of idealized innocence.[1]

Russell Hoban's *Mouse and His Child* appears apt for such a reading. Its theme, a child's longing for a home and family, is familiar enough, while its happy outcome echoes any number of stories in which an inventive and persistent youngster succeeds where adults have given up or have already failed.[2] However, Hoban's text, rather than affirming familiar ideas, in fact reevaluates the status of children and childhood, rejecting ideas of wholeness and innocence in favor of struggle and empowerment. Interpreted in this way some of the apparent difficulties in the book, such as Hoban's allusions to existential philosophy and modernist writing, as well as his use of narrative repetition, are demystified.[3] It is in these details that the book's careful reworking of the theme of childhood develops much of its argumentative power and generates the conditions in which a radical rethinking of the idea of an innocent child can be undertaken.

Hoban's book is not an easy read; nor is childhood an easy time as Hoban remembers and reimagines it. It is a time when the child is beginning to create a self, a me, and to find a place in the world into which (willy-nilly) she or he was so abruptly born. The chal-

*Children's Literature* 21, ed. Francelia Butler, Christine Doyle Francis, Anne K. Phillips, and Julie K. Pfeiffer (Yale University Press, © 1993 The Children's Literature Foundation, Inc.).

lenges of self-creation are met by Hoban's protagonist with verve, dignity, and determination: the mouse-child's progress is something like a pilgrimage. Its ending is not easily thought of, however, within the conventional frameworks of reconciliation and affirmation that bring other childish success stories to a close: the selfhood the mouse-child achieves is the site of loss as well as gain, and the "happy ending" is shown to be provisional. Nor is Hoban's rethinking or reimagining of childhood limited to the characters and events in the book; as the reader imagines this text and creates its meanings, she or he must also struggle to become its reader, its partner in narrative. The reader's struggle interweaves with that of the mouse-child: both reader and character are trying to find a place—the reader in the book, the mouse-child in his world. What, then, is offered? What sort of world, what sort of place, can the child reader find in Hoban's work?

No human child is represented directly in *The Mouse and His Child*. Instead, the narrative of the coming-into-being of a human subject takes as its protagonist a clockwork mouse-child, attached by his hands, apparently for ever, to his father. Born into the world in a toy shop, the mouse-child wants to know what and where he is. His father cannot help; they must "wait and see" (14). The child hears the word "mama," and although he does not know what the word means, "he knew at once that he needed one badly" (17). In an interesting reversal of a well-established psychoanalytic view of childhood development, Hoban's mouse-child encounters language, the system that will enable him to represent, and thus to some extent overcome, his primary loss of the mother before he is aware of his lack of her. So, in a moment of remarkable power and economy, the text indicates both that the mouse-child's existence begins with lack (expressed here as the absence of a mother) and that his attempts to remedy this will be made within language, a system that precedes him (he has language as soon as he is aware) and, to some extent, defines him (he knows what he wants within its frameworks: "He had no idea what a mama might be, but he knew at once that he needed one badly"). The narrative of human subjectivity brought into focus here suggests that human beings find and locate themselves in a world in which there is an imperfect match between what their unsocialized selves demand and what the social structures of their world will allow them to have or to be.

The mouse-child, who doesn't know who or what he is, who

doesn't know what being someone means, sets out from the toy store in which he comes into being. Made of matched halves of tin held together with tags, he and his father have no place, society, or name to call their own. Their only family is each other. What the mice lack is summed up in their desire to be self-winding and to have their own territory. With a nice irony Hoban's metaphors point to the contradiction in their situation: mechanical, they seek to carve out a place for themselves within the plenitude of an organic world. As the text contemplates their mechanical state it questions oppositions which appear natural, asking what in the organic is mechanical, where in clockwork can we find a human face?

The mouse-child's entry into history as an independent subject is made in a meditative mode. Submerged at the bottom of a pond, he has been staring for months at a nearby tin can that once contained Bonzo dog food. The label on the Bonzo can shows a dog carrying a tray upon which rests another can showing a dog bearing a tray, and so on, until the dogs "become too small for the eye to follow" (30). The toy mice encounter Bonzo cans soon after being sent out into the world. But then it was the father who faced a can filled with clockwork dumped after being torn from the bodies of toys worn out in the service of a tyrant rat called Manny. The mouse father knew only that he and his son must try to escape: "He could not look beyond that, and did not attempt to" (32). When their positions are reversed and it is his son who faces a Bonzo can, the mouse-child also wants to escape, but to do so he contemplates infinity.

By the time the mouse-child confronts his own Bonzo can in the water an exploration of the relation of container to contained, one of the book's central themes, has found expression through the agency of the cans. In a literal reading, the cans are a double of the mice, who are also made of tin. Like the mice, the cans undergo a subtle transformation. Originally receptacles for dog food, then containers for clockwork, the cans next appear unlabeled, props in a Becket-like play entitled "The Last Visible Dog."[4] They later provide armor for Manny Rat and a mirror for the mouse-child. Initially both can and label depend for their meaning upon something inside. The can that the mouse father contemplates when he stands immobile and helpless in Manny Rat's camp has meaning as a container of mechanical spare parts, similar to those he bears inside himself. By the time it is his son's turn to stand staring at a can, meaning has been transferred from an inner essence to an outer representation. What is important for the mouse-child is not what the can contains but what is on the outside: its label. This label, which shows the dog and its tray, contains all the meaning that the mouse-child will allocate to the can. For him it becomes both sign and symbol: the last visible dog.

One day the tattered label is gone, and the mouse child sees that beyond the last visible dog, "on the other side of nothing," as he puts it, is his own reflection (116). It is a moment doubly inscribed. On the other side of nothing lies the child himself, a knowing subject, recognized, in Kantian style, through the play of his own faculties. At the same time the child sees himself reflected in a mirror. He is also, then, in Lacan's psychoanalytic account, the narcissistic infant who, having until this moment experienced his body as fragmented, suddenly sees himself whole, apparently coordinated and in control. The infant then "jubilantly assumes" the plenitude seen, mistaking representation for reality. The development of the Lacanian mirror-stage, we are told, "projects the formation of the individual into history"—that is, sets in motion the subject's activity of anticipation and retroaction, of placing her or himself within chronology (Lacan 1–4). For the human subject this is a moment, as one of Lacan's commentators puts it, of "high tragedy," since the unity the child sees is illusory. It is nevertheless one that will haunt his life forever as he attempts to recapture, to live up to, the idea of wholeness he once had. Gallop calls the mirror-stage a "lost paradise" and sees it in terms of a rewriting of the tragedy of Adam and Eve (85). It is an innocence short-lived indeed, both for the human child and for Hoban's young toy mouse.

The mouse and his child are surrounded by minor characters who provide a set of relations in which the toy mice can find a place. These relations are envisaged by the text in both an embodied form (the mice find a wife and mother, uncles, and a sister) and an abstract one. The necessary correlation of these concrete and abstract forms is achieved in a remarkable way through the bodies of the toy mice. The mice are broken and remade three times during the story. After their first awakening in a toy shop they are sold, broken, and thrown out in the rubbish. They are found by a tramp, the same person who witnessed their coming-into-being as they danced in circles in the toy shop window. He refashions them, ensuring that they will walk in a straight line instead of a circle. After their adventures in a wider world the toy mice return to the rubbish dump in the claws of a hawk who, discovering that they will make no sort of meal, drops them. The impact breaks them apart: never again will father and son be joined. But their individual bodies are remade, and "as his two halves came together the mouse child *returned to himself*" (131, emphasis added). In their final remaking, Manny Rat implants in the mice the clockwork mechanism that will make them self-winding. The mice then "return to consciousness" (167): their evolution seems complete. It is this idea of a completeness that the text interrogates.

Hoban's analysis of identity takes account of misidentification, of the sort of mistake represented by the mouse-child's appropriation of the reflection he saw in the Bonzo can as his "self" rather than a representation of it, and of the assumption by father and son of a "self-winding" that is really nothing of the kind. Such mistakes are important enough to warrant an allegory of their own, one that warns against taking things literally.

The mouse and his child spend some time in the company of a muskrat, a scientist manqué. The muskrat has a project: to fell a tree. His elaborate thinking on the subject finds eventual embodiment in a formula to do with teeth and gnawing—he has in mind the way beavers get wood for their lodges. The muskrat, who is lame, can only think when he walks. He sends the mice on circuits of his room; they walk so that he can think. The result is a formula: $XT = T^f$ (89). The muskrat then harnesses the mice to an ax; they act as a motor, going round and round like clockwork. When the tree falls, the muskrat misidentifies the role his formula has played: he thinks the tree is felled because he produced the formula. The text makes it absolutely clear however, that the relation of formulated thought to result is not causal and that the muskrat's formula is neither an explanation of the tree's felling nor a recipe for repeating the effect.

The mice, in their turn, retrospectively "identify" what they achieve with what they set out to do. They reinterpret the past in the light of the present and identify events as grounded in an originary moment, as something they were "wound" to do (17). This interpretation depends, as the muskrat's formula shows, on an arbitrary allocation of significance or meaning to events that, rather than being linked in a causal chain, are contiguous and contingent.

In other words, the relation of event to event is not one of "because" but rather of "then." It is an abstract point that has concrete results: the mouse and his child interpret a series of events as deterministic when in fact the relation they attribute to them is their own creation, part of the story they tell of their own subjectivities and their lives. In revealing this misidentification the text is at pains to illustrate the retrospective and retroactive nature of self-understanding, as well as the disjunctive nature of the self. It does so not only in the allegory of signification that is the muskrat's story but in its narrative of the bodies of the mice themselves.

Each time the mice are broken and remade their appearance changes, and importantly, while they are being reconstituted, the mice cease to exist. So what the mouse-child experiences as a return to himself is in fact a fresh beginning, a resurrection. Each time the mice come back to life they are changed beyond the possibility of a return to their former state, and each return marks a new stage in their life experiences and possibilities. A gap opens between the mice who existed before remaking and those who "return" to life. In a clear subversion of certain humanistic accounts of the subject that stress continuity and the presence of some essential and unchanging core, Hoban introduces the idea of a subject created by disjunction and discontinuity. Again, this idea of the subject can be usefully imagined within the interpretive frameworks of Lacanian theory.

The mirror-stage, which we imagine the mouse-child entering when he sees himself in the Bonzo can, marks the first step in a process that will impose a gap, or splitting, within the child's psyche, a splitting that results in the creation of the unconscious. This gap or disjuncture, according to Lacan, will never be closed. The child will henceforth experience itself as split between "me" and "I," where the child's "I" is a representation of self created in the mirror of language. The idea of wholeness, of a complete, unsplit entity that includes unproblematically both me and I is therefore, according to this account, a fantasy. Yet, it is a fantasy in which the subject continually indulges, imagining a past moment of primordial wholeness with the world—a wholeness that can, by association with ideas of anterior perfection, become a synonym for innocence. It is such a fantasy of subjectivity that this text interrogates: an interrogation made not only within the narrative itself, but in the position it makes available for its reader.

The story of the toy mouse and child is embedded within a narrative frame that describes the margins of the world of the toys and their friends. The frame finds expression in the tramp who utters the text's last words: "Be happy." The tramp, we recall, was first encountered in the book's opening paragraphs, and it was he who saw the mice come into the world. His return at the end of their story points to the possibility of return, of closure. But in narrative terms this is a promise unfulfilled. The omniscient and therefore authoritative narrator, who introduced the reader to the tramp as well as to the mice, leaves us looking over the tramp's shoulder into the toys' world without returning us to the toyshop window, where we looked at the tramp looking at the toys. The reader, in other words, is left in an immediate relationship with the tramp and given no final narratorial guidance about how to read him or what he says. Is "Be happy" a command or entreaty, a statement of fact or the invitation to another pilgrimage?

This ambiguous moment represents a revelation long deferred in the cause of narrative, of telling a story: just as the reader has been shown how the mice mistake the source of their "identity," so the source of the text's authority is reassessed. The frame that is the text, and the textual frames that were opened at the book's beginning, fail to close over the characters created, fail to shut them into a fictional world held in the eye of omniscience. Instead, as the text inhibits the expected closure, the narrator relinquishes his power, inviting the reader to engage even more closely with the book, whose ending now depends not on the past of the narrator but upon the reader's present. So as the mice are dependent upon their relations for self-winding and the tramp is dependent upon the narrator, the narrator, absent at the end, reveals that the novel's meanings are dependent upon the reader.

Hoban's book positions its reader as an active partner engaged in the creative work of the text. In recognition of the partnership required for reading, texts have been likened to musical scores.[5] Just as a musician must bring creativity to bear upon a score, so, it is argued, must the reader invest creativity in the story. This model of reading is particularly useful when applied to a complex narrative with great possibilities for interpretation; in which, for example, the reader can apply intertextual knowledge (for example, recognize the reference to Becket) as well as respond to unusual turns in narrative technique, such as repetition within a realistic discourse, and such overt textual devices as framing. It is, of course, precisely the inclusion of such possibilities within Hoban's text that have led to discussions of its difficulty for younger readers. Yet although it remains unlikely that many younger readers will have enough intertextual knowledge to be able to take up the allusion to Becket, to read this reference as a shortcoming or as a sign of misunderstanding or miscoding at the site of the implied reader is to reconstruct the narrative in terms of an interpretive strategy that the text itself has investigated and found wanting.

The story of a subject who is perpetually becoming rather than being, who is in a process that ensures that he will continually reassess, rework, and reconstruct his own identity, will be told in conventional narrative form at its peril, particularly if its implied audience is of all readerships the least experienced. The way Hoban's book tackles the narrative difficulties and opportunities afforded by telling such a story has been outlined in part here. Many of the strategies discussed point to the text's desire to interrogate received ideas about what it means to be a person or subject, the role of history in that project, and the reader's role in textual interpretation. Intertextual references that may or may not be available to the child implied reader (or an adult reader, for that matter) form part of the text's web of cultural reference, which is at times overt and at times worked out in terms of metaphor and simile, as, say, the muskrat's story speaks indirectly about misidentification of cause and effect. Whereas the audience of the Becket-like play in which the toy mice become involved, however, was not "ready for this yet" (71), according to the fieldmouse critic, it is clear that Hoban's implied reader is ready or, rather, is made ready by the struggle that is involved in creating a meaning and a place in this text.

Hoban's messages about the retrospective and retroactive nature of understanding demand that the reader continually reassess where she or he is in the text, both in terms of the narrative and of the subjectivities suggested within it. *The Mouse and His Child* is a modern allegory of subjectivity; the role of allegory is not to make each of its discrete utterances plain but rather to enable its audience to make meaning under its guidance. Hoban's writing and use of symbolism are certainly more self-conscious than is generally expected in contemporary children's novels.[6] As we have seen, however, the text is at pains to avoid conventional reconstructions of its meanings; what may be thought of as heavy-handed can also be read as the text's determination to disrupt a too-simple reading of its representations, symbolic or narrative. The reader is forced to pick a way through the complications of Hoban's story, through difficult language, obscure symbolism, and the disruptions in the lifeline of the protagonist. How the reader strings this together to make a story is explained by the text in its own story of the mice, who are joined by their relations. This analogy, complex in the abstract, is lived by the reader in the concrete, who connects one element of the story to another by relating language, theme, and narrative to create meaning. That this work is not easy is in itself a warning against a natural or straightforward reading both of narrative and of symbol. Hoban's book makes the reader aware that knowing what or where one is and what it means to find a place in any story, including the one we tell about ourselves, is as difficult as it is necessary.

*Notes*

1. See Rose for an account of how the idea of the innocent child affects the criticism and reception of children's fiction.

2. For a recent account of this text that adopts a view of the child as innocent or the site of hope, see De Luca, 211–21.

3. For the text's difficulty, see, e.g., Rustin 182.

4. In one of the text's meditations on the difference between organic and mechanical, the label on the Bonzo can resembles, or repeats, the little black-and-white dog that accompanies the tramp who first saw the mouse and his child.

5. See Riffaterre 4.

6. See Inglis: "But it is a heavy-handed as well as an obscure little message if you try to unpack its meanings" (304).

*Works Cited*

De Luca, Geraldine. "'A Condition of Complete Simplicity': The Toy as Child in *The Mouse and His Child*." *Children's Literature in Education* 19 (1988): 211–21.

Gallop, Jane. *Reading Lacan*. Ithaca: Cornell University Press, 1985.

Hoban, Russell. *The Mouse and His Child*. Harmondsworth: Penguin, 1976.

Inglis, Fred. *The Promise of Happiness: Value and Meaning in Children's Fiction*. Cambridge: Cambridge University Press, 1981.

Lacan, Jacques. *Ecrits*. Trans. Alan Sheridan. London: Tavistock, 1977.

Riffaterre, Michael. *Text Production*. Trans. Terese Lyons. New York: Columbia University Press, 1983.

Rose, Jacqueline. *The Case of Peter Pan, or The Impossibility of Children's Fiction*. London: Verso, 1987.

Rustin, Margaret and Michael. *Narratives of Love and Loss: Studies in Modern Children's Fiction*. London: Verso, 1987.

# Metafiction and Interpretation: William Mayne's Salt River Times, Winter Quarters, *and* Drift

## John Stephens

William Mayne has long been considered one of the more "difficult" of contemporary children's writers. Studies of his work focus mainly on books for older readers and tend to begin by remarking on their difficulty (Sarland 107; Walker 31; Rees 94). The essence of the "problem" of Mayne, first isolated by Charles Sarland and Aidan Chambers, is that he cultivates a narrative stance that distances reader from text, demanding that analysis predominate over empathy. With hindsight, we can see that in the novels discussed by Sarland and Chambers the narrative stance is part of Mayne's use of the strategies of modernist fiction (Stephens "Modernism"). In the early eighties, Mayne began to emphasize further the process of analysis (and thereby to reflect an increasing use of postmodernist modes) by including in his books substantial metafictional episodes that simultaneously advance the story and act as models for interpreting the narrative techniques that inform it. The function of those episodes in *Salt River Times, Winter Quarters,* and *Drift* is examined here. All three have again generally been regarded as "difficult" (a reviewer remarked in *Horn Book,* with some hint of relief, on the "less difficult and complex" prose of *Drift*), but readers prepared to take up the challenge will not only find the books rewarding in themselves but may also discover that the experience broadens their awareness of how fiction works.

Metafiction—the strategy of suspending the illusion of fiction in some way in order to direct attention to the processes of making fiction—is often regarded with suspicion; at worst, it can seem merely a postmodernist self-indulgence. In Mayne's hands, though, it can play an important part in a reader's understanding of his fictions. When they are not being guided through a book by an omniscient and interventionist narrator, readers are subject to less constraint but must also take more responsibility, and this has two notable consequences. First, by drawing attention to aspects of the process

*Children's Literature* 21, ed. Francelia Butler, Christine Doyle Francis, Anne K. Phillips, and Julie K. Pfeiffer (Yale University Press, © 1993 The Children's Literature Foundation, Inc.).

of text production, Mayne invites his readers to share his delight not just in the end-product—at a simple level, the story—but also in the process of production. Second, by focusing on *how* the text means, he is able to offer analogies to how meaning is ascribed to events in everyday reality. Events in life, as in fiction, may not have a particular and obvious significance, but they acquire it by interpretation, and this in turn depends largely on the presuppositions of the interpreter.

The responsibility of the interpreter is enlarged in these three books by the way each involves the representation and interpretation of minorities or subcultures, and each shows to varying degrees how the presuppositions of an outsider result in misinterpretation. The distance Mayne maintains between text and reader reminds us that we, too, are interpreters outside the text. The analogy between interpreting human situations and reading fictions is expressed by the strategy of placing at the center of each narrative some element of mystery, a concealed center that the protagonists strive to reach as they struggle to interpret events and the world in which they live, and then building into the narrative the metafictional episodes, which represent this quest for the center as analogous to a reader's struggle with the text.

One of the ways Mayne signals the presence of this metafictional element is by his handling of levels of narration, whereby he virtually eliminates narrator presence in favor of character focalization—that is, presenting the world of the fiction as perceived by one or more of the characters in it. Theories of narrative have for some time distinguished between primary narrators, who tell a story and present a framing point of view; secondary narrators within that story, who may narrate segments of story from a different point of view; and focalizers, characters who do not tell their own story but whose point of view nevertheless prevails because they are presented as the lens through which ideas, events, and other characters are perceived (see Martin 142–46; Stephens "Middle of Being"; Stephens *Language* 67–69). Broad movements in narrative level among these possibilities are obvious and commonly indicated by words denoting perception or communication. By overtly exploiting these differences in narrative levels Mayne draws attention to the process of narration, particularly to how narration shifts reader attention from story to theme.

In each of these books, Mayne has minimized the extent to which narration presents the point of view of an omniscient, primary narrator, preferring character-focalized modes instead. The result is a narrative stance situated close to events, in the sense that it enables readers little more, or no more, insight into what is taking place, and what it means, than is seen to be available to the focalizing characters. At the same time, though, the emphasis on narrative process draws attention to the essentially limited points of view represented by such focalization and hence heightens reader awareness of the different ways reality is filtered by story-telling: biases are imputed to a character because his or her perception is transparently selective, or else it is distorted or obstructed by simple misinterpretation or miscomprehension. When the intrusive forms of omniscient narration do appear, their function is no longer straightforwardly directive. In *Winter Quarters,* for example, narrator comment establishes a good-humored irony toward the characters' attempts to make sense of the world. Thus, such a direct address to readers as "It was [Lall's] worked-out thought. It was to be found wrong" (119) neither has a genuine prospective effect nor directs reader attention to "story," for the simple reason that the preceding chapter has already shown that Lall is wrong. Instead, it focuses ironic attention on the process of logical deduction (as Lall exemplifies it), which concentrates on circumstantial details and fails to penetrate to inner meaning.

The books offer many more substantial and more obviously metafictional comments on their own narrative processes. Of the metafictional scenes in *Salt River Times,* two are of particular interest, the first because it models how texts may obstruct reception, and the second because it shows how readers must decode this particular text. The primary narrator is here substantially effaced, since only six of the twenty-one chapters are presented from his point of view (7, 11, 12, 18, 20, 21), whereas the rest are narrated or focalized wholly or partly through one of the several children who are the principal characters. Indeed, in a remarkable tour de force, Mayne has welded together a narrative presenting the points of view of eight characters apart from the narrator.[1] Such focalization is not merely a matter of particular chapters focusing on one of the characters but of locating perception of events within the mind of that character; this is achieved by restricting presentation of thought (as opposed to speech) to the one character, and by presenting the text's pervasive gaps in information as impinging specifically on that character.

The process is imbued with a metafictional effect in chapter 1, which moves between omniscient narration and limited perspective character focalization (through Mel). The act of observation is rendered more immediate by the use of the present tense:[2]

> An old woman is telling a story. She says it happened long ago, and she has had a cold ever since. Her nose runs on cold days, so there is a drop on the end of it now. She leaves it there.
> Mel is listening. He has his hands in his pockets.

There is a narrator present who "sees" Mel as much as the old woman is "seen," but as the chapter proceeds, point of view shifts between the narrator and the boy, so that by page 2 Mel has become focalizer: "Mel thinks that can't be true, because there's a Safeway one side of the road and McDonald's the other, and there must always be something there first. And what's a tram doing in a paddock? But the old woman is saying something about that." The use of present tense narrows the distance and blurs the distinction between reported indirect thought (signaled by "thinks") and the free direct thought marked by the interrogative. This shift to character focalization enables Mayne to establish a more restricted narrative vantage point. At the same time, it discreetly begins the novel's metafictional unfolding. The narrator begins the book with an account of story-telling, "An old woman is telling a story. . . . Mel is listening," and this is framed by the Narrator-Narratee relationship, which implicitly suggests, "A narrator is telling a story about an old woman telling a story. . . . The narratee is listening." This story-within-the-story immediately highlights a dialogic strategy characteristic of all three novels: there are internal dialogues between the various stories—or versions of a single story—that are told, and there is an external dialogue between reader and text. Mel's attempts here to decode and interpret the story mirror those of readers, in that Mel is overhearing the narrative, rather than being its direct audience (since, as it soon emerges, "The old woman is talking to Mrs. Anghelidas"), and readers likewise "overhear" (since the narrator addresses the narratee); further, Mel's reception of the text is fragmented because passing traffic periodically drowns the old woman's voice, and this in turn parallels the way the text's various restricted narrative stances withhold information from its readers.

An extension of the metafictional effect of this scene in the later part of the opening chapter suggests an obvious model for a reader's overall experience of *Salt River Times*. The old woman's story is continued, but now with Joe as audience: a crucial piece of information, that she chooses Joe because he is of Chinese descent, is held back until her story is completed; that Joe is the grandson of one of the Chinese involved in her story is not revealed until chapter 17. The "story"-line of *Salt River Times* is very fragmented, and although there is one mystery that runs through it, connecting most of the strands, and that is solved, the task the book poses for its readers is not simply that of solving this mystery; the apparent clues do not function only toward that end but also direct attention toward the book's themes—the important processes of perception, interpretation and communication, and the role these play in the development of a sense of self in relationship to a sense of place (and its history) and to the evolution of a multicultural society.

Perhaps the most intensely self-reflexive section of this rich novel is chapter 7, which functions as a *mise en abyme*. (I am using *mise en abyme* here in the sense of a small narrative segment which, embedded within a larger narrative, indicates how that larger narrative might be interpreted.)[3] Chapter 6 had described how "One day Mr. Lee came into River Street and burned down Mr. Young's house"; chapter 7 re-presents the burning of the house as retold by Jack to his wife, Mary. The ironical title of the chapter, "The House That Jack Built," should alert readers to its game-playing aspect in two ways: first, because the old, well-known narrative it alludes to is one that is linear and simply accretes facts and assumes causality, and as such could hardly differ more from the convoluted and evasive narration attempted by Jack; second, because the title is metaphoric, as Jack's story about the destruction of a house is presented as an act of building—indeed, of fabrication—on his part. While Jack purports to describe an event that is factual, in the sense that it has already occurred in the previous chapter, his story radically exemplifies how narrative can filter and reshape fact, since he is actually attempting to conceal from Mary that in his hurry to reach the scene of the fire he has wrecked their car. But Mary adroitly decodes his narration and extracts from it the "story" of the car. This may be classified as a narrated chapter, and although the narrator has very little actual presence, since the chapter is constructed almost entirely as dialogue, the presence of a narrator point of view has a significant function in underpinning Mary's dominant role in the dialogue. The speech reporting tags are generally restricted to "said Jack" and "said Mary" (there are only five examples of marked tags—"said Jack, crossly"; "said Jack, taking no notice"; "Jack bellowed"; "said Jack. Shouted."; "said Jack, offended"), and the narrator's only other presence is in three short sentences concluding the chapter.

The chapter clearly connects with the rest of the book as a mise en abyme: it relates to the surrounding narrative at story level because it deals with the burning of the house, but it also has a metafictional function because Mary's decoding of Jack's story reflects the way a reader of *Salt River Times* decodes the narrator's apparently unco-ordinated narrative to perceive significances beyond that of mere story. It thus becomes important that all marked speech reporting tags pertain to Jack, whereas the narrator remains totally neutral toward Mary, the interrogator of Jack's text and the image of a reader's relationship with the larger narrative. Mary's re-reading is sustained throughout the chapter, but the following extract is symptomatic:

> "I just backed up in the space behind this ute, and, whammo, there's the fire engine."
> "Just making this little scratch," said Mary. "Whammo?"
> "This little scrape," said Jack. "Little whammo."
> "This dent you mentioned," said Mary. "Was that it?"
> "Just a little hole, you know," said Jack. "Soon fix it, no worries."
> "Whammo," said Mary.
> "You keep finding out things I never said," said Jack. "I suppose you think you can tell me about the two old boys. Because I haven't managed to tell you anything about them yet. I suppose you know about them already."
> "Leaning on the gate watching the bullocks," said Mary.
> "There aren't any bullocks in Iramoo," said Jack. Shouted.
> "Just a guess," said Mary. "You leave such a lot out of your stories, Jack."
> "I don't believe you listen," said Jack. "Only to the bits I leave out."

This duologue explores the constitution of narrative as a bundle of linguistic and literary structures (henceforth the "text") that encodes the story and then, by means of such features as textual organization and textual attitudes toward story, further implies thematic meaning or other such ulterior significances. As "story" is encoded as "text," various kinds of choice operate at the level of lexis. A particular lexical slot can be filled in a number of possible ways, suggesting various overtones and even hierarchies of degree, as in "little scratch . . . little scrape . . . dent . . . little hole"; or else a particular signifier may be invested with a shifting signified, as in the varying scales of impact indicated by "whammo." Such choices influence not just the "story" reconstructed from them but also the attitude toward and significance of that "story." Another crucial aspect of narration is the process of "finding out things I never said" by listening to "the bits I leave out," that is, reading in such a way as to move beyond "story," the primary abstraction from the surface text, to the secondary abstraction of ulterior "meaning." To effect this move, a reader must formulate hypotheses as he or she reads ("Leaning on the gate watching the bullocks." . . . "Just a guess"); Mary is teasing Jack with her reference to bullocks, but its absurdity foregrounds the point that the process of extrapolation that enables her to discover the truth about the car before Jack reaches the intended significance of his story is the same process that readers carry out to perceive significances in the narrative at a higher level of abstraction than that of the "story."

Jack's narrative discloses a double commentary on narrative point of view. On the one hand, his story is motivated by a point of view that is no more than narrow self-interest,[4] as he attempts, unsuccessfully, to use story for an exemplary effect, to modify the behavior of his audience:

> "Think of those two old boys, house burning down, not a worry in the world."
> Mary said something Jack didn't want to hear.
> Just walked away calmly. At full speed.

That is, he wishes to present the behavior of the old men as a model for Mary's response to the destroyed car. An implication to be drawn from this is that the author recognizes a reader's capacity to resist being manipulated by the text and regards the author-reader relationship as one of subtle cooperation, a cooperation readily apparent here in the joke of the contradiction between "calmly" and "At full speed," which is available to readers but not to the character in the text. If, for example, the text's propositions are then a distortion of the world as readers know it, those propositions will become the object of careful scrutiny.

Such a limitation is revealed, in the example of Jack's story, by the second implied comment on point of view: Jack's physical vantage-point is restricted because he was trapped within his wrecked car during the fire, and so lacked access to the main actors within his story. Readers, with prior and superior knowledge, are aware of the further undermining effected by Jack's limited understanding of events and by his ignorance that the fire was deliberately lit. This further irony thus functions as another sign of the restriction placed on a narrative when it is focalized through the limited perceptions of a character within the text. The task of interpretation is passed back to readers with the chapter's final sentences, since a "something" left unstated has to be inferred from its impact on its hearer-audience. Just as the book as a whole encodes its interlocked stories as text but never overtly discloses the meaning(s) of the events described, so accordingly its mise en abyme chapter ends with a minute example of the larger task presented to its readers.

The other books employ comparable strategies, though they are not so clearly separated from the larger narrative. In each a crucial episode also functions as a mise en abyme, indicating how readers can extrapolate from text not only to story but also to meaning. The pertinent episode in *Winter Quarters* is that in which Issy enters the Hall of Mirrors. *Winter Quarters* is a thematically complex book, concerned with identity, responsibility, memory, perception, and understanding. By making his principal characters Travellers, people with a culture situated outside the hierarchies of mainstream, sedentary society (which dismisses them with the pejorative name "gypsies"), Mayne is immediately able to defamiliarize ways of looking at the world, thus making it harder for readers to formulate facile judgments by applying conventional social ideologies to the text. Indeed, strategies of defamiliarization are used to this end in all three books. *Winter Quarters* narrates a double quest: Lall, the Traveller, and Issy, the "housey," must exchange ways of life, families, and, in part, identities to carry out their interconnected searches. To Lall falls the task of being stationary and finding what is concealed in a single place; to Issy, who dreams of wandering to distant cities with romantic names, comes a wandering much more restricted and less romantic, in search of the Travellers' missing chief. Both quests are more than a merely physical searching, being also an exploration into the customs and traditions of a people in order to recuperate the past and make the present possible.

The book opens with the Travellers locked out from what they regard as their traditional winter quarters, an exclusion that becomes a metonymy for their separation from the core of their culture. On a larger scale, the Travellers' plight functions as a metonymy for any society that forgets its past and becomes rootless and fragmented. It is significant, then, that the Travellers are wary of their unofficial scribe's practice of preserving records in writing: "Clark Riston had papers on which things were written. It was a thing not approved of by the people of the coffle" (38). Riston's given name, Clark, preserves his function as a meaning trace (early English *clerk*, "scholar"), and some readers will recognize in this figure—the Bird Man with his cloak of feathers—the Egyptian god of writing and scholarship, Thoth. One of the important effects of *Winter Quarters*, indeed, is to show how the past can be recovered through a cooperative compilation of oral tradition and written records.

As the past is reflected in the memories of the present like images in a distorting mirror, and as people interpret signs and phenomena according to experience and expectation, so also fiction poses problems of interpretation for its readers. More specifically, as the questers in the novel have to turn clues into signs and signs into meaning, so the novel's readers have to progress from text to the meanings beyond story. How this is done is mapped out explicitly in the Hall of Mirrors, at that point in the novel when Issy achieves the major part of his quest by seeing and identifying Shemer, the Travellers' lost chief. The episode's double procedure of advancing "story" and of commenting on text-reader relations begins when, having been admitted to Shemer's compound, Issy rings the bell on his caravan but gets no response:

> This is what happens, the nothing, thought Issy, when you get to Chimborazo, the Gold Coast, Samarkand. No one comes to the door. There isn't anything at the end, after all. You get there, and that is all there is. [110] . . . [Issy then gazes at the marquee that houses the Hall of Mirrors.] Issy looked. A thing is hard to see until you know what you are looking at. You have to be able to imagine it at the same time. Issy felt clearly the distinction between seeing and understanding. Somewhere between seeing and knowing is Samarkand.
>
> However, you are not in Samarkand very long. Behind him, in the road, a street lamp gave a sulky glop, and began to cast

a sullen light. The result was that the rest of the world became darker. When it did so Issy understood what was taking
place at the marquee. It was merely lit from inside; light shone
through the canvas. He had seen the same effect before, at the
tent in the woods. In the woods there had already been darkness; here there had been light all round, and at the moment
of balance he had been looking but not seeing, seeing but not
understanding.

It was clear now that he was to walk down to the marquee.
It had been obvious all the time, in fact, but that was another
instance of seeing and not knowing what you look at. [111]

Constantly slipping, once again, between narration and character focalization, Mayne here asks his readers to perceive their task
as comparable with Issy's. Both character and reader must perform
a double mental process involving, on the one hand, the temporal
progression from "seeing" to "understanding" or "knowing," and,
on the other hand, the capacity to comprehend perceptually and
conceptually (or imaginatively) at the same time. Issy's dream countries, represented here by Samarkand, are reinscribed not as goals
or ends but as moments of transition, just as a passive reading of
a book needs to be replaced by the kind of imaginative interpretive reading that goes beyond escapist dwelling on "story"—that is,
which goes beyond "seeing" to achieve "knowing." Otherwise, if the
step beyond story is not taken, textuality is emptied of significance
and exists only in the moment of reception: "There isn't anything
at the end, after all." What this metafictional episode asserts, however, is that the text will insist on the progression so that its readers
will "not [be] at Samarkand very long," and the way it does this is by
using foregrounding techniques to elicit significance. In this case,
the gradually altering relativity of the light of the marquee and the
fading light of a late afternoon in winter functions as a metaphor
for the way artistic foregrounding techniques focus audience attention, so that what is "obvious all the time" can be "known" as well
as "seen."

But the relationship between text and reader is not quite that
simple, since it is also in the nature of texts to cultivate indirection
and to make readers work at finding meaning:

[Issy has entered the marquee.] He took three or four easy
steps towards the carpet, then rammed hard into something
solid. It was as if a door had been slammed against him. It

hurt. There was no need now to wonder about the difference between seeing and understanding. He understood that he was hurt, and saw nothing. . . .

He had walked straight into a large sheet of something like glass. He put his hand on it, and felt it flex in an unforgiving way. He could see it now he had understood it, like glass, but not so. It is like that with Samarkand: you can't get through.

He got up. Now he knew he was in some sort of joky trap. It was necessary to look, see, know. [112]

The further reference to 'Samarkand' here functions to play out the process the incident is exploring, in that rephrasing the impene-trability of the perspex as the Samarkand-metaphor brings out the metaphor also implicit in the perspex barrier. Text is also "like glass, but not so"; it can be a transparent window onto "story" but, "like Samarkand," the text-story relationship is not an end in itself but a means to a further end whereby significance ("understanding") changes the nature of text ("seeing").

The quest pursued by Issy (as also that pursued by Lall) gains meaning for him only in retrospect, when understanding pulls together all that has been seen and experienced into a fresh con-figuration that actually alters the meaning of the individual parts. This, of course, also models how readers experience the text. The prerequisite for decoding the text is understanding that it is like a mirror maze, "some sort of joky trap," and that the process of read-ing demands the progression "look, see, know." Ultimately, though, there are limits to understanding, as a work may always withhold some part of its mystery:

[Issy wanders, lost in the maze of mirrors, seeing numerous distorted images of himself.] Then he came upon mirror-sided steps, and went up slowly, beside himself, being edged off by his own double as the glass encroached on the treads. Then he came to the top, and walked on a strip of carpet, with wide glass either side. This glass started reflective, and with more mirror overhanging it there was an immense void either side, deeper than depth, going down to places the eye could not see, or mind ever understand. [114–15]

While text order here emphasizes spatio-temporal linearity (espe-cially by means of the temporal adverbs and correlative clauses), the progression is toward an ever-increasing self-reflexivity as the

mirrors reflect in one, then two, and finally three dimensions, culminating in the infinity of inter-reflecting mirrors, which confounds
notions of time and space, affirming the existence of places beyond Samarkand but which, situated in the paradox "deeper than
depth," remain unseeable and unimaginable. A text cannot yield up
answers to all the questions a reader may ask of it, and neither can
a reader conceive all the possible questions.

The gap between perceiving and knowing is further explored
in *Drift,* but here through a different kind of double narration,
a telling of the same "story" twice. This metafictive strategy, long
familiar from such early postmodernist texts as John Fowles's *Col-
lector* (see Donovan 296), draws attention to the fact that a narrative
is a process of representation. A complex model of reading is developed as, again eschewing narrator omniscience, Mayne focalizes
the first two-thirds of the novel through Rafe, a white boy lost on
the Canadian frontier and taken up by two Indian women. Unable to communicate with his captors through language, Rafe does
not understand what is happening to him, and there are few clues
available to a reader to enable any "reading" of events that differs substantially from Rafe's own misreading. The last third of the
novel then re-presents events now refocalized as the experiences
of Tawena, the young Indian girl with whom Rafe had originally
become lost.

The episode in this novel that I identify as specifically metafictional is that in which, under cover of darkness, Tawena pretends
to be a bear and in that role orders the women to return Rafe to
his village and then stages her own apparent death. Henceforth,
shadowing the others, intervening at crucial moments, she becomes
a deus ex machina similar to the author behind the text. Further,
her own survival depends on her success in creating an incentive
for the women to preserve Rafe's life and return him to his village,
since this is also her village and she, too, is lost. The analogy between these central aspects of the story and the author-text-reader
relationship lies in the area of the hermeneutic gaps that induce a
reader to continue reading.[5] Because Tawena's "play" is twice narrated at length, first focalized through Rafe as receiver and then
through Tawena as author, the novel can present two very different
perspectives on the event and in so doing can comment on the difference between creation and reception of a text. Tawena intends
Rafe to know that the bear tells the Indian women to take him

home and to think that the bear has also eaten Tawena. Here is the episode as Rafe perceives it:

> Somewhere in the woods beyond, behind them, there was more noise, louder shrieks, and screams. And with the screams came the growl of the bear, the great noise of it moving about, and something like the snapping of its teeth. There was a shout of pain, and then, echoing among the trees, a last scream from Tawena, stopping suddenly. Tawena's talk with the bear was over. In Rafe's head the noise stayed. It seemed to echo back from the distant trees.
>
> There was a fearful crunching noise now. Rafe remembered how he had eaten whole caterpillars, and at this minute the bear was eating Tawena in the same way, straight with its teeth.
>
> And now, he thought, the bear would not tell the Indian women anything, because it had not been told. . . .
>
> Rafe slept. He had stopped being able to think, and his eyes closed by themselves. He was woken for a third time that night, this time by a deep and loud shouting from close by. He heard Hareskin and Deerskin get up, because the deep shout had words in it. The words came slowly out from the trees. Now and then among them was the snuffling noise of the bear. Rafe knew the sound well from the fisherman's hut on the ice, the snuffing, sniffing, large breathing, and the noise of claws on wood. The bear had come back and was talking, telling them all something.
>
> Deerskin and Hareskin were listening. They were attending and obeying; they were answering quietly. After all, the bear was telling them what Tawena said it would. Rafe knew now that the only way to tell the bear anything was to let it kill and eat you, and that was how Tawena had given it the message. She had died, she had been torn apart by a wild creature, just to save him, Rafe. He knew it must be so, though he did not understand a word the bear said. [37–38]

Even though much of the description of the bear's behavior seems factual ("there was more noise . . . came the growl. . . . There was a shout") and lacks the kind of signs, especially verbals and deictics, needed to shift point of view from narrator to character, many indicators show that Rafe acts as a focalizer (but not *narrator,* as Donovan [298] argues): the verbals "remembered, thought, heard, knew, did not understand"; the phrase, "in Rafe's head"; emotive point of view in "a *fearful* crunching noise"; and suggestions of free indirect thought, in the segment beginning "After all." Readers will perhaps only grasp the point of this gap between the apparently objective account and the character's interpretation once they review the episode after having read the second version of it (109–11), where it is revealed that there was no bear. A major difference between the two accounts is that the second is indeed factual, filling in the story elements missing from the first, and that it lacks the emphasis on perception and interpretation evident in the earlier version.

The process of "seeing, knowing, understanding" is thus given a whole new slant. From Rafe's point of view, all he failed to understand was the words spoken by the "bear" in the Indians' language. In fact, he has constructed a completely erroneous story from what he heard, on the basis of his recent experiences ("Rafe remembered how he had eaten whole caterpillars, and . . . the bear was eating Tawena in the same way"; "Rafe knew the sound well") and of the gender relationships presupposed by his cultural tradition (female dies so that male might live). At this stage in the text readers face a hermeneutic gap: there is insufficient information to explain what has taken place, but in line with the realistic mode of the text so far, a reader is apt to remain skeptical of the proposition that bears convey verbal messages to humans even though the Indians believe it and Rafe has been convinced.

The gap is repeated in other ways as the novel progresses: someone lights a fire for Rafe while he sleeps; when he loses his way collecting wood, he is driven back to camp by bear noises; and something creeps into the camp on occasional nights to snuggle against him. First-time readers will probably realize that Rafe, motivated by hope and fear, misinterprets all such actions, and the retrospective re-reading explains how Tawena is involved in each. One thing Rafe is sure he does know—"that the only way to tell the bear anything was to let it kill and eat you"—stands as a type of self-surrender to the text; it is a procedure the novel's retrospective re-reading of the episode rejects as misreading. In her secret visit to Rafe just before her bear play, Tawena had told Rafe that the bear would tell the women to take him home, yet Rafe concludes that he is to be sold into slavery because he can't believe Tawena and assumes the worst out of his ignorance of the Other. Traveling under this illusion,

Rafe has to discover that what he thinks is a journey away and into slavery is a journey home to freedom. It is more than a physical journey, however: as affection slowly grows between him and the women, he gains insight into an Other (a way of life, of communication, of seeing the world) that has the potential to extend his mental and emotional boundaries.

On the level of "story" the book ends happily for Rafe, since he is returned to his home, but its meaning is more pessimistic. The last meeting between Rafe and Tawena, back in the village, takes the form of a third version of the bear-play, which Tawena partly acts out and partly narrates as she explains to Rafe how she had saved him to save herself. Rafe thus finally attains the same knowledge of the "story" as a reader has, but not the same knowledge of its meaning. He is left "startled and wondering" (155); he has made little progress in human understanding, and his potential for growth, it is suggested by the closing sentences of the book, will be restricted by his cultural milieu:

> Rafe went in. But always he remembered the noise of the bear in the woods, the fire mysteriously lit, the footprints of bear; and mostly the presence once or twice by night of Tawena beside him.
>
> Tawena went away with other Indians during the summer. Rafe was never sure whether she came back. She never spoke to him again, if she did.
>
> "Women." said his father, when he spoke of it; and Mrs Considine said, when Rafe angered her again, "Wouldn't I rather have the bag of meal and them Indians have kept you!"

His experiences thus stay with him as a memory of the things he badly misread at the time, but they have not altered his life; he was granted an insight, as a reader of a text might be, and the possibility of an inner transformation, but the experience does not noticeably bring him and Tawena together—his sense of loss expressed in the last few lines is brushed aside by the conventional responses of his society (in his parents' sexism and racism). Readers, though, have seen that potential for growth and can move on into a realm of more generous values.

The ending of *Drift* foregrounds the relationship between fiction and society in another interesting way. With Rafe's return home and Tawena's explanation of events the "story" has been neatly rounded off in the manner of a classic realistic well-made plot, with its concomitant suggestions of shapeliness and meaningfulness. But by focusing on the problem of meaning through the metafictional use of the recurring accounts of the bear-play, the novel suggests that meaning that inheres only in story is not meaning at all, or at best is so only on a very limited scale. By pitting the well-made plot against thematic inconclusiveness, *Drift* challenges the conventional forms of endings in children's literature, with their tendencies either to strong closure or to the currently fashionable open-endedness. (Other writers have also done this, of course: John Gordon's *The House on the Brink* is a pertinent analogy.) The conventional fictional frame is broken more obviously by *Salt River Times,* which, beginning with its story-within-a-story, ends, after the "mystery" has been solved, with an apparently inconsequential chapter that flaunts a refusal to tie up loose ends. The implication in these handlings of the endings is that shapeliness is imposed on fiction, and by exposing the narrative frame Mayne makes the point, often made by metafictions, "that neither historical experiences nor literary fictions are unmediated or unprocessed" (Waugh 30).

The books I have been discussing are difficult in the way they draw attention to their own fictionality in order to involve their readers in an active decoding of text. While textual process is so insistently present, whether by the metafictional or focalizing strategies, it is impossible to treat the text as a mere cipher through which one passes to the "story." If the text *seems* to be transparent, it turns out to be like the perspex barrier in *Winter Quarters;* attempts to construct "story" will be hampered by the fragmentary and elliptical representations of experiences mediated through focalizers who characteristically misinterpret the significance of what they observe.

But an understanding of the events depicted is not simply obstructed by this narrative strategy, since it operates in tandem with the metafictional reflections on obstructed reception and decoding. The metafictions inform a reader's observations of how the characters deduce wrong meanings from signs and events and subsequently arrive more or less successfully at better meanings, and by means of this process the reader is confronted with a commentary on how people impose presuppositional meaning on life, based on assumptions about race, sex, and culture. Literary and social codes exist in parallel. In everyday reality, people create fictions about others (just as fictional characters do in *Salt River Times* and *Drift*) or about themselves (as in *Winter Quarters*), and by reflecting on the process whereby fictions are made, and on their final arbitrariness, Mayne seeks to disturb his readers' literary presuppositions, and then through that their social and moral presuppositions, as he transforms the glass wall of fiction into a mirror.

### Notes

1. Chapter focalizers are as follows: Mel (1, 5, 9, 17); Gwenda (2, 10); Joe (3); Sophie (6, 15); Elissa (8); Dee (13, 15); Kate (16). Two chapters (4, 19) are first-person narrations by Morgan.
2. Present tense is used only here and in chapters 4 and 19, where it is used to further the rendering of Morgan's re-encoding of immediately present phenomena as fantasy.
3. Discussions relevant to this use of mise en abyme are: Tadeusz Kowzan, "Art En Abyme,'" *Diogenes* 96 (1976): 78–88 (on "autothematism"); Moshe Ron, "The Restricted Abyss: Nine Problems in the Theory of *Mise en Abyme*," *Poetics Today* 8 (1987): 432–34; and Gerald Prince, *A Dictionary of Narratology* (Lincoln: University of Nebraska Press, 1987), 53.
4. For types of point of view, see Seymour Chatman, *Story and Discourse* (Ithaca: Cornell University Press, 1978), 151–52, and Stephens, *Language*, 26–29.
5. This aspect of narrative is summarized by Shlomith Rimmon-Kenan, *Narrative Fiction* (London: Methuen, 1983), 125–29.

### Works Cited

Chambers, Aidan. "The Reader in the Book." *Signal* 23 (1977): 64–87. Reprinted in *Booktalk*. London: Bodley Head, 1985, 34–58.
Donovan, Ann. "Narrative Strategy in *Drift* by William Mayne." Pages 295–307 in Charlotte F. Otten and Gary D. Schmidt, eds., *The Voice of the Narrator in Children's Literature*. New York: Greenwood, 1989.
Martin, Wallace. *Recent Theories of Narrative*. Ithaca: Cornell University Press, 1986.
Mayne, William. *Salt River Times*. New York: Greenwillow Books, 1980.
———. *Winter Quarters*. Harmondsworth: Puffin Books, 1984.
———. *Drift*. Harmondsworth: Puffin Books, 1987.
Rees, David. "Enigma Variations: William Mayne." *Children's Literature in Education* 19 (1988): 94–105.
Review of *Drift*. *Horn Book Magazine* (July–August 1986): 457.
Sarland, Charles. "Chorister Quartet." *Signal* 18 (1975): 107–13.
Scutter, Heather. "Fantastic Imagery in William Mayne's *Winter Quarters*." *Papers: Explorations into Children's Literature* 1:2 (1990): 87–94.
Stephens, John. "'In the Middle of Being in Two Places at Once': Perception and Signification in William Mayne's *All the King's Men*." *Ariel* 19 (1988): 59–71.
———. *Language and Ideology in Children's Fiction*. London: Longman, 1992.
———. "Modernism to Postmodernism, or The Line from Insk to Onsk: William Mayne's *Tiger's Railway*." *Papers: Explorations into Children's Literature* 3:2 (1992): 51–59.
Walker, Alistair. "Landscape as Metaphor in the Novels of William Mayne." *Children's Literature in Education* 11 (1980): 31–42.
Waugh, Patricia. *Metafiction*. London: Methuen, 1984.

# Arabic Adventurers and American Investigators: Cultural Values in Adolescent Detective Fiction

Sylvia Patterson Iskander

> The international smuggler Kent was able to slip through the hands of the police in many countries. Suddenly Inspector Sami received a message stating that this dangerous smuggler had arrived in Egypt. . . . The five adventurers appeared in the heart of the chase. Were they able to reach John Kent? Were they able to succeed where police from all over the world had failed? [*International Smuggler,* preface]

With this opening Mahmoud Salem hooks his adolescent readers into one of the Five Adventurers series; other contemporary series in Arabic—the Three Adventurers and the Four Adventurers—begin in similar fashion.[1] These contemporary Arabic Adventurers series, set in Egypt, invite comparison with the American Three Investigators series, particularly the earlier volumes by Robert Arthur.[2] Arabic series of detective fiction, a fairly recent development, have become popular among Middle Eastern children, who have not had their own children's literature until this century (Ghurayyib 17), much later than European and American children.[3]

John Cawelti's description of "the world of a formula . . . as an archetypal story pattern embodied in the images, symbols, themes, and myths of a particular culture" (16) and Dennis Porter's belief that Western detective fiction is a "valuable barometer of [a] society's ideological norms" (1), although written about detective fiction for adults, are both valid concepts for adolescent fiction whether Eastern or Western.[4] The formula for detective fiction largely remains constant, but cultural differences clearly distinguish the Eastern Adventurers series from the Western Investigators; furthermore, techniques for creating suspense subsequently produce a slower pace in the Arabic stories.[5]

Stories from both cultures generally adopt the viewpoint of the youthful detective, never that of the criminal. Because romanticiz-

*Children's Literature* 21, ed. Francelia Butler, Christine Doyle Francis, Anne K. Phillips, and Julie K. Pfeiffer (Yale University Press, © 1993 The Children's Literature Foundation, Inc.).

ing crime or criminals is not acceptable in Middle Eastern culture, the Arabic stories do not focus on the criminal;[6] Western stories for children also do not romanticize the criminal, though some adult American stories may. The attitude toward crime, however, can be significantly different in Eastern and Western detective fiction. The attitudes that crime is a social problem and that criminal acts are "not evil deeds but the result of defective social arrangements or heredity" (Cawelti 57) do not coincide with Islamic law, which, rather than faulting society, generally punishes the individual doer of the act.

In spite of their different attitudes toward criminals, both Eastern and Western youths with prior experience in reading detective fiction enjoy the contrast between the "safely familiar" and the "tantalizingly new and different" (Billman 37), the rarity of the crime, the clever solution to a common crime, the development of suspense, and the arousal of the reader's emotions (Porter 236). As Anne Scott MacLeod has written, "The real protagonist of [formula fiction] is the reader; the real plot is a satisfying vicarious experience that also—and not incidentally—conveys messages the reader wants and is able to hear" (129). Both Eastern and Western tales affirm their readers' beliefs; indeed, "the persistence of certain recognizable national cultural traditions within the large corpus of detective fiction" is, according to Porter, "remarkable" (127). Although Porter speaks of fiction for adults, his remarks prove valid for children's fiction in which cultural differences permeate the characterization, action, and setting, as well as the methods for creating suspense and the resulting pace of the story.

All detective stories obviously require a victim, a criminal, a detective, and others who, though involved with the crime, are incapable of solving it. The victim must not be so prominent as to overshadow the detective's role, but the reader must know enough about the victim to care about the crime's solution (Cawelti 91). In some Arabic stories, such as *The Bride of Sinai*, the reader knows almost nothing about the bride but can sympathize with her having been kidnaped from her wedding without knowing her more intimately. Rules exist for the creation of the criminal as well; his or her motives must not be probed too deeply, the goal of the detective story being to establish clearly the criminal's guilt (Cawelti 92). In the Arabic and American stories discussed here, the motive is usually simple greed, a universal motivation.

In regard to characterization, both Eastern and Western stories for adolescents usually have multiple detectives, but the five sleuths of the Five Adventurers series are unusual. In the Arabic stories *The Mystery of the International Smuggler* and *The Mystery of the Dead End Street,* two of the more than two hundred books in the Five Adventurers series, the five protagonists range in age from seven to fifteen. The oldest, Tawfiq, whose nickname "Takhtakh" appropriately means "tubby," excels in logic and ratiocination; he bears no stigma in the Middle East for being a little overweight. In contrast, Jupiter ("Jupe") Jones, the brains of the American Three Investigators series is often taken for dumb because of his weight problem.[7] Takhtakh's companions, two brother and sister pairs, Mohib and Nousah, Atif and Lozah, lack the same intellectual prowess. The girls Nousah and Lozah play small roles, not because of their gender but because of the difficulty of sustaining roles for five detectives. Because boys and girls generally are educated separately, except in small villages, in most Middle Eastern countries, children usually know few members of the opposite sex outside the extended family. And so the adventurers are usually related, emphasizing the role of the family in Middle Eastern society. The American detectives, in contrast, are usually friends rather than relatives, the Hardy boys being an exception.

Even though detectives in juvenile fiction customarily work in groups, some of the children in the Arabic stories are so much younger than their leader Takhtakh that they cannot assist in the same ways that Bess and George, Nancy Drew's friends, can aid Nancy or that Pete and Bob, Jupe's friends, can help Jupe. In fact, each of the three American investigators has an area of expertise: Jupe is intellectual and efficient, good at solving codes; Pete Crenshaw is athletic and expert on directions and following trails (Arthur, *Stuttering Parrot* 164); Bob Andrews is studious and thorough. The combination of talents makes each a valuable part of the whole, whereas in the Eastern series, the younger children contribute to the solution of the crime only occasionally.

Nousah and Lozah perform traditional female functions, such as preparing food, but they also accompany their brothers, indicating a move toward female equality, since young Middle Eastern girls are traditionally more closely supervised and protected than boys.[8] In *The International Smuggler,* for example, Takhtakh sends Mohib to follow three suspects, a potentially dangerous assignment, while Lozah volunteers to collect cigarette butts from beneath the balcony of the cottage of the three men after they have departed for the day, a safer task.

On rare occasions the girls help solve the mystery;[9] in *The Dead End Street*, the detectives know that a key was used in a robbery but that the keeper of the keys is innocent. Nousah's theory that the key was duplicated months earlier when someone substituted for the keeper on vacation proves correct. In *The Bride of Sinai*, one of the Four Adventurers series, the girl Filfil (Pepper) is regarded as the leader, perhaps because the three cousins are visiting her or traveling as guests of her family when the adventures occur, or perhaps because she is clever and innovative. When she is captured along with her three cousins (two of them boys) by kidnapers, Filfil conceives the idea of dropping items of clothing, leaving a trail for the police, as the children are transported on horseback across the desert. The scheme enables the police to rescue the children and the kidnaped bride.

The boys' behavior in every Arabic detective book is a model of decorum, indicating respect for the girls and each other. In *The International Smuggler,* the five adventurers, chasing three criminals, find themselves in trouble on a small boat during a storm:

> The tempest had become mad, and water was entering the boat. Lozah [the youngest] cried, and Zinger [the dog] howled sadly. . . . In the midst of all this horror Takhtakh thought only of Lozah and Nousah; he was afraid the water might pull them into the lake and drown them. He rushed to . . . [the girls], tied them with one end of the rope, and tied the other end around his waist in case the waters pulled one of the girls in. In less than a minute what he feared happened. [chapter 5]

He rescues Lozah, who has fallen overboard, and then, realizing that the boat will soon sink, he tries to rescue all of them. A large wave lifts the boat, smashing it on the beach. The group is thrown onto the sand dunes. Takhtakh without hesitation carries Nousah (he is the strongest boy, and she the larger girl), Mohib carries Lozah to safety, and Atif and Zinger follow. The author mentions this rescue and continues the story without comment. The girls do not even thank the boys, not because they are ungrateful, but because the boys' helpful actions were automatic. No doubt, both American and Arab boys would try to save their younger relatives if the need arose; the difference is that the thanks are understood without words by the Middle Eastern children. Clearly, the girls are grateful, and the boys performed admirably.

Takhtakh next uses his handkerchief to bind a wound on Atif's head and then searches for a haven for the wet, hungry, and thirsty group. After finding shelter in a cave, the children converse:

> Lozah asked while drying herself in the sun, "How will we return?"
>
> Mohib answered, "Nobody can answer this question right now, especially since our boat was smashed."
>
> Nousah inquired, "Where did the three men go?"
>
> Atif said, "Either they have drowned or their boat has smashed like ours."
>
> Mohib added, "But it is possible they were able to control the boat and reach the beach safely." [chapter 6]

The boys answer politely. Even when Atif has obviously omitted a very real possibility—in fact, the one that did occur—Mohib simply states it with no personal criticism of Atif's error in logic. The dialogue here and in the other books reveals a lack of competition and jealousy among the youths that is unusual by American standards.

In every book in the American series, good-natured kidding about Jupe's "diets" and, in the later books, rivalry about girls show the three investigators to be normal American teens. In contrast, there is no kidding in the Eastern series, and when the rare disagreement occurs, quiet discussion with deference shown to Takhtakh as the smartest resolves the issue.

This decorous behavior is probably no more unrealistic than some other assumptions behind juvenile detection, such as child sleuths solving crimes that adults cannot solve. Margery Fisher enumerates the child-investigators' natural advantages for detection: "curiosity, an eye for insignificant details, the power to lurk unseen, and an awareness of environment as intense as that of a policeman on the beat" (284).

One child investigator extraordinaire is Alia, a principal character in the Three Adventurers series. Called "the mother of ideas," Alia bases her theories on careful attention to detail and ratiocination. In *The Phony Policeman,* her observation of the tight coat and short trousers on a policeman leads the detectives to believe he might be the phony officer they seek. Alia's role equals, or even surpasses, that of her brothers. She could be an Eastern Nancy

Drew, except for her younger age, her restricted independence, and the danger factor. Always accompanied by someone—a brother, a cousin, or one to four police officers—who respects her ability but feels the need to protect her, Alia is never in jeopardy, the protection of females being integral to Moslem society, but neither does she have the freedom of Nancy Drew. Nancy and her friends, as well as the three investigators, display more independence and have more freedom to act, and as a result they often find themselves in life-threatening situations. When Alia deduces that trailing the gang's messenger will lead to the gang, "Everybody looks at her with appreciation, respect, and admiration. Colonel El-Amari [a high-ranking policeman who doubtless already knows the shadowing technique] says, 'What a sharp girl you are!'" (chap. 6). The Egyptian author clearly respects Alia. Female roles, then, are not stereotyped in these stories, but Eastern heroines are more limited in initiating action and in acting independently than such Western sleuths as Nancy Drew.

Alia's suggestion of following a character and Filfil's idea of leaving a trail of clothing are clever but not as unusual as the *Ghost-to-Ghost Hookup,* in which the three American investigators each call five friends to ask if they have seen a car and driver the boys are seeking; then each friend is to call five other friends, and the network should canvass the area effectively. All are given the telephone number of the trio, can remain anonymous if they wish ("ghosts"), or can receive a reward of a ride in a gold-plated Rolls-Royce for assisting the three youthful detectives (Arthur, *Stuttering Parrot* 46–47).

The detective hero's qualities are determined at least in part by culture.[10] The detective story "celebrates traditional heroic virtues and expresses many of the attitudes associated with an ideology of hero worship" (Porter 126). The hero is the one whom the reader lives vicariously through and whose values the reader tries to emulate, and so most youthful detectives come from middle-to-upper-middle-class families. The three American investigators are middle-class but not as wealthy as Nancy Drew, who drives her own roadster and is the daughter of prominent attorney Carson Drew. In fact, Jupe's guardians, his aunt and uncle, own a junkyard. The three youths establish a headquarters complete with phone and four hidden entrances inside the junkyard. In the early books of the Three Investigators series, Jupe has won the use of a Rolls-

Royce and a chauffeur for thirty days, although in later books Jupe and his two colleagues in the detective business ride bikes, borrow cars, or use whatever they can acquire. Similarly, Takhtakh and his partners are middle-to-upper-middle-class: they live in a villa, employ a maid, and own a telephone, phones at the time being fairly uncommon in Egypt outside major cities. Although the criminal may travel by Peugeot or Fiat Ritmo in the Arabic series, the heroes, like their American counterparts, go by bus, bike, or small car, such as a Volkswagen—the usual middle-class modes of travel. The Eastern hero, however, seems more modest, thoughtful, and soft-spoken than the Western hero, who is more sophisticated, as clever, and more willing to take chances and face danger. In return for their sometimes dangerous missions, the heroes and heroines of each culture receive similar rewards: praise, local fame, and the gratitude of police and community.[11]

The communities demonstrate their thanks in part because the detectives have been successful where others have failed. In addition to victims, criminals, and detectives, Cawelti lists as essential characters in a detective story a group involved with the crime but unable to solve it; he divides this group into three types: friends or assistants of the detective; incompetent police; and false suspects (96). The Arabic stories rely largely on the first type: numerous friends (or relatives) who assist the detectives. These stories do not refer to the incompetence of the police; rather, they stress the superior thinking, observation, and intuition of the youthful sleuths. Although false suspects do appear, they fade from the story as the detectives progress in solving the crime. An example of this narrowing of suspects is found in *The Pounding in the Night,* in which Filfil determines that only one of the two night watchmen at the museum could be involved with the theft of a golden crown from a "civilization" fair because the crime occurred while the electricity was cut. If both guards had been involved in the night-time theft, there would have been no need to cut the electricity. The field of two suspects is thus narrowed to one.

The three American investigators, unlike Nancy Drew, have few friends who play a role;[12] the police are usually unaware rather than incompetent; and many false suspects appear in the course of the American series, adding further interest and challenge for the reader. In *Funny Business,* for example, possible suspects include a comic-book illustrator, several comic-book dealers, a critical reviewer, a beautiful young model and her mother, an editor, and the comic-book convention boss.

The relative balance of action to thought also distinguishes Eastern from Western detective fiction; in the West the central characters are involved in more action and the theoretical solving of the crime receives less emphasis; in other words, many minor climaxes occur as the heroes extricate themselves from various situations or explain various minor points leading to the main climax or solution. In the Egyptian series, ironically in light of the titles in the series, ratiocination predominates over the few "dangerous" adventures of the protagonists.[13] The reader observes Takhtakh thinking and assigning tasks to his companions:

> That evening Takhtakh sat on the palace balcony watching the nearby cottage where the two hunters lived. He knew from Awad that their names were Moussa and Othman. Takhtakh hoped that the third man would come and visit them at night so that he could follow him. He felt that behind this nightly visit was a secret. Who was the third man? Why didn't he come except at night? Was he one of the four hunters?
>
> Takhtakh wanted to have the answer to all these questions. The only solution was to follow that man on his nightly journey to know where he came from. [*International Smuggler*, chapter 4]

This passivity predominates; only on rare occasions do the characters find themselves in "dangerous" situations, such as when they are stranded in the desert (*International Smuggler*), or when the heroes, but not the heroines, are briefly captured and imprisoned in a villa (*Dead End Street*), or when both males and females are kidnaped, tied up, and imprisoned in a cave (*Bride of Sinai*).

Both Eastern and Western stories are similar in that their heroes survive all danger and in their belief in deductive reasoning and the establishment of moral order, but the laws and the notion of criminality may differ from society to society. Such crimes as murder, theft, kidnaping, and smuggling, however, seem to be abhorred by all cultures as antisocial acts. Theft, perceived to be victimless, is a popular crime in these stories. The thievery of an international syndicate, such as the one operating in *The International Smuggler*, probably excites both Eastern and Western readers; in that story, the five detectives solve the crime after several unusual adventures. They discover a most unusual cartridge that has been shot from a large flare gun used to light a target all around and under it. What is the connection, if any, between the flare gun and the secret opening, deep in a water well, they have discovered? The tunnel in the well leads to a series of caves in which members of the smuggling team have hidden stolen pharaonic statues. The detectives discover the stolen property, but they are cold, hungry, and stranded (a violent storm has left them alone in the desert with no means of escape, the only nearby people being armed criminals). This situation engages the reader's empathy and anticipation, irrespective of culture.

*The Dead End Street* also requires a more sophisticated reader to perceive that a friend of the detectives participated as a gang member in a daring payroll robbery. A Mr. Karam, offering to watch for the criminals who have disappeared somewhere in his neighborhood, perhaps in the villa across the street, fools most of the youthful detectives and readers alike, but Takhtakh keeps his own watch and traps Karam, whose in-depth portrait opposes the generic tradition of relative anonymity for the criminal and thus is particularly challenging for the reader. In fact, of the Arabic books discussed here, only this story makes a double impact not only in the solution to the crime but also in the revelation of an error in past assumptions, such as the sleuths trusting Karam. This story breaks the "least-likely person" convention because the concept normally refers to someone whose shadowy presence in the story has been virtually overlooked (Cawelti 90), but Karam has played a substantial role, one of trustworthy friend, and so his part in the crime is doubly surprising for the reader and demonstrates clearly the detectives' ability. In both *The International Smuggler* and *The Dead End Street,* moral order is ultimately restored to the respective communities.

The communities or settings of both the Arabic and the American series reflect their respective society's customs and values in addition to offering local color. The calm and ordered abode of the detective contrasts with the chaos of the crime scene in both series. Both the Four Adventurers and the Five Adventurers series have scenes set in the homes of the youthful sleuths Filfil and Takhtakh, respectively. Although the crimes often occur in ordered public places, such as a museum or at a wedding ceremony, these scenes become chaotic as a result of the crime. In both Nancy Drew and the Three Investigators, the readers "visit" the homes of the detectives and learn about their families; almost nothing is known, however, about the families of the Arabic detectives.[13]

The crimes are also determined in part by the setting. Egypt, for example, is the most likely place to find pharaonic statues to steal (*International Smuggler*) and an open wedding that allows unknown criminals entry in order to kidnap a bride (*Bride of Sinai*). By the same token, America, specifically Hollywood, is a more likely place to find the Three Investigators mysteries involving the owner of a fast-food chain (*Murder to Go*), the movie industry (*Haunted Mirror*), and the recording industry (*Reel Trouble*). The settings differ widely, but both provide background and pique interest, although the Arabic series moves at a slower pace, largely because of the techniques used to create suspense.

It is a challenge to develop suspense. Cawelti, again writing about adult fiction but also stating a truth about adolescent fiction, maintains that the good detective story writer will "sustain uncertainty until the final revelation, yet at the same time assure [the reader] that the detective has the qualities which will enable him to reach the solution" (17). Traditional methods for developing suspense, such as delaying the action through descriptive passages, dialogue, authorial intrusion, or the inclusion of details about everyday life, are employed by both Eastern and Western authors. Both create suspense by giving and withholding information. The Arabic story, however, usually contains fewer red herrings, more repetition, and more characters whose portraits are almost Flemish in detail. Because the detectives are seldom alone, perhaps indicative of the large families and crowded conditions of many Egyptian cities, the author must delay the action by identifying the speeches by speaker and perhaps by listener. The plurality of characters, each required to speak on occasion, produces frequent interruptions and sometimes tedious reiteration.

Another type of delay for suspense occurs in *The Dead End Street* when Takhtakh meets Inspector Sami:

> T: "Something must have happened in Ma'ady [a Cairo suburb]."
> IS: "I have news—fifty thousand Egyptian pounds worth!"
> T: "Don't you want to have a cup of coffee before we talk?"
> IS: "Indeed, I left my house without having anything."
> Takhtakh leaves and asks the maid to make a cup of coffee.

Then he phones his friends . . . and asks them to come to his house after telling them about Inspector Sami's presence.

When the maid serves the coffee, the four friends come and greet the inspector warmly. It has been quite a while since they last saw him. After his first sip of coffee, the inspector commences talking. [Chapter 1]

This meeting is typical of many gatherings that enable the youthful detectives to discover crimes, pool information, formulate moves, and deduce solutions. Suspense is generated from the delay caused by the polite inquiry about the coffee, the request to the maid, the phone call, the serving of coffee, the arrival of the friends, and their greetings to the inspector—all before any further explanation of the fifty thousand pounds. The Arab reader's patience, which might be contrasted with the American child's demand for action, is indicative of the slower pace of life in Middle Eastern society as compared with that of the United States.

These stories also reveal many Middle Eastern customs. The quoted passage, for example, indicates the importance of welcoming and serving guests before conducting business, and it emphasizes the importance of attention to elders and their positions, for throughout the series each officer is accurately and repeatedly addressed by his appropriate title. And in *The Bride of Sinai,* the four adventurers, on vacation in El-Arish in the Sinai, wish to sample the local culture. A hotel employee suggests they attend a wedding being held across the street from the hotel. They may attend without an invitation because the wedding is open to all, a custom of less populous towns; in this case, the bride's father opens the wedding to shower her with attention because she is an only child. Similarly, the three investigators in one of their later books are given access to a comic-book convention (*Funny Business*), but it is a public function, not a private one opened to the public.

The Arabic Adventurers and the American Investigators series provide provocative insights to readers interested in hermeneutics, logic, subtleties of detection and ratiocination, and Eastern and Western culture, respectively. Though controlled by the criteria for detective fiction and affirming existing social constructs, the series substantiate and extend the theories of Cawelti and Porter about adult detective fiction to adolescent detective fiction. These theories might profitably be extended to detective fiction of other cultures or to other types of formula fiction.

## Notes

1. Both the Three Adventurers and the Four Adventurers were written by multiple authors, whereas the Five Adventurers was written primarily by Mahmoud Salem. The series, which ended in the mid-1980s, were published in Cairo in modern standard Arabic rather than in Egyptian dialect, presumably to attract a wider reading audience. These formula stories consist of approximately sixty pages (in English translation) and traditionally conclude with a puff for the next book in the series.

2. These earlier books also hook the potential reader with exciting prefatory remarks (as well as concluding ones) by that master of suspense Alfred Hitchcock; and they make a better comparison with the Eastern series because the protagonists in both are only thirteen, whereas in the most recent American books, the male detectives have "aged" to seventeen and acquired cars and girlfriends. The earlier American volumes also reflect a pre-1960s culture, which possessed values closer to those of modern Egypt.

These Arabic series might also be compared to Donald Sobol's Encyclopedia Brown series in their clever solution of crimes, but they are much longer and more fully developed (approximately 15,000 words [in English translation] compared with about 1,000 words for the Encyclopedia Brown stories), possess a wider range of developed characters (especially adults), and involve crimes that are potentially dangerous, not just mysterious.

The Eastern series might be compared more profitably, however, with Erick Kastner's *Emil and the Detectives* than with the Encyclopedia Brown series. First, in terms of length, *Emil* is longer (about 26,000 words) than the average Arabic story; a sizable portion at both beginning and end concerns family relationships, unlike the Arabic tales, which do not focus on the families of the youthful detectives. The crime-solution part of *Emil* is thus similar in length to an entire Arabic story, although the solution is based more on numbers of children shadowing and then surrounding the criminal so that escape is impossible than upon ratiocination. Emil is a good boy and a model son, but he is not noted for his powers of deduction, as Takhtakh is. Although the child detectives of the Arabic series are not, like Emil, initially victims of a crime, they are often captured by the criminals and thus become victims before the inevitable rescue. At the end of *Emil*, only Emil, who comes from a poor family, receives a large monetary reward; the other children who aided him do not receive anything. None of the Arab children receive tangible rewards.

3. The term *adventurers* is used throughout to refer to Arabic characters and *investigators* to refer to American protagonists.

4. Other hallmarks of adolescent detective fiction in both series are: improbably young heroes and heroines solving crimes that adults have been unable to unravel; villainy limited to smuggling, theft, or perhaps kidnaping, but usually not murder or terrorism; the dilution of current danger (Fisher 280, 278, 283); the affirmation of moral order; the belief in deductive reasoning; and the creation of a culturally acceptable hero.

The sequence of events that define a children's detective story includes the introduction of the hero, the commission of the crime, its discovery, the search for clues (including some red herrings), the recognition of the criminal, the chase and capture, and the explanation. Arabic stories for adolescents, like their Western counterparts, possess only the briefest denouement, the climax being the solution to the crime.

5. These series are not available in translation.

6. One of Nobel laureate Nagib Mahfouz's stories for adults, *The Thief and the*

*Dogs*, does, however, somewhat romanticize a thief, but only because he is not considered the real criminal in the story.

7. In later books in that series, Jupiter's weight becomes a source of humor; although he does not diet, he participates in what he calls an "eating program" (Stone, *Reel Trouble* 39). He must eat melon with every meal in *Murder to Go* (7), a dietary program that changes to "[a]lfalfa sprouts and a two-mile walk every day" in *Funny Business* (31).

8. It is easy to generalize about young girls, but difficult to do so about women in the Middle East because of the diversity in female customs: in such Westernized countries as Egypt, Jordan, Lebanon, and Syria women are freer to dress in Western clothes and drive cars, whereas in Saudi Arabia, the most conservative country in the Arab world, they cannot.

9. Although a few female writers contributed to the Adventurers series, there appears to be no connection between the author's gender and the books that feature female protagonists. All the Adventurers books mentioned here happen to be written by males.

10. Abdul Fattah (1973) observes in regard to Arab youths reading about a Western hero: "The presentation in foreign children's literature of the all-powerful hero who is victorious due to his intellectual and physical strength leads to the young [Middle Eastern] person's imitating such heroes in order to make headway in a society in which he has an inferior position and in order to convince adults that young people have a right to a suitable place within this society. This offence against existing customs and relations has led to a movement against the influence and use of foreign literature" (32). Unfortunately, Fattah does not elaborate or explain the movement; his observations do, however, explain in part the development of a literature (including detective fiction), for Arab children that reflects the mores and philosophy of Arab culture, which often differs from those in America.

11. Once when the three investigators receive a one-thousand-dollar reward, they give it to a poor Mexican boy and his sick uncle, who helped them solve the crime (*Stuttering Parrot* 181).

12. In juvenile fiction the detective seldom acts alone; thus Nancy has friends George and Bess and occasionally Ned to help her, but the Arabic adventurers and the American investigators seldom rely on friends because they are already a group.

13. Perhaps little is known about the families because Middle Easterners are generally more reserved about revealing personal information than most Americans.

### Works Cited

Arthur, Robert. *Alfred Hitchcock and the Three Investigators in the Mystery of the Stuttering Parrot*. Alfred Hitchcock Mystery Series 2. New York: Random House, 1964.
———. *Alfred Hitchcock and the Three Investigators in the Secret of Terror Castle*. Alfred Hitchcock Mystery Series 1. New York: Random House, 1964.
Billman, Carol. "The Child Reader as Sleuth." *Children's Literature in Education* 15:1 (1984): 30–41.
Carey, M. V. *Alfred Hitchcock and the Three Investigators in the Secret of the Haunted Mirror*. Alfred Hitchcock Mystery Series 21. New York: Random House, 1974.
Cawelti, John G. *Adventure, Mystery, and Romance: Formula Stories as Art and Popular Culture*. Chicago: University of Chicago Press, 1976.
DiYanni, Robert. "The Expectations of Genre: A Review of *The Pursuit of Crime* by Dennis Porter." *Children's Literature Quarterly* 8:3 (1983): 32–33.
Fattah, Abdul Razzak. "Arabian Children's and Juvenile Literature." *Bookbird* 11:3 (1973): 29–32.

Fisher, Margery. "The Sleuth—Then and Now." *Quarterly Journal of the Library of Congress* 38:4 (1981): 277–84.

Ghurayyib, Rose. "Children's Literature in Lebanon and the Arab World." *Bookbird* 4 (1981): 17–19.

Kastner, Erick. *Emil and the Detectives: A Story for Children.* 1929. Trans. May Massee. Garden City, N.Y.: Doubleday, 1943.

McCay, William. *The Three Investigators in Funny Business.* Crimebusters 4. New York: Random House, 1989.

MacLeod, Anne Scott. "Secret in the Trash Bin: On the Perennial Popularity of Juvenile Series Books." *Children's Literature in Education* 15:3 (1984): 127–40.

Porter, Dennis. *The Pursuit of Crime: Art and Ideology in Detective Fiction.* New Haven: Yale University Press, 1981.

Saber, Magdi. *The Four Adventurers in the Mystery of the Pounding in the Night.* The Four Adventurers Series 162. Cairo: Dar El-Ma'aref, 1985.

Salem, Mahmoud. *The Five Adventurers in the Mystery of the International Smuggler.* The Five Adventurers Series 22. Cairo: Dar El-Ma'aref, 1985.

———. *The Five Adventurers in the Mystery of the Dead End Street.* The Five Adventurers Series 27. Cairo: Dar El-Ma'aref, 1986.

Sobol, Donald H. *Encyclopedia Brown, Boy Detective.* Illus. Leonard Shortall. New York: T. Nelson, 1963. [The series consists of sixteen collections of short stories published after *Boy Detective.*]

Stine, Megan, and H. William Stine. *The Three Investigators in Murder to Go.* Crimebusters 2. New York: Random House, 1989.

Stone, G. H. *The Three Investigators in Reel Trouble.* Crimebusters 7. New York: Random House, 1989.

Suleiman, Hassan. *The Four Adventurers in the Mystery of the Bride of Sinai.* The Four Adventurers Series 161. Cairo: Dar El-Ma'aref, 1984.

Wali, Esamat. *The Three Adventurers in the Mystery of the Phony Officer.* The Three Adventurers Series 161. Cairo: Dar El-Ma'aref, 1986.

# Varia

# "A Hard Night," a Contemporary Chinese Story by Yu Chai Fang

## Translated with an Introduction by Wang Lin

### A Note on "A Hard Night"

Chinese pupils are busy enough with school during the daytime. They long for a relaxing and warm evening at home with their parents. But many of them fail to get this. *A Hard Night*, a contemporary children's story with a strongly sympathetic tone, provides a picture of the everyday lives of many pupils and their young parents.

In China, it is easy to be a child but hard to be a pupil. When children enter primary school, they must be top students, as their parents desire. To be excellent pupils, they study many difficult lessons during the day, and must finish homework under the supervision of their parents at night. With such hard work, the parents hope, their children will place into one of the key middle schools (about one key middle school in a county, three to five in a city). But less than 10 percent of pupils gain entrance. And entering the key middle school is just the first step. The next one is to become a college student. The rate of enrollment to college from both the key and normal middle schools is about 2 percent, while only some 40 percent of the students from the key middle schools can expect to pass the entrance examination.

Most of the pupils' parents are in their forties. They experienced a period of restriction under the decade of Cultural Revolution during their youth. In those years, 1967–76, most schools were closed; no colleges existed. The students from middle schools, then called "intellectual youths," were sent to the countryside to work as new peasants and to be re-educated by the peasants. After 1976 they were able to return to the cities and get jobs. Now the vast majority have become parents and their children are studying at primary schools. On the one hand, the parents think too much of their children, desiring them to learn much and better in order to be somebody in the future. So they treat the children strictly. On the

*Children's Literature* 21, ed. Francelia Butler, Christine Doyle Francis, Anne K. Phillips, and Julie K. Pfeiffer (Yale University Press, © 1993 The Children's Literature Foundation, Inc.).

other hand, they lose no time in following modern fashions, trying to catch up with today's youth. This they call "seeking the lost youth." Although they exhibit concern for their children, in fact they are not at all considerate of them. They take no notice of what their children truly desire or need.

This gap between parents and children is a hard fact in China. Many writers have composed stories, papers, and plays in order to help parents better understand their children. Although neither the government nor publishing houses in China has set rules for materials appropriate for publication (government subsidies are rare and are offered only to the most established authors), editors usually choose stories for publication on the basis of their potential for instruction. Adult books, sold in bookstores in cities, towns, and counties, are more highly regarded if they encourage contemporary readers to learn, think, and even criticize. Stories for children can also be disseminated in schools; the most successful ones may be adapted to fit school textbooks. Both teachers and parents are encouraged to read to their children.

The story that follows is regarded as one of the best on this difficult problem, because it helps to bridge the gap between parent and child. It warns parents to ask a friend or relative to keep an eye on school-age children rather than leaving them home alone; it also provides a means for children to understand and appreciate their parents as people who work hard and may have been deprived, by former political circumstances, of enjoying their lives as young people.

### A Hard Night

After supper, father and mother went out together.

On their departure, the mother addressed the children: "We have something to do. You little ones stay at home to finish your homework carefully and review your lessons. Don't make too much noise."

These words were not new to them.

Under an electric lamp, the brother and younger sister sat face to face at the desk. The brother was twelve, and the sister was a

*A Hard Night* is taken from a collection of stories, *Growing Up Together*, by Yu Chai Fang (Beijing: China's Literary Association, 1989).

little over seven. It was very quiet in the room where they sat bending over their exercises. From the neighbor's radio came the steady voice of a male broadcaster.

After a while the sister raised her head and said: "Brother, I have done my written work already." The dominant member of the family when the parents were away, the brother, at present busy at his math, paid no attention to her words.

"Brother, I have to read my Chinese text. Would you please listen and count how many times I've read it over?" asked the sister. "Our teacher asked us to read it over at least ten times. You can sign the number in my text book." (Signature is really the most efficacious way for teachers to supervise their pupils and even their parents.)

"Don't bother me," the brother said impatiently. "I'm busy myself and have no time; you'd better ask our parents to do that." Many times before the brother had signed his sister's exercise or text book as a "tiny" head of the family.

"They come back so late . . . and tomorrow morning I'll go to school in a hurry, so we have no time to postpone it. I have been criticized for this several times by the teacher." The sister pronounced the words in a sad voice.

"Well, well, now you just read and I'll count." The brother gave in at last and listened attentively to his sister, who began to read the text—*A Small Horse Crosses the River.*

The brother still remembered those days when he had been with his grandmother, who would stop everything to listen carefully to his reading of the text, one, two, three, and more times, carefully counting the number of times he had gone over it. Then, under her grandson's guidance, she would sign on his text or exercise book the only three words she was able to write all her life long: "Huan Xiou Yin," her name.

Suddenly, the light went out. The world around them fell into total darkness.

There came a hubbub of voices from the nearby lane; and it grew louder and louder. Among the noises, they caught the sound of someone crying: "Help, help! The house is on fire!"

Hearing these words, the brother and sister were disturbed and frightened. Without hesitation, the brother ran to fetch a basin and dashed towards the door, while the sister shouted, "Wait for me, I'll go too."

They rushed together to the outdoor spigot and filled the basin.

The crowded lane lit up with a burst of flames from the fire in a single-story house.

"Go back! Go back, little ones, you might be hurt here," some adults said, and pushed them along. Out came the water from the basin, and the sister was thoroughly soaked.

The brother stood there with an empty basin in his hands; beside him was his sister as wet as a drenched chicken. They could find no way to approach the burning house yet.

The fire was wiped out in no time. They heard people talk about the cause of the fire—children playing with matches at home while the parents were out working.

The brother and sister went home with the other people. As they came near the door, they both had a dreadful shock, for the door was wide open. They had forgotten to close it.

They went fumbling into the dark house. Lighting a match would be a fine thing, but they couldn't find one. They felt about again, touching a bed at last. They sat on the bed.

The sister said: "Brother, I'm getting a bit scared."

"What is there to be afraid of?" the brother asked, although he had hardly any confidence himself.

"The mouse, the cat and . . ."

"Why, they are not scary!" While saying so, the brother thought in terror about the thief and scoundrel, who might have come to hide in this room while they were away just now.

With tears in her eyes, the sister murmured, "How happy we would be if grandmother were alive." Both the brother and sister had been brought up by their grandmother, who remained in their eyes a figure of comfort.

"Why haven't our parents come back yet? Where have they been?" asked the sister as she leaned closer to her brother. The brother said: "They told us they had something to do, didn't they?"

"They always say that they have something to do. What is it? Do they have a meeting or go to work? My classmate Xiou Li's parents do not go out at night to do things," the sister wondered.

"Father and mother have to work hard in order to earn us a better living." These were the words the grandmother used to speak, and now the brother said them to persuade his sister.

The sister still grumbled. "But they are so strict with us. We aren't allowed to play games. They themselves go out every night to 'play' instead."

"How can you speak like that? Mother often tells us they didn't have a good time when they were young. Especially during the Cultural Revolution, they left the big city for the countryside, where they worked together with the peasants. Now, things are getting much better. They want to enjoy everything they have missed—'to seek the lost youth,' as they like to say." But the sister didn't quite catch the meaning of these words.

Without electricity, it was still dark everywhere.

The brother said, "We'd better light a candle and do our unfinished homework."

So they went fumbling again to look for the candle. They searched every room, including the kitchen, but could not find one.

"Sister, it's already nine o'clock. Time for you to go to bed."

"No, I haven't done my reading yet."

The brother thought about it for a moment and said: "It's no use waiting here. We'd better go out to look for our parents."

"Where shall we go?"

"To their places of work."

"To mother's place or to father's?" The sister knew quite well that their parents worked in two different places.

"To mother's; it's nearer."

"All right, let's go!"

Shutting the door behind them, the brother and sister stepped into the darkness. Through the dim narrow lane, they came to the broad street. Walking on the bright shining sidewalk, they didn't feel dismayed any more.

It was a tranquil night; only a few pedestrians wandered up and down the street. From far away came sweet music. It relaxed them.

Passing by an evening club, they noticed an old man keeping a watch on rows of bikes in front of the club door.

"Five, ten, fifteen, twenty-five. . . ." The sister counted the number of the bikes. Suddenly she drew back as if she were hit by electricity.

"Look, brother, that bike is father's."

The brother went up to the bikes; to his delight, he saw on one of them the plastic rope he once used to fix his father's bike. Well, we could easily find them here, thought the brother.

Knowing that they came to look for their parents, the old man felt sympathy for the two children. He let them in.

The club hall was filled with melodious music; many a pair of people were dancing to it. Among the dancing couples, the brother and sister found their parents. Their dancing was beautiful, and it attracted a number of people who stood looking at them. Now the brother understood what the parents meant by the phrase "seeking the lost youth."

The sister complained again, "They let us stay at home while they themselves go out to play."

The brother continued: "They don't care about us, and take no notice whether the house in our lane is on fire, whether there is a scoundrel hiding under our bed, or whether the electric lamp is on . . . ."

The sister tried to call her mother and father, but something choked in her throat. She burst into loud weeping. The brother managed to hold back his own tears and soothed the sister, "Don't cry, don't cry. You can speak to them."

But their father and mother were deeply immersed in the dance. They were good partners to each other, swaying to pleasant light music, intoxicated with satisfaction.

# Additional Thoughts on East Slavic "Dirge" Lullabies: The Hunting Song

Sheryl A. Spitz

In an earlier piece ("Social and Psychological Themes in East Slavic Folk Lullabies," *Slavic and East European Journal* 23), I argued that East Slavic folk lullabies are often closely related in form and content to—indeed, modeled on—other Slav folksong genres, including the *koljada* (solstice) song and the wedding song. In a kind of reciprocal resonance, some wedding songs even include the interesting image of a cradle in a tree, in which the bridegroom is rocked and swung. This naturally evokes, especially for Westerners, one of the most popular of lullabies, "Rockabye Baby": a song scarcely soothing to any infant who might happen to understand the lyrics, but perhaps calculated on at least one level to assuage some of the child-minder's tension at being trapped in attendance on a demanding infant.

Slavic culture has its own version of the "Rockabye Baby" lullaby, and these Slavic songs may be grouped under the general heading of "dirge" lullabies. Two examples typify the genre. The first might be called a "semi-dirge," in that no funeral rites are described. Instead, the song describes how the child's death comes about, in terms that almost parallel the Western song. A cradle is hung up (likely from the rafters) and rocked by the child-minder; the string holding the cradle breaks; down crashes cradle and infant; both are destroyed. A concluding verse describes the mother or child-minder's grief at the infant's death:

> Taj ne zhal' meni kolison'ki novoj,
> Til'ko meni zhal' ditinochki i maloj.
> Bo kolsochku za den' za dva zabuduju
> Malu ditinu za rochok ne zguduju. . . .
> Ditina umre—matika ne zabude.[1]
> [Klymasz 178]

*Children's Literature* 21, ed. Francelia Butler, Christine Doyle Francis, Anne K. Phillips, and Julie K. Pfeiffer (Yale University Press, © 1993 The Children's Literature Foundation, Inc.)

> I don't regret the new cradle,
> I only regret the little child.
> For I can build the cradle in a day or two,
> But I can't raise a child in a whole year. . . .
> If the child dies—the mother doesn't forget.

In his article "Social and Cultural Motifs in Canadian-Ukrainian Lullabies" (*SEEJ* 12), Robert Klymasz, as I have pointed out earlier, suggests that such songs express the mother or child-minder's resentment at being bound to the cradle of a sleepless child, at being held captive by child-duties in general. To this notion, I suggested as well that out of what may be superstition or ambivalence or both, a concluding verse seeks to negate the implied destructive "curse" by protesting the singer's real grief should such an event occur and, by extension, her innocence of any such destructive wish or act.

The "full" dirge lullaby begins more or less where the "semi-dirge" leaves off, describing the child's funeral rites:

> Spi, spi,
> Khot' segodnja umri
> Skolochu grobok
> Iz sosnovykh dosok.
> Snesu na pogost.
> Poplachu, povoju,
> V mogilku zaroju.[2]
>     [Chicherov 347]

> Sleep, sleep,
> If you die today,
> I'll make a little coffin
> Of pine boards.
> I'll carry you off to the churchyard,
> I'll cry, I'll wail,
> I'll bury you in the little grave.

Again, the singer's real grief at an event that in moments of extreme frustration she might covertly wish, is expressed in detail. And as if to underscore the point, the chant provides a careful catalog of funeral preparations and rites.

A psychosocial interpretation of this lullaby form could focus on repressed individual desires and frustrated needs. But, extending an earlier idea, one can also find a parallel with another folksong genre, one recently discussed at length in Jonathan K. Smith's *Imagining Religion: From Babylon to Jonestown* (University of Chicago Press, 1982). This is the hunting song. As Smith points out, from Africa to America to Siberia, hunting songs often follow set formulas and assumptions. And although Smith does not point this out, these formulas and assumptions seem to parallel rather closely those of the East Slavic "dirge" lullabies.

A pygmy elephant-hunting song recounted by Smith is typical of this genre. "The progression," says Smith, "is clear: (1) We did not mean to kill you; it was an accident. (2) We did not kill you; you died a natural death. (3) We killed you in your own best interests. You may now return to your ancestral world to begin a better life" (62). The animal must be killed to satisfy the human need for food and materials. But the songs sung to the animal before the kill, directly after the kill, and when its corpse is brought to the village, go to great lengths to "rationalize" the death and distance it from human wishes and actions. "Among almost all of these northern hunting groups," Smith points out, "there is a disclaimer of responsibility recited over the animal's corpse immediately after it has been killed. 'Let us clasp paws in handshake . . . . It was not I that threw you down, nor my companion over there. You, yourself, slipped and burst your belly.' Even responsibility for the weapon will be disclaimed: 'Not by me was the knife fashioned, nor by any of my countrymen. It was made in Estonia from iron bought in Stockholm'" (59). As Smith notes, in many instances a bloodless kill is the ideal, no matter how much blood is actually shed. In these songs, the animal offers itself for sacrifice and stumbles or tumbles to its death, absolving the hunters of blood-guilt.

Once the animal's body is brought back to the village, there is a "continued need for etiquette in the treatment of the corpse, in the reintegration of the hunters into human society, in the eating of the flesh and in insuring that the animal's soul will return to its 'Supernatural Owner.' The corpse may be adorned and carried in solemn procession. The hunters continue to disclaim responsibility, reminding the animal that now its soul is free to return to its spiritual domicile and assuring it that its body will be treated with respect" (60).

Of great interest in the present case is the fact that "women play a prominent role in ritually greeting the men, reintegrating them into the domestic world" (60). Lullabies, too, are the special province of women, and the lullaby situation can give women an opportunity to express feelings males may express in other, more public settings. In a sense, the lullaby enables women to integrate—"domesticate"—the male hunting song, adapting its formulas and assumptions to their own needs, just as, in the same sense, solstice and wedding songs are pressed into the service of the lullaby setting. Males nourish by providing food, females by nurturing children, so the paradigm has it; and in both cases the object of concern is a "wild thing" that somehow must be bent to society's needs.

Parallels between the hunting song lyrics and Slavic "dirge" lullabies are clear. The animal comes to its death "accidentally"; the cradle and infant fall, not by human intervention or negligence, but by chance: the string breaks, the cradle falls, the child is killed. Additional verses in both genres disclaim responsibility for the death. And just as the animal's corpse is promised proper treatment, so the infant's "corpse" in the lullaby is promised full funeral rites. In contrast to the child's "accidental" death, its coffin is even made by the singer's own hands.

Smith concludes that rituals establish a kind of psychological balance, an expression of the tension between consciousness of reality, with its accidents and variables, and wished-for control. The satisfaction comes in the dual consciousness that things ought to be one way yet they are as they are. This is a more subtle form of relief than mere threat, which occurs so often in child-raising. And there is a sly humor in it, as well: an acknowledgment, at once, of human power and human limitation. Initiation of a child into this communal understanding becomes part of the lullaby situation, just as acknowledgment of the child and its profound needs reinforces that understanding for the singer. The lullaby chant focuses this multilevel consciousness, drawing on familiar rituals, social patterns, and individual expression.

*Notes*

1. See also Mixail I. Belous, *Russkoe-narodnij kolibel'nj pesni* (Kolomyja, 1913), available in electrostatic reproduction at the New York Public Library.

2. V.I. Chicherov, "Kolybel'nye pesni," in *Russkoe narodnoe tvorcestvo* (M: Moskovskij Universitet, 1959).

# A Lithuanian Folk Tale

Feenie Ziner

Before I left on a trip to Lithuania last March, the editors of *Children's Literature* asked me to bring back a children's book. I found *The Orphan Elenyte and Joniukas the Lamb* at the Ciorlonis State Art Museum, in the city of Kaunas, and was drawn to it at once by its stunning graphic design (fig. 1). An amalgam of sophisticated contemporary typography and a distinctly medieval style of manuscript illumination, the book was a beautiful puzzle begging to be deciphered, for I do not know a word of Lithuanian. Nor could I guess my way through the text because, unique among European languages, Lithuanian's closest relation is Sanskrit.

Even less could I deduce the content of the story from the illustrations, except for the central figure on the title page, an organ grinder in a flowered hat who reappears many times throughout the text and makes a final appearance in the lower left-hand corner of the last page (fig. 4). There, he has just cut the story-tree off at the trunk with his right hand, and he holds the whole marvelous invention aloft, intact, with his left. So he is the artist himself, who has told us "a pretty tale" and severed it from its source.

In summary, *The Orphan Elenyte and Joniukas the Lamb* tells of an orphan boy who quenches his thirst by drinking water from the footprint of a sheep, and is turned into a lamb. His sister, Elenyte, mourns his transformation but continues to love and protect him in his new shape. The two are taken into the care of a benevolent king, who marries Elenyte when she grows up (fig. 2). But Laume Ragana, who bears the generic Lithuanian name for witch, envies Elenyte her good fortune, and pushes the girl into a pond. Elenyte does not drown. Instead, she becomes a golden fish. The king does not notice that his dear wife, Elenyte, has been replaced until Laume, feigning illness so that she may hide in her bed, insists on butchering and eating the meat of the innocent lamb (fig. 3). While the servants sharpen their knives for the slaughter, Joniukas the lamb goes to the fish pond and sings to his sister of his

The folk tale was kindly translated by B. Maciuka of the University of Connecticut. *Children's Literature* 21, ed. Francelia Butler, Christine Doyle Francis, Anne K. Phillips, and Julie K. Pfeiffer (Yale University Press, © 1993 The Children's Literature Foundation, Inc.).

peril. Elenyte replies that the villagers must weave a silken net in which to catch her and bring her into the presence of the king. The king, who has overheard all that has been said or sung, orders his people to do Elenyte's bidding. Drawn from the water, Elenyte spontaneously resumes her human form. Simultaneously, the little lamb becomes Joniukas again. The king orders the witch killed, and Elenyte, her brother, and the king all live together in his castle, happily ever after.

For me, the action of the story seems arbitrary, preordained, governed by a set of rules I do not understand. Elenyte and Joniukas are vulnerable because they are orphans, but their devotion to each other enables them to communicate without human speech. The king is a protector of his people but he is gullible, easily deceived. Lauma Ragana is evil and jealous by nature, but her power to make mischief is limited. The psychology of the story is of the type, rather than the individual. It is as if events are being recounted that everyone already knows, and it is not necessary to explain them. The characters DO what they ARE, play the role inherent in their identity. We get the feeling that something important has been left out, that what drives the story forward is not clear causality—"this happened, and as a consequence, that happened"—but causality of another, hidden order.

For instance, if you believed that a footprint retains the spirit of the creature who made it, if indeed a footprint lies in wait for its absent maker to return, then it is quite logical for a boy who thoughtlessly drinks water lying in a sheep's footprint to be claimed by the spirit of the departed sheep, and consequently to be turned into a lamb.

But if you don't believe it?

In short, the story depends upon a knowledge of magic, of taboos, upon understanding and respecting the gods and the demons who inhabit and rule the natural world. It depends upon a belief system to which we do not possess the key.

I would imagine that this is a well-known story in Lithuania, and that its origins and meaning have been subjected to a good deal of analysis and interpretation, for Lithuania is passionate about the preservation of its cultural heritage. The University of Kaunas has a Department of Folklore that produced, in the 1930s, a ten-volume reference work identifying 132,000 items of distinctly Lithuanian origin. But since I have no access to this resource, my guess is that *The Orphan Elenyte and Joniukas the Lamb* is a story whose roots lie in Lithuania's pagan past. According to *Mythology* (University of Chicago Press, 1991), "The Baltic peoples were dedicated to a personified cult of natural forces, for, being agricultural tribes they primarily revered trees, forests, fields, lakes and rivers that their demons and their gods 'inhabited.' A kind of tutelary animism reigned in their mental universe. As late as 1606, the Jesuit Stribling relates the Livonians made offerings to certain trees and to certain woods. . . . Fate shapes a cult of nature and the dead. Life, still rough and primitive . . . is worshipped in a raw state. It has not yet been made into law, order or science." Indeed, although 98 percent of its population is now Roman Catholic, Lithuania was among the last countries in Europe to embrace Christianity, and one still sees statues of Perkaunas, the pagan god of thunder, in Lithuania's parks and along its roads. A child's prayer addresses Perkaunas obliquely: "Black clouds, go to the land of the Russians. Mother dear sun, come to our land. Bring cakes. Drive away the clouds." The name of this most powerful of Lithuania's nature gods is believed to derive from the Indo-European name for oak tree, possibly because of the affinity of the oak tree for lightning. And lest we think ourselves far beyond such connection to the spirit world, we do the same thing when we "knock on wood."

In fact, some relative of Perkaunas seems to appear on almost every page of this little book for children. Barren tree limbs are woven into garlands of love. Branches of trees twist and intertwine, giving rise to humans who turn into beasts and back again. Severed tree trunks bloom and flourish as if they were independent of their roots—as if they had another, separate source of life. Some trees support birds' nests strong enough to hold horses. Birds devour lizards twice their size. Oak trees, oak leaves, and the acorns of oaks are everywhere in this enchanted world. There are savage dogs and runaway cows and peacocks who preempt the throne of the king. Evil and chaos are loose in this world, and the reader had better beware.

But if the specific graphic symbols of the text suggest pagan origins, the interwoven text and pictures immediately recall medieval Christian and Hebraic manuscript illumination, in which botanic and animal imagery, presumably divested of magical properties, adorn and enliven the text. Although the belief system in these religious books is modified, the illustrations serve the same purpose:

to enhance the power of the Word by invoking the familiar forms of natural phenomena. Some might call this magic. Others would call it art.

Admittedly, this is heavy freight for an apparently innocent little story to bear. If we cannot resist the temptation to discover contemporary wisdom in *The Orphan Elenyte and Joniukas the Lamb,* the weaving of "a silken net" by the common people of the village might offer a clue, a suggestion of social solidarity. Perhaps. Even though Elenyte suffers a long, silent immersion as a lovely golden fish, when at last she speaks out in her own voice she is restored to her full humanity. Conceivably, Elenyte is Lithuania herself, and the jealous witch is . . . well!

Whether the artist-illustrator of this beautiful book intended to suggest an archaic source for this story or whether these illustrations arose spontaneously from the unconscious seems unimportant. The story and illustrations combine in a seamless whole, and together they bear the indelible stamp of their country of origin.

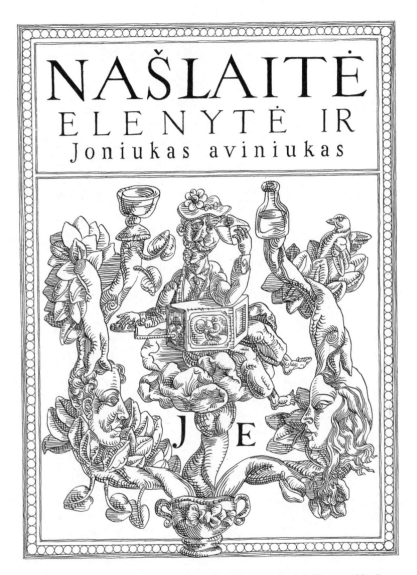

# NAŠLAITĖ
## ELENYTĖ IR
### Joniukas aviniukas

J E

Figure 1. Title page of *The Orphan Elenyte and Joniukas the Lamb*, illustrated by Petras Repšys, copyright 1971 by Vyturys Publishing House, Vilnius.

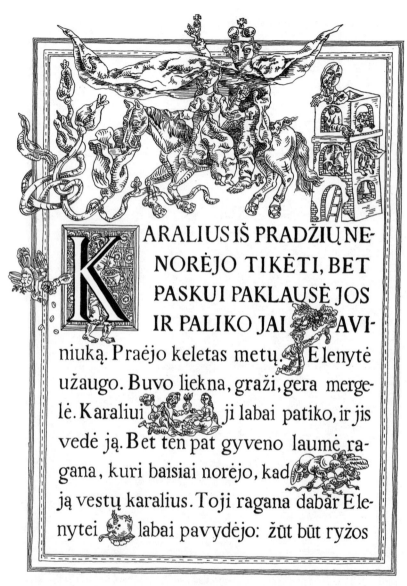

**K**ARALIUS IŠ PRADŽIŲ NE-
NORĖJO TIKĖTI, BET
PASKUI PAKLAUSĖ JOS
IR PALIKO JAI AVI-
niuką. Praėjo keletas metų. Elenytė
užaugo. Buvo liekna, graži, gera merge-
lė. Karaliui ji labai patiko, ir jis
vedė ją. Bet ten pat gyveno laumė ragana, kuri baisiai norėjo, kad
ją vestų karalius. Toji ragana dabar Ele-
nytei labai pavydėjo: žūt būt ryžos

Figure 2. "Several years passed. Elenyte grew up and turned into a tall, slim, beautiful, and pleasant young woman. The king liked her very much, so he married her.
However, nearby there also lived a witch who had wanted to marry the king very
badly. The witch was very envious of Elenyte and decided to do her in somehow."

nori aviniuką pjau-
ti! Tu juk
visados saky-
davai,
kad čia
tavo
brolis Joniukas... ir jį
taip tausojai, mylėjai!" Laumė ragana
atsakė: „Aš tuomet kvaila buvau... aš
tyčia taip sakiau... argi
avinas bus mano
brolis! Aš dabar
sergu, ir jeigu
to

Figure 3. "The witch pretended to be very ill and told the king that he must kill the sheep. The king didn't understand her change of mind and asked: 'Are you out of your mind? You want to kill the sheep?! You always said that the sheep was your brother Joniukas . . . and that you loved him so very much!' The witch answered: 'At that time I was stupid. . . . I made all of that up. . . . How could a sheep be my brother?' "

Figure 4. An old rhymed Lithuanian folk-tale ending: "I am telling you a tale, the wolf was swallowing a husk. Wasn't my tale pretty?"

# Reviews

# An Ambivalent Revolution

Ian Wojcik-Andrews

*The Pleasures of Children's Literature,* by Perry Nodelman. New York: Longman, 1992.

In *Criticism, Theory and Children's Literature,* Peter Hunt observes that "the last ten [years] have seen a revolution in critical thinking in universities, which has, paradoxically, thrust children's books and their critics into the limelight" (6). One such critic and his book is Perry Nodelman and *The Pleasures of Children's Literature.* His aims are twofold: "to provide adults with contexts and strategies of comprehension" that will enable them to understand and enjoy children's literature, and to show that "children too can be taught—and would benefit from—these contexts and strategies" (1). Perhaps most important of Nodelman's objectives is his courageous insistence that we "defy" (4) his opinions and become resistant readers. Indeed, Nodelman states that "to facilitate your dialogue with my ideas and opinions, I have included short 'Explorations' throughout the book. . . . They are meant to help you think actively about the issues and ideas" (4).

In his opening chapters, Nodelman offers the reader traditional contexts and strategies: childhood is a recent invention (20); the Puritans influenced children and children's literature (23). These conventional ideas call forth an equally conventional list of names— Locke, Newbery, Rousseau, Harvey Darton, Piaget—past scholars who, in Louis Althusser's words, interpellate students of children's literature, inculcating them with a certain "know how" that ensures the circulation and reproduction through schools and in society of the traditional ideas we have about children's literature. Once past this familiar roll call, though, Nodelman introduces two radically new contexts: popular culture and contemporary critical theory, both of which will ensure the circulation and reproduction among students and teachers of a revolutionary set of ideas about children's literature, one that empowers students to dissent.

Making a significant break from traditional anthologies of chil-

*Children's Literature* 21, ed. Francelia Butler, Christine Doyle Francis, Anne K. Phillips, and Julie K. Pfeiffer (Yale University Press, © 1993 The Children's Literature Foundation, Inc.).

dren's literature—those by Sutherland, Norton, Russell, and Lukens, for example—Nodelman argues that "the context in which children look at picture books and read novels includes not only their dealings with parents, teachers, and other adults who might make some of the assumptions outlined in Chapter 4; . . . it also includes their encounters with video games, Barbie dolls, and Saturday morning cartoons. Toys, TV shows, and movies intended for children are the most immediate background of many children's responses to literature" (43). Many contemporary critics would agree with Nodelman's argument that, because these "products of popular culture have a powerful influence on children's expectations and attitudes . . . they deserve particular attention" (43). Thus, chapter 5, "Children's Literature in the Context of Popular Culture," includes brief essays on such subjects as "The Culture of Childhood" (43–45) and "TV, Movies, and the Literary Education of Children" (55–56). Within these sections are even shorter pieces in which Nodelman simply raises an issue. In "Toys and Games: Their Effect on Children's Enjoyment of Literature," for instance, Nodelman examines in one paragraph the narrative elements in video games (47), a controversial aspect of the relation between children's literature and popular culture.

Though brief, these sections will surely stimulate discussion. Nodelman includes a brief assessment of the Disney controversy in "Disney Films: An Appraisal" (53–55), bringing together the different points of view of such children's literature critics as Frances Clarke Sayers, Jill May, and Lucy Rollin. He swiftly summarizes their positions, an important task for the beginning student who might not be aware of the Disney corporation's influence on children's literature specifically and popular culture generally. Unfortunately, Nodelman makes little effort to build on the Marxist framework he invokes at the beginning of this chapter in a section called "Ideology and Hegemony" (43–44). The anthologizing of theoretical contexts for understanding popular culture, particularly those that emphasize ideology and hegemony, are important; it is a shame to see them treated so briefly.

Still, using Nodelman's "Explorations," a teacher who wishes to resist the reduction of what Eagleton calls the "complex into the simple" (619) should be able to initiate further discussions about the infantilization of bourgeois culture ideologically implicit in the Disneyfication of children's literature, the narratives of extinction that shape the latest video games, or the relationship between an insurgent American patriotism and the militarization of recent toys for girls and boys. In fact, this chapter will surely interest students of children's literature, many of whom were raised during the Reagan years and who thus have grown to maturity amid the rapid technological developments that led to Nintendo and other electronic games: in discussing children's literature in the context of popular culture, they are, in effect, discussing themselves as cultural products. Understanding the subjects of children's literature and its contexts in popular culture is a provocative way of understanding ourselves as subjects defined in terms of popular culture.

That an entire chapter devoted to children's culture is built upon a Marxist and cultural theorist framework suggests another potentially exciting aspect of Nodelman's *Pleasures of Children's Literature:* its extensive use of critical theory, a feature sadly lacking in current anthologies in children's literature and one sure to produce more critically aware students. In Zena Sutherland's *Children and Books* (8th ed., 1992), Kay Vandergrift's essay "Types of Literary Research" is heavily indebted to M. Abrams's famous "Some Coordinates of Art Criticism" in *The Mirror and the Lamp* (1953). Following Abrams, Vandergrift says that children's books can be read in terms of the Work, the Author, the Audience, and the World (Universe, Work, Artist, and Audience for Abrams). Rebecca Lukens's *Critical Handbook of Children's Literature* (4th ed., 1990) provides equally traditional strategies for reading children's literature; her glossary of terms suggests a basic New Critical approach, while her introductory chapters about the nature of children's literature, written in quasi-religious rhetoric, suggest a naive Expressive Theory: "Finally, literature forces us, leads us, entices us, or woos us into meeting a writer-creator whose medium, words, we know; whose subject, human nature, we live with; whose vision, life's meaning, we hope to understand. We are the student-novice before the artist" (8). Nodelman's presentation of a range of modern critical theories for the student of children's literature significantly updates the relation between children's literature and critical theory.

In his sixth, seventh, and eighth chapters Nodelman offers the reader examples of how specific theories might work in relation to children's literature. In chapter 6, while discussing E. B. White's *Charlotte's Web,* Nodelman reminds students that the basic elements of literary texts (character, plot, theme, and point of view, for example) employed by most students to evaluate literature are, in fact, "elements of our repertoire of strategies for responding to texts" (62). These elements are not just inevitably in texts: they are the basic ways readers approach texts. They are the tools of the critic's trade, and we must become apprentices and work at them.

Nodelman outlines more sophisticated theoretical ideas in chapters 7 and 8. In chapter 7, for example, he employs famous texts by Sendak, White, Andersen, Joyce, and Lewis, and well-known critical essays by Hollindale, Moss, and Smedman, to show students how intertextuality works. Chapter 8, the most controversial of the three, makes some disappointingly brief remarks about class, gender, and race in relation to Kenneth Grahame's *Wind in the Willows,* L. M. Montgomery's *Anne of Green Gables,* and Paula Fox's *Slave Dancer* (91–98). It then examines a variety of critical positions: psychoanalytic (Freud, Bettelheim, Lacan), archetypal (Jung, Frye), structuralist (Lévi-Strauss, Propp, Barthes), deconstructionist (Derrida). Nodelman applies these theories to such canonical texts as "Cinderella," *Where the Wild Things Are, The Tale of Peter Rabbit,* and *Charlotte's Web.* Beatrix Potter's *Tale of Peter Rabbit,* for example, is read using Barthes's five codes: proairetic, hermeneutic, semes, symbols, cultural (105–06). No longer a mere adventurous rabbit, everybody's furry friend, Peter Rabbit is reduced, using Barthes's antihumanist schema, to a series of questions. The plurality of meanings brought into being by critical theory, what we might call the democratization of children's literature, will frighten more conservative students, but it will empower those prepared to risk the approbation of a conservative professor by arguing for radical ways of reading and understanding themselves through children's literature. A revolution in the classroom is surely under way here: a revolution in ideas.

Nodelman's *Pleasures of Children's Literature* represents a significant departure from traditional anthologizing: because of this book, popular culture and critical theory will surely remain integral to the study of children's literature. But although it is an important book—indeed, perhaps because it is such an important book by a recognized scholar—it remains a problematic book for me; and, in the spirit of Nodelman's "Explorations," his dialogue with his readers, I wish to say why.

First, though the book includes two radically different contexts —popular culture and critical theory—it remains an immensely conservative, reactionary work. The canonical children's literature texts Nodelman uses, despite being deconstructed, privilege the same hegemonic ideologies, what Nodelman calls the "values and assumptions that many North Americans take for granted" (43). Nodelman's position here seems contradictory. He celebrates the value of a literary canon, or a series of touchstones "which have proven to be so satisfying or important to us that we can use them as schemata for judging other books" (108), but then argues for the importance of introducing students to a range of literary texts: "The most successful literature curriculum . . . exposes children to as many different kinds of books as possible . . . and not just texts that children can understand but more unusual ones" (217). What is excluded from the democratic vision that structures Nodelman's *Pleasures of Children's Literature* are all these "unusual" (217) texts and their relation to theory: Jamaica Kincaid's *Annie John* read from the radical theorist perspective of Hélène Cixous's "The Laugh of the Medusa," which emphasizes that women writers "write the body"; or Mildred Taylor's *Roll of Thunder,* read from the perspective of black critics like Bell Hooks or Cornel West. The interrogation of heterosexist and racial ideologies by Cixous, Hooks, or West would truly empower students, would truly arm them with the weapons of dissent. Without these significant others, the book unintentionally becomes a metaphor for the discriminatory practices of democratic systems that claim to produce equity.

Second, Nodelman writes in one of his "Explorations": "The literary theories we have considered in this chapter . . . reveal my own bias. Having read through the last three chapters you might go back and consider what my biases are and how my writing reveals them" (108). These are soon discovered. Although Nodelman quotes Raymond Williams in the "Ideology and Hegemony" section mentioned earlier and cites Williams's *Marxism and Literature* in the bibliography, there is no sustained analysis of the relation between Marxism and children's literature, particularly in the context of children's culture, which is increasingly commodified along hegemonic lines of race, class, and gender. Nodelman's bibliography contains brief sections on theory, minorities, media and popular culture, and film; but just as there is more to psychoanalysis than Bettelheim, Freud, and Lacan (what happened to French feminism and American feminist psychoanalysis?), there is more to Marxism than Williams, Eagleton, and Zipes. What of Marx's original writings on how the bourgeois imperative is to make the world over in its own image and to do so through children's culture? How is this bourgeois imperative part of the New World Order? What of Walter Benjamin's essay on the reproduction of art through technology, an essay that has direct links to the reproduction of art through film, video, and television? What of Marxist feminists like Nancy Harstock, whose *Money, Sex, and Power: Toward a Feminist Historical Materialism* theorizes about the relations among capitalism, power, and domination through hero myths. Yet Nodelman's writing reveals that, although the Marxist tradition is more or less excluded, it cannot be forgotten; indeed, it shapes much of Nodelman's thinking and writing. In his discussion of stereotypes, for example, Nodelman notes: "It is clearly in the interest of those whom the current state of affairs benefits that we see these limited depictions as the norm" (44). Deconstructing this, Nodelman argues that ruling class elites (which include academics) benefit from the cultural production and reproduction of stereotypes.

Subsuming Marxist rhetoric and ideas beneath anemic academic prose insults the Marxist tradition, as do Nodelman's reductive comments about Marxist critic Jack Zipes and feminist critic Ruth Bottigheimer. Speaking of truth and meaning in the fairy tale, Nodelman says, "It is interesting to note that the truths these critics find in the tales seem to represent fulfillments of their personal wishes. The Marxist Zipes finds the truths of Marxism; the feminist Bottigheimer, the truths of feminism. Thus, even for interpreters the tales are wish-fulfillment fantasies" (169). Presumably, by the same specious logic, the reader-response theories used but never acknowledged by Nodelman to structure his book are wish-fulfillment fantasies. Pierre Macherey writes: "A work is tied to ideology not so much by what it says as by what it does not say" (34). *The Pleasures of Children's Literature* perfectly reflects a democratic-sounding rhetoric that makes the correct gestures toward a politics of inclusion but actually puts into practice a politics of exclusion. Often reactionary, *The Pleasures of Children's Literature* is an important but disturbing book.

*Works Cited*

Abrams, M. H. *The Mirror and the Lamp: Romantic Theory and the Critical Tradition.* London: Oxford University Press, 1953.

Eagleton, T. "The Critic as Clown." *Marxism and the Interpretation of Culture*. Ed. Cary Nelson et al. Urbana: University of Illinois Press, 1988.

Harstock, Nancy C. M. *Money, Sex, and Power: Toward a Feminist Historical Materialism*. Boston: Northeastern University Press, 1983.

Hunt, Peter. *Criticism, Theory, and Children's Literature*. Oxford: Basil Blackwell, 1991.

Lukens, R. *A Critical Handbook of Children's Literature*. 4th ed. Oxford, Ohio: Harper-Collins, 1990.

Macherey, Pierre. *A Theory of Literary Production*. Trans. Geoffrey Wall. London: Routledge and Kegan Paul, 1966.

Vandegrift, Kay E. "Research in Children's Literature." *Children and Books*. 8th ed. Ed. Zena Sutherland, et al. New York: HarperCollins, 1991.

Williams, R. *Marxism and Literature*. Oxford: Oxford University Press, 1977.

# Changing Agendas

Ruth B. Bottigheimer

*Engines of Instruction, Mischief, and Magic: Children's Literature in England from Its Beginnings to 1839,* by Mary V. Jackson. Lincoln: University of Nebraska Press, 1989.

Frances Fairchild and Margery Meanwell inhabit the pages of Mary Jackson's study, along with Goody Two-Shoes and Primrose Pretty-face. In prose with a bite, Jackson pithily characterizes authors of seventeenth- to early nineteenth-century English children's literature who, like Sarah Trimmer, viewed their world "through a lens ground between the stones of religious and social orthodoxy" (132). This observation follows from and is amply demonstrated by Jackson's thesis, that children's literature was rooted in the conditions and imperatives of the adult world, and its corollary, that children's literature was regarded as a tool to shape the young to the needs of the adult world (xi). Some years ago Geoffrey Summerfield's *Fantasy and Reason: Children's Literature in the Eighteenth Century* (University of Georgia Press, 1984) covered much the same ground. Summerfield's emphasis on the lives of children's literature authors complements Jackson's study, but his tone differs profoundly from Jackson's, for his work reflected and incorporated the newly awakened awareness of the 1970s about the socializing intent of children's literature, against which he reacted with acerbic criticism.

Three major clusters of literature for children dominate Jackson's analysis: those works that express John Locke's vision of the child; those that incorporate Rousseau's views; and those occasioned by the French Revolution and Terror. At a stroke, Jackson suggests, John Locke's thoughts on human understanding erased original sin from the pedagogical imperative by declaring the child's mind to be a blank slate. Hard on its heels, charity and Sunday schools developed in England and introduced forms of reading material that incorporated and implicitly expounded Locke's vision of the growing child. In Jackson's view, Enlightenment concepts thus entered English awareness simultaneously from two direc-

*Children's Literature* 21, ed. Francelia Butler, Christine Doyle Francis, Anne K. Phillips, and Julie K. Pfeiffer (Yale University Press, © 1993 The Children's Literature Foundation, Inc.).

tions: from the top down via intellectuals and from the bottom up through children's literature, like that used in charity and Sunday schools. Effective agents of instruction, the schools of the Sunday School Movement had 23,421 pupils in 1,327 schools in 1723, numbers that continued to grow for the next eighty years.

Enough has been written about Rousseau's Emile to last a life-time, but far too little attention has been paid to his enraging creation Sophie, whose education was designed to produce the perfect wife for Emile. Jackson redresses that omission and in the process pinpoints the eighteenth-century moment in which children's literature became gender-specific. In an insightful discussion (96–99) of humor and irony, "license, freedom, an entitlement of sorts" (96), she concludes that girls were soon to lose this entitlement, as their idealized literary counterparts became the earthly angels their readers were supposed to imitate (139), in part, at least, modeling themselves on Rousseau's ideal, Sophie (149ff.). Not all doors closed on docile maidens, however, for society rewarded Sophie-clones with highborn husbands, at least in tales about Primrose Prettyface and her mid- to late-eighteenth-century English ilk.

But the French Revolution and the Terror that followed put an end to plots with poor-but-worthy children rewarded with "estate and esteem," for an intractable conservatism within the middle classes produced a new literature for English children designed to maintain class distinctions and to restrain class crossovers like those that had benefited poor Primrose Prettyface. Charity and Sunday school education had fostered a "growing conviction of the rights of the individual among the lower-middle classes and artisans" (169), a conviction suddenly perceived as bloodily dangerous when tumbrels lumbered toward Parisian guillotines. Hence, from the 1790s onward, Jackson asserts, artists and literary figures joined the conservative middle classes and the recently liberal aristocracy in favoring a new direction for the content of children's books. "Many attitudes and ideals that had flourished in trade books during the freewheeling transitional years were now suspect as potential seeds of revolution. The books of Newbery and his colleagues from 1740 to 1765, and socioeconomic developments between 1750 and 1785, had encouraged children to believe that the handicaps of birth might be overcome by action—industry, virtue, learning, even luck. Environment might be so arranged as to outweigh 'blood.' . . . This explains the vitriolic criticism of books like Primrose Prettyface, Goody Goosecap, and even Goody Two-Shoes and also accounts for the mounting religious propaganda directed at children and the poor by Trimmer, More, and many other writers between 1780 and 1815. Censuring dangerous books and reinforcing religious restraints were complementary lines of attack pursued to restore fealty to the infallible and essential established order" (171). Characters with such socially critical names as Farmer Graspall or Sir Timothy Gripe were replaced by unwaveringly self-serving portrayals of the beneficent rich like Lady Bountiful and the virtuously stingy Mr. Johnson.

Conservative fear of social upheaval also gave birth to the castigation of fairy tales because of their subversive and terrifying promise of class-crossover. They would not return to favor until nationalist views about the nature of the "people" as "folk" superseded conservatizing efforts and until publishers recognized that the time was ripe to react against the grinding sobriety of reformist and Rousseauist children's literature.

The work of authors for the adult market frequently found its way into the hands of the young, albeit in much reduced form. *Pilgrim's Progress, Robinson Crusoe,* and *Gulliver's Travels* were on the child's bookshelf, of course, and so were Richardson's *Pamela, Clarissa Harlowe,* and *Sir Charles Grandison,* not to mention Smollett's *Roderick Random.* Other authors dipped their nibs directly into childish ink, as did Mary Wollstonecraft with her *Original Stories from Real Life* and Oliver Goldsmith, the probable author of *Goody Two-Shoes.* Yet, Jackson informs us, "very little of the early literature was belletristic, in the tradition of adult literature" (245). In fact, as Jackson asserts in her concluding remarks—remarks that are fully justified by the wealth of material introduced in her study: "Especially in its early stages, English children's literature was rooted in complex social, religious, and political conflict. It was yoked to the service of this or that party, faction, class, dogma, or philosophy and was constantly buffeted in controversies over who should control the child's world and mind" (245).

I have looked at many of the same books as Mary Jackson has done, and in some of the same libraries. The books' crumbling fragility and their caretakers' necessarily watchful and forbidding care of them deny access to these books to many of those who would gladly see them. All the more valuable, then, are her richly illustrated pages, which literally bring these rare survivors from past centuries into the reader's hands, one or two pages at a time. The illustrations provide a parallel running text of images and partial narratives from these old books on the pages of Jackson's study. Similarly, prose snippets excerpted from old stories wrench us from habitual notions about former times and raise up a ghostly past when corpses still swung in the wind. This form of punishment was not, of course, a dead metaphor in early nineteenth-century England, as is reflected in the grisly morality tale Mr. Fairchild told his children about fraternal love, illustrated with a ghastly walk to a neighboring gibbet.

Jackson views publishing history as a defining component of the study of children's literature. Changes made from one edition to another, like Mary Sherwood's 1820 revision of Sarah Fielding's 1749 *Governess,* reveal attitudinal shifts with efficient precision. Yet readers must beware of phrases like "sold well" without attendant figures, such as print-run sizes. For example, the twenty-year interval between two printings of an edition of *Aesop's Fables* could indicate sales of 50 copies per year to upwards of 300 (based on a probable print run of 1,000 to a phenomenal and unlikely one of 6,000 volumes, hitherto known only for Bibles). May we understand 50–300 copies per year as selling well in a nation of approximately twelve million English-speakers? A host of auxiliary—and mostly currently unanswerable—questions about publishers' expectations, the number and identity of potential buyers, and comparative sales for other types of books clamor for attention, and unalterably condition our perception of the concept of selling well.

It is abundantly clear that the patterns Jackson identifies in English children's literature reflect developments in the children's literature common to France and Germany. For example, some *Bibliothèque bleue* productions for adults also addressed young audiences; and the development of magazines for children in England, like Newbery's short-lived *Lilliputian Magazine,* was matched, slightly later, by Joachim Heinrich Campe's German periodicals, themselves contributing to the internationality of children's literature by being translated into French. Nor should we forget the mid-eighteenth-century French-language *Magasin des enfans,* published both in England and Germany, parts of which were later translated into the vernacular in both countries. Jackson rightly includes children's Bibles, a genre of great importance in the early eighteenth century, and she touches tantalizingly on children's drama, a subject similarly ripe for investigation.

Driven by the commercial imperatives of expanding publishing enterprises that were themselves fueled by an increasingly literate population whose well-being was intimately related to expanding domestic and overseas markets, eighteenth-century children's literature responded to calls for new kinds of child populations (as precursors to future adult populations). After two centuries of children's literature devoted principally to soul-saving or artisanal instruction, eighteenth-century children's literature represented an unorganized and chaotically diverse set of attempts to reform populations. Agendas changed, and children's literature was bent to meet new requirements. Those bends—reworkings, new plots, new characters, new names, even—provide "invaluable insights into the evolution of taste, moral values, reading habits, and the applications of books to real lives" (15).

# Questions of Power

Gary D. Schmidt

*Criticism, Theory, and Children's Literature,* by Peter Hunt. Cambridge, Mass.: Basil Blackwell, 1991.

*Children's Literature: The Development of Criticism,* ed. Peter Hunt. New York: Routledge, 1990.

As a critic of children's literature, I have recently written about two books that were childhood favorites: Robert McCloskey's *Make Way for Ducklings* and Hugh Lofting's *Voyages of Doctor Dolittle.* That each had won the most prestigious award in their genre was of no moment to me as a child. I loved them for the way they were. And if you were to go with me now, hand in hand, I could still take you down the stairs of the Hicksville Public Library—I am not making up the name—to where they stood and, I hope, remain on the shelves.

Writing in the last year, I detailed McCloskey's use of the island as a metaphor for wholeness, Lofting's portrayal of the gentle doctor as an emblem of peace and tolerance, and both writers' circular structuring of a journey motif so that the very form of the work pointed toward the thematic concern of the security engendered by a family, however broadly defined.

Now Peter Hunt's work asks me to rethink these interpretations. As an adult critic, I read *The Voyages of Doctor Dolittle* carrying with me one bag full of critical concerns and another loaded with the weight of criticism—mostly negative—that Lofting's novel has accrued. But when I plucked it from the Hicksville Public Library's shelves—when I was, in Hunt's terms, a peer reader—no such folderol mattered. The tension of the spine; the dry feel of the pages; the smell, the wonderful smell of an old book—these mattered. The adventures, the delight of a man who could talk to animals, the poignant ending, the identification with Tommy Stubbins—these mattered. How shall I, as an adult critic, ever reconcile my non-peer reading with my peer reading? Is such a reconciliation possible?

*Children's Literature* 21, ed. Francelia Butler, Christine Doyle Francis, Anne K. Phillips, and Julie K. Pfeiffer (Yale University Press, © 1993 The Children's Literature Foundation, Inc.).

For that matter, is it even possible to reconstruct that peer reading?

These are precisely the kinds of foundational questions Peter Hunt asks in *Criticism, Theory, and Children's Literature.* Beginning with the observation that criticism and theory can help us understand not what we read but actually how we understand what we read, Hunt proposes to establish methods by which we might "see what happens when we read, and at each stage . . . qualify what is happening with what may be happening with a child" (3). This may give some pause. It does this reviewer. Is audience reception and perception necessarily the business of the literary critic? Some may believe that a critical focus which concentrates on how the child perceives rather than on the work itself can become a siren's call, leading further and inevitably further from the work itself. Yet just such a focus leads, instead, to Hunt's fascinating and incisive analysis of how we can understand children's literature.

Hunt begins his exploration with the astonishing claim that contemporary literary criticism has broadened access to children's literature, so that "all specialists"—from teachers in nursery schools to university academics—"now contribute vitally" (10). Modern literary criticism—particularly those schools that have come under so much recent attack—are more often damned for speaking to a smaller and smaller audience, an audience that, for example, is privy to the jargon of the deconstructionist or the structuralist, or that finds affinity with the ideology of the feminist or Marxist. But here Hunt suggests the opposite: modern criticism has broadened the audience that tries to understand how literature does what it does.

But this is not the only astonishing claim. Two pages later, Hunt poses the question, Is Jane Austen a better writer than Judy Blume? His response might dispose nineteenth-century specialists to raise an eyebrow. And hardly three pages later Hunt asserts that all canons—the work of the Children's Literature Association's Touchstones Committee notwithstanding—are idiosyncratic; one's perceptions of any canon are based on mere personal responses.

Depending on which preposition one chooses, one will be provoked by or at such claims. If criticism has validated the responses of "all specialists," it has also rarefied the atmosphere about a work. If canons are based merely on personal likes and dislikes, it is also true that there are standards of artistry that point to merit or its lack. And I side impenitently with those who believe that Jane

Austen is a better writer—not just different—but *better* than Judy Blume. To say that Austen is merely different is to say nothing. To say that she might only be considered better in certain contexts of group power is hardly defensible.

But here, Hunt might say, I am only responding out of my own idiosyncratic canonization of Austen. And this is precisely what his text does again and again: it makes readers ask how they understand what they understand. To this end, Hunt explores fundamental questions that any critic of children's literature will have to answer before approaching a work. What is children's literature? (Preliminary to that, what is literature?) How does a peer reading of a children's novel differ from a non-peer reading, and how might such readings be reconciled, if indeed they should be? How does a child decode a text, and what implications do the limitations that a child reader brings to a text have for the author's use of language, allusion, and narrative strategy? What expectations do genres establish, and how does a child reader anticipate or use such expectations? How does a children's book reflect an author's attempt to cope with competing ideologies and politics? How does the market affect authorial strategies?

In spite of enormous gains in the past decade, the questions Hunt poses are precisely those that critics will need to tackle in a field that has no theoretical and hardly a working definition to classify its texts. As other fields struggle to redefine a canon, children's literature has yet to define one with a broad consensus that may then be subject to redefinition. It is the only field in which audience seems to play a major role in defining what texts might be considered part of the field's purview. How that audience affects the field is still an open question. And then there is the fact that some works, like those of Randolph Caldecott, John Newbery, and Mrs. Molesworth, seem to shift in and out of the field. The works of these and other earlier writers have departed the field, at least in a practical sense, for all but academics. Certainly they have departed as far as peer readers are concerned.

The need for definitions and foundational theory is examined in the collection of essays Hunt has edited, *Children's Literature: The Development of Criticism*. The essays range from mid-eighteenth-century discussions of the task of the children's book writer to recent theoretical examinations of the nature of the field. (This should be qualified by noting that the group of pre-1900 pieces is so small as to seem tokenish, including as it does only short selections by Sarah Fielding, Charles Dickens, and John Ruskin.) The majority of the collected essays have been published since 1970, and each of these aims toward a "coherent poetics for children's literature" (6–7). What these essays demonstrate is that such a coherence has not been reached; perhaps it never will be. But they also show how contemporary critical schools have contributed to our understanding of how children's literature does what it does.

Included in this collection are passages from classic statements about children's literature: G. K. Chesterton's "Ethics of Elfland," J. R. R. Tolkien's "On Fairy Stories" and even Charles Dickens's less accessible "Frauds on the Fairies," the point of which any enemy of Mr. Gradgrind will be able to predict: "a nation without fancy, without some romance, never did, never can, never will hold a great place under the sun" (25). But Hunt also collects more sharply focused essays that demonstrate how the academic community has been analyzing children's literature. Hunt includes those suspicious of critical trends—Roger Lancelyn Green, for example—and notes the effects of such criticism on reviewing: a general vagueness, a dependency on biography, a tendency to describe rather than to analyze. Against this position, Hunt contrasts the views of critics like John Rowe Townsend, whose focus on the text represents a step away from Green's suspicion, as well as Felicity Hughes, Aidan Chambers, and Margaret Meek, who have embraced contemporary theory and contributed enormously to the acceptance of children's literature in academia. Though the pieces by the last three critics are wide-ranging, Hunt demonstrates the contributions of specific schools of literary criticism in articles by William Moebius, who examines elements of design and characterization in picture books in order to discern visual codes; Hugh Crago, who writes of reader responses out of a combined interest in literary criticism and psychotherapy; and Lissa Paul, who writes out of the discourse community of feminist criticism.

The names in the last paragraph will be familiar to critics of children's literature. And the pieces themselves are not unfamiliar. What is important about this collection is its cumulative effect. It demonstrates how critics have wrestled—are wrestling—with fundamental questions of children's literature, perhaps the most important of which remains its definition. The volume as a whole addresses the usefulness of theory to counter impressionistic and emotion-laden responses. Further, Hunt's book shows the difficulties of engineering criticism for a body of literature in which the critics are not the primary readers in any real sense. If the collection tries a mite too hard to demonstrate that the criticism of children's literature is indeed a valid academic enterprise, it may be forgiven because of its insistence on asking rigorous questions of a literary form that has not always received such questions.

In *Criticism, Theory, and Children's Literature,* Hunt tries to deal with some of these questions on his own terms. His answers are often stated in terms of power, as when he argues: "We need to take on board the obvious, relative idea that 'literature' is the writing authorized and prioritized by a powerful minority . . . that 'canon' has been influenced by universities, and if children's literature is to accede to this privileged status, it must either become part of the power structure or that power structure must change" (54). A book, Hunt claims, becomes literature only after it is accepted by its power structure. So Austen is literature, Blume is children's literature, the adjective assigned by the power structures of the academic world which points to lower status.

Though the word *power* appears with astonishing frequency in this study, the word *aesthetics* never does. Has Hunt considered that Judy Blume's work is not judged to be literature not because of a powerful minority's circling of the wagons but because Blume's work is not aesthetically masterful? Hunt will claim that it is indeed a powerful minority that defines what is aesthetically masterful, but if one pushes that assumption, one is led willingly to the useless observation that there is no such thing as a bad book (in aesthetic terms) since at any time the powerful minority might shift, and suddenly Judy Blume is a classic, Austen a footnote. (Hunt's own observations on the remakes of *The Tale of Peter Rabbit,* the "predigested style" of *First Term at Trebizon* [82], and the narrative voice of *Goodnight Mr. Tom* [88] suggest that he, too, makes evaluative judgments of a book's aesthetic worth.)

Hunt claims that "instead of saying 'better/worse,' or 'suitable/ unsuitable,' criticism would be more profitably employed in saying 'this text has certain potentials for interaction, certain possibilities for meaning'" (83). Certainly it would be helpful if criticism could show such potentiality, but if Hunt is suggesting that this should come about to prevent the "confusion of 'good' with 'good for,'" a confusion leading to "lazy writing" and "indifferent texts" (83), he must also note the possibility that preposterously bad writing might also have "certain possibilities of meaning," and if it is not valid to make aesthetic choices, since doing so would be to ally oneself with an arbitrary power group, then how indeed are we to judge a book's aesthetic merits?

Hunt's answer might again be phrased in terms of power. Midway through his study, he questions Enid Blyton's use of a powerful, omniscient narrator who is "so obviously present and dominant and more knowledgeable than the implied audience, that the interaction cannot seem to be between peers" (106). Here Hunt assumes that such interaction between peers is what the author is striving for. But what if it is not? What if the author wishes such a narratorial stance? If such a stance is to be questioned, it seems more fruitful to examine your aesthetic, rather than power, principles. At least Hunt would need to show why an interactive narrator is better than an omniscient, non-interactive narrator. I doubt that such an argument would be useful without reference to aesthetic terms. (Those uninterested in an attack on Blyton's art might turn the page and find a similar attack on the narrator of *The Lion, the Witch, and the Wardrobe.*)

Certainly, if we are to consider how readers understand what they understand, we must consider as well how readers might respond to aesthetic qualities. For these must go hand in hand with the concerns for power in narrative voice, and how that power affects understanding. To neglect one in favor of the other is to lead to inextricable contradictions.

Hunt calls for what he terms a "childist" criticism: an examination of the codes that texts contain and how it is that a child reader—as opposed to an adult reader—deciphers or is unable to decipher those codes. As Hunt puts it, "The 'realization' of a text, especially a text for children, is closely involved with questions of control, and of the techniques through which power is exercised over, or shared with, the reader" (81). The call for a childist criticism is an important summons to deal with the fundamental questions he poses. If at times this reviewer is frustrated by an omnipresent concern with power, coupled with a too-quick analysis of texts (*Make Way for Ducklings* and Graham Oakley's Church Mouse series each receive only a single analytic sentence despite their prominence as examples [182, 187]), it is much more often the case that the book invites reexamination of how critics of children's literature do what they do. Hunt calls for a criticism that examines readers and their abilities to understand and decode *before* that criticism examines the text; it is a criticism that examines the context of the act of reading. In one respect, he compels one critic to remember the Hicksville Public Library in a different way, and in a larger sense, he raises questions that will shape the future of the academic field of children's literature.

# A Committed, Passionate Voice

Peter F. Neumeyer

*Climb into the Bell Tower: Essays on Poetry,* by Myra Cohn Livingston. New York: Harper & Row, 1990.

The underlying questions of this volume are inescapable: What *is* children's poetry? Is it somehow different in *kind* from adult poetry? Do stanzas by Eleanor Farjeon, A. A. Milne, Aileen Fisher, and Elizabeth Madox Roberts represent a genre of their own and, basically, of a sort that no adult would pick up for solace, insight, or understanding? (Be honest when you answer that.) Or is children's poetry essentially no different from adult poetry? Is it simply that stratum of adult poetry which, at some level, a child can respond to—Dickinson's "I like to see it lap the miles," Tennyson's "Eagle," Langston Hughes's "Dreams"? Do Valerie Worth's or N. M. Bodecker's writings rank as good poetry by any criteria, or do we judge them more leniently because they're either written or marketed for a different audience? Do Ted Hughes's "My Sister Jane" or "My Uncle Dan" really rank with "Pike" or "View of a Pig"—or are they, as it were, written for the left hand?

Even as I have taught graduate seminars in children's poetry, I was unsure of my answers to these questions. Sometimes, in my puzzlement, I turned to the writings of Myra Livingston, whose first book *about* children's poetry I reviewed almost twenty years ago. Reading Livingston on children's poetry, I am still not sure I always find the answers to my major questions, but I do know I am listening to the most knowledgeable, thoughtful, responsible voice—sometimes the most astringent voice—in America today on the subject. The voice is astringent because Livingston is committed and passionate about the seriousness of the subject of children and poetry, because when we give a child a book—she quotes George Steiner— we take in hand "the quick of another human being" (191).

Myra Livingston is herself an esteemed poet ("children's poet," if such a thing there be), and by the time of this publication, she may have published her fiftieth book of or about poetry for and con-

*Children's Literature* 21, ed. Francelia Butler, Christine Doyle Francis, Anne K. Phillips, and Julie K. Pfeiffer (Yale University Press, © 1993 The Children's Literature Foundation, Inc.).

nected with children. She is one of the two or three wisest and most industrious anthologizers of children's poetry (not a hack assembler but a master synthesizer). She is a thoughtful, subtle teacher and lecturer whose message is ever a balance of concern for poetry, poets, and children. And finally, as more than one significant contemporary poet can attest, Myra Livingston has been an invaluable sponsor and mentor of new poets.

Livingston's collections of original poems range broadly from eclectic assemblings of "Worlds I Know" to thematic volumes on such subjects as trees and the seasons; frequently her books have been illustrated by our best artists, among them Leonard Everett Fisher, Antonio Frasconi, and Peter Sis. Her anthologies likewise range from the inclusive (*Anthology of Children's Literature*) to the topical ("poems of the unknowable"). Her *The Child as Poet: Myth or Reality* is an important book for parents, teachers, and all others who think about poetry and children—an examination of the poetic imagination, a scrupulous study of acclaimed (or, "notorious") "child poets," as well as a plea for common sense and honest appraisal, a valiant barricade against mindless mediocrity, and a tonic for the cheap and condescending sentimentality that is such a danger to those who, with good intentions, attempt to foster "creativity" in children with the poetical equivalent of coloring books.

Myra Livingston is a necessary voice from outside the academy and its often institutionalized opinions. At the same time, academics trust her because she is subtle, serious, passionate, and fully professional as a poet-scholar. While some write single-mindedly about the craft of poetry and others write fondly of children, Livingston is knowledgeable about and dedicated to the tradition and art of poetry at the same time that she cherishes no romantic illusions about "genius" children. For these reasons I have kept Livingston's widely scattered essays permanently on reserve for my students.

You may imagine, then, what a godsend it is to have *Climb into the Bell Tower*, eleven essays or lectures (all having appeared or been delivered on earlier occasions) available in both hard and soft covers. Let me say at once that the collection is repetitive. Nor do the essays develop toward a revelation in any way that I could discern. Nor is it a summation of Livingston's far-ranging explorations. That's still to come, we hope, in the next decade. But for what this collection is—a gathering of eleven representative essays by perhaps the most knowledgeable writer on poetry and children—the collection is essential.

One of Livingston's missions has ever been perhaps the happiest task of the critic: to shine light on remarkable poets and their works. And she is fine on specific writers and individual poems. In this volume, her writing on David McCord, Edward Lear, X. J. Kennedy, Valerie Worth, and a number of other poets makes us read them with new care. Her admiration for Jack Prelutsky is more circumscribed, as she notes his technical facility, and makes the true and original observation of his "echoes of the German school, of *Struwwelpeter*" (92), noting in his works a frequent direct threat to the reader. Here, her juxtaposition and exposition of the modulated, humorous, benign moralism of Shel Silverstein is instructive and persuasive.

Along with introducing poets and instructing her audience in reading and writing poetry, for years Myra Livingston has also been doing two other needful things. She has championed the free poetic imagination, stressing the crippling limitations of those who, like Jarrell's Mockingbird, mistake poetical machinery and prosodic techniques for the creative, imaginative act that is itself the poetic experience. Her first essay ("The Poem on Page 81") sets the tone. Here she stresses that poems are to be experiences, lived, felt in the marrow. Poetry leads, she shows us, to a special knowledge felt on the pulse, perceptible to the emotions, rather than to the ratiocinative self. Or, in Livingston's words, "We should allow ourselves the time to stop, occasionally, and become 'right readers,' not through analysis . . . not through rhyme, but in the giving of our feelings and sensitivities to what lies behind the words" (20).

Yet Livingston has ever bravely swum against the tide in her insistence that not every word uttered from the mouths of babes is poetry (even though it may be underwritten by the sacred Writers in the Schools). Having intensively, "clinically," studied child poets (as few have done), having thought long on the nature of metaphor, on what Coleridge deemed the *synthetic* ("and magical") power of the poetical imagination, and on the creations evolving from observation and contemplation, Livingston has eloquently alerted us to the distinctions between poetry and Kenneth Kochian pump-priming devices. Further, she has delineated for us the difference between a child's actual spiritual explorations and the "Oh Wow!" exclamations of the Richard Lewis *Miracles* vein. (Sadly, though, one of Livingston's clearest, sharpest, most useful essays on this topic, with the apt title, "But Is it Poetry?" is not included in this volume.)

Yet Livingston's critical "Bell Tower" is not built of ivory or set in a desert. She has spent ample time in classrooms and encouraged hundreds of children to develop their poetic muscles. Frequently quoting John Ciardi, she disdains "the spillage of raw emotion" (40); she eschews "can't miss" Haiku gimmickry. What, then, one might ask, does she offer in their stead? The answer is supplied by another recent volume in her ongoing project, *Poem Making: Ways to Begin Writing Poetry* (1991), a teaching book for parents, teachers, and bright youngsters that goes sensibly, rationally from "Voice" to those prosodic devices that are the scales, the finger exercises if you like, that one has to master before one can make the music of poetry.

The only quarrel I have with *Climb into the Bell Tower*—actually, the difficulty I have had for many years with Livingston's arguments—is her so seemingly useful distinction between *poetry* and *verse*. *Poetry* obviously has the "synthetic," "imaginative" unity and power of which Coleridge spoke—the insight or maturity or depth —and *verse*, the lesser genre, is apparently something like doggerel aspiring to the condition of poetry. One understands her point, obviously. And like-as-not, one even agrees with virtually any example Livingston cites. And yet, knowing what Livingston and we all know about the co-creative act of the reader, and sensing, even while confident in our well-tutored judgment, the anxiety of influence, the burden of canon, and the historical fickleness of taste and literary reputation, we just aren't comfortable with an argument based solely on rhetorical assertion, on tacit understanding, on a wink and a nudge.

Still, *Climb into the Bell Tower* is a necessary collection. That is, you need it. It argues for the centrality of the free imagination in poetry. It argues for the necessity of inculcating that free imagination by way of the poetical education of children. By considering the cases of Eve Merriam, Norma Farber, Harry Behn, and six other poets, it instructs us in the reading of poetry—enriching our lives and those of our students. It exhorts us to be honest and not to elevate mindlessly any child-generated effusion simply because we have not the wit or courage to insist that a true poem is high art and is no more accidentally "found" than a sonata. In Livingston's words, it "takes hard work and time to write a poem, and the mistaken notion that writing is 'easy,' that anyone can do it, continues, unfortunately, to flourish" (31). (To the detriment of our children, says Livingston; to the detriment of the innocents who flock to our "Creative" writing classes, says this reviewer.)

With learning, skill, and dedication, Livingston has for years labored so that we and our children will not, as William Carlos Williams feared, "die miserably every day for lack of what is found" in poems.

# Reappraising the Puritan Past

Anne Scott MacLeod

*The Discovery of Childhood in Puritan England,* by C. John Sommerville. Athens: University of Georgia Press, 1992.

Given our history, it is strange how little most Americans know about Puritanism and how much of that little is at least half wrong. Conventional opinion holds that Puritans were religious fanatics obsessed by the question of eternal salvation, convinced of predestination and infant depravity, and rigidly harsh in their attitudes to children and childhood. H. L. Mencken's profoundly silly definition of a Puritan as a man living in constant fear that "someone somewhere is having fun" has survived all scholarship to be quoted endlessly, including by the president of the United States in a recent State of the Union speech.

C. John Sommerville's *The Discovery of Childhood in Puritan England* is a major contribution to the ongoing discussion of the history of childhood. This study carefully and persuasively documents the origins of a new concept of childhood in seventeenth-century England. Arguing that Puritans promulgated that new concept, Sommerville looks closely at Puritan attitudes toward children, comparing them with both earlier and later views of childhood. Though his purpose is to trace the beginnings of an intellectually liberalized approach to children, in the process he rehabilitates the conventional image of Puritans. His evidence not only restores Puritans to humanity but elevates them in many respects above their contemporaries in their treatment of children.

Sommerville's story begins with new names. In the 1560s, some parish birth registers began to record names quite unlike those used in England for hundreds of years. The ancient, familiar Johns, Williams, Henrys, and their many variations gave way to Thankful, Chastity, and even Tribulation Wholesome. The namers were Puritan parents, whose decision to give their children new names symbolizes for Sommerville the attitudes that made Puritanism the major influence in the transformation of the seventeenth-century

*Children's Literature* 21, ed. Francelia Butler, Christine Doyle Francis, Anne K. Phillips, and Julie K. Pfeiffer (Yale University Press, © 1993 The Children's Literature Foundation, Inc.).

English view of childhood. Puritans, he says, broke with the past, rejecting the old bondage of family and tradition, and looking toward the future. The new names indicated a fresh start.

It is Sommerville's thesis that "an interest in the subject of childhood . . . arose within a particular religious subculture"—that is, with Puritanism. Historians of childhood have generally conceded the importance of Puritanism in bringing about a new interest in childhood and have tried to account for it with analyses—largely hostile—of Puritan psychology, theology, and class position. None of this convinces Sommerville. The root of Puritan concern with childhood, he argues, lay in "the most obvious fact about Puritanism,—that it constituted a reform movement" (9). Indeed, in defining Puritanism, Sommerville avoids even theology, identifying as Puritans "all those who made their dissatisfaction with the church known" (12). Puritans wanted to purify the Church of England, and thereby to reform the institutions of English society. When the Elizabethan Church of England successfully resisted their efforts, the movement had to take a longer view. Puritans began to see children as future agents of reform, and this created a crucial difference in attitudes toward children between Puritanism and established religion. Puritans were the first to direct serious attention to childhood because they were Outs: "Those groups that have no secure institutional basis are most likely to sense the importance of reaching children" (24). Oriented to the future, hoping to secure their ideology in the rising generation, Puritans tried to understand children and childhood, with, ultimately, momentous results for education, children's reading, child nurturing, and almost everything else having to do with children in society.

Sommerville covers the years between 1560 and 1660, during which the Puritans created a movement, achieved a short-lived political triumph, and were displaced. After the Restoration, some returned to the Anglican church, but more did not, and Puritanism became one sect among many dissenting groups. As Dissenters, Puritans retained their interest in children as their only hope of survival, but Sommerville senses a hardening in their attitudes toward the young. It may be, he suggests, that "the Puritan reputation for harshness with children was actually earned in those later generations," adding later that "if the picture of 17th century attitudes presented in the present study is surprising in its mildness, that may be because it stops short of the period in which Puritanism changed from a movement to a sect" (11, 14).

As a group, Puritans were scholarly, opinionated, and loquacious. Sommerville draws on a wide variety of sources: biography, catechisms, literature on raising children, treatises on education and theology, and children's books. In biography he finds Puritans taking a newly realistic look at children. Humanist biographers evinced little interest in the childhood experience of their subjects. Because they valued mature development, their greatest praise was reserved for a child prematurely old. Anglicans, too, generally assumed that childhood was a brief period of uneventful contentment, quite unimportant to adult life. They dwelt on childhood only when telling premonitory stories—the future warrior whose first word was "sword"; the future royalist whose first step was toward the king's picture. Such prophetic stories, Sommerville points out, represent the traditionalist's desire to suggest a static order preordained by God. Similarly, hagiographers depicted saints as religiously extraordinary even in infancy, "icon[s] of holy simplicity," signaling their future greatness. Such biography aimed at inspiring devotion, not emulation; realism was irrelevant. In fact, "the farther removed [these biographies] were from everyday life, the better they served their purpose" (44).

Puritans, in contrast, gave childhood serious attention because they had a compelling interest in developing children's inner spiritual convictions. They showed children as less than perfect in order to demonstrate that they could (and should) improve. In one of the many contradictions of Puritanism, Puritan authors, even as they embraced the doctrine of predestination, designed biography to inspire action. Puritans and Dissenters often used children's words and realistic details, testifying, Sommerville says, "to the author's belief that these child biographies represented real possibilities for young readers" (53). In Puritans, children at last had chroniclers willing to see them as they were and as they might become.

Turning to theories of childhood as expressed in theological treatises, children's books, and child-rearing advice, Sommerville finds surprises. "[The] authors defeat our expectations and mitigate the central beliefs of English Calvinism" (71). In most direct contests between theological purity and the need to accommodate the child's nature, Puritans accommodated children. Children "left a mark at every stage in the development of Puritan doctrine, from Covenant corporatism through evangelical conversionism to an individualistic moralism" (71).

A summary can only suggest the detailed examination of sources in this chapter, which forms the core of Sommerville's claim for Puritan sympathy toward children. One example, however, shows the direction of the theological argument. Strictly speaking, Protestantism's theoretical insistence on faith freely and consciously avowed—a kind of religious informed consent—would seem to restrict baptism and church membership to those able to make a mature decision. But where did this leave the many children who died before reaching maturity? And what of their anguished parents, left to contemplate their children denied salvation for eternity? Protestants looked for ways to include children in "the shelter of the church," and many decided that God's covenant allowed infant baptism. The theological arguments may not have been watertight, but even Calvin made them rather than exclude children from all hope of heaven: "What [is] the danger . . . if infants be said to receive now some part of that grace which in a little while they shall enjoy to the full?" he wrote. "Infants are baptized into future repentance, and faith" (73). If this was a politically practical stratagem to retain and enlarge adult membership in the church, it was also a measure of tenderness toward children.

As for children's books, Sommerville shows that for nearly a century Puritans and Dissenters had the field virtually to themselves. Books of courtesy and instruction existed, but books written to reach children at their own level and to encourage inner spiritual direction in children were new forms in seventeenth-century England. Puritan writing for children was, of course, wholly didactic, meant to convey religious doctrine, yet here, too, the results were less unsympathetic than such a purpose would seem to promise.

The literature, Sommerville points out, tried to guide and encourage; it was designed to offer hope. If doctrine stood in the way of this goal, doctrine was often shaded: "Calvinist piety was bent by the effort to appeal to the older children and to make sense to the younger ones. . . . Even the doctrines of depravity and predestination were made compatible with a respect for the child's freedom and moral value" (78). Sommerville finds most Puritan children's literature attentive to children's capacities and respectful of their moral autonomy.

Puritans also reformed advice literature for parents, moving away from the casual brutality of medieval treatment of children toward moderation in discipline. Sommerville corrects the conventional idea that Puritan parents set out to "break the will" of the child. The phrase, he says, belongs not to the seventeenth but to the eighteenth century, "when doctrinal and social patterns had changed" (94). Puritans wished "to produce free-standing individuals who could operate in any circumstances with only the guidance of a religious conscience" (95). John Locke's essay of 1693 on children's education is close in tone, Sommerville argues, to many Puritan and Dissenting authors (101).

Puritan initiatives induced Anglicans to put forth, tardily, their own ideas of childhood in children's books, child-rearing advice, and educational theory. In a reversal of conventional opinion, Sommerville characterizes Anglicans as more repressive in their attitudes toward children, less trusting of a child's capacity to grow and improve, and far less willing to grant a child's right to autonomy than were Puritans. Education, especially, became contested territory. A debate long raged over whether schooling was to be indoctrination or a search for truth, with Dissenters finally making the child's intellectual and moral autonomy a settled principle of their theory of education.

In an epilogue, Sommerville traces some of the wider social and personal ramifications of the Puritan discovery of childhood. Attention to childhood had a dynamic effect on Puritans; it influenced their theology, approach to education, and family life. Families and movements, observes Sommerville, "represent the opposite poles of stability and movement" (158). Movements promote social change, which puts them in opposition to society's most deeply traditional institution, the family. Moreover, movements and families compete for the loyalty of their members, and compromise, if it can be reached, will change both. Sommerville reviews the journey of Christianity from a radically individualistic movement that threatened family solidarity to a traditional faith that accommodated family needs and wants. Puritanism, too, began with religious individualism, even intimating that each child represented itself before God, an idea that threatened parental authority. Family, however, wins most contests between doctrinal purity and family claims, as it did with infant baptism and the American Half-Way Covenant. Moreover, in the end, Dissenters had no alternative to dependence on the family. After the Restoration, they were Outs, without any realistic hope of becoming Ins, and they had to convert their children if they were to survive as a religious group.

Sommerville's book is as full of meat as a walnut, and his argument is detailed, lucid, and well-documented. He writes clearly, and when he takes issue with historical theories and received opinions, he does so equably. *The Discovery of Childhood* is a key chapter in the intellectual history of the idea of childhood, and Sommerville's careful, consistent focus on documentary evidence is one of its strengths. Yet I could wish that the context in which Puritanism worked its curious miracle had been sketched in, even in broad outline. The general break-up of medieval corporatism in the face of Protestant individualism, the relative prosperity of the period, the growth of commerce, the expansion of the middle class, and the fluidity of social status—all these made up a social and economic environment in which the discovery of childhood could not only take place but take root. A climate of change and possibility meant that the Puritan discovery of childhood, so thoroughly documented in this fine book, was the beginning of a social revolution.

# A Soaring Look at the Picture Book

## William Moebius

*The Picture Book Comes of Age: Looking at Childhood through the Art of
Illustration,* by Joseph H. Schwarcz and Chava Schwarcz. Chicago
and London: American Library Association, 1991.

Joseph Schwarcz would have had much more to say had he lived to
complete the making of *The Picture Book Comes of Age.* It is a measure of his generous spirit that even now, four years after his death
in 1988, the reader encountering his latest and last book must from
time to time feel his passing acutely, and with each turn of the page
mourn the loss to all of this teacher whose insight into the images
in picture books and into the feelings and needs of children went
so much further than most contemporary critics of the genre have
managed.

When Joseph Schwarcz died at age seventy-one in 1988, he had
published *Ways of the Illustrator: Visual Communication in Children's
Literature* (Chicago: ALA, 1982), as well as a host of articles in German, English, and Hebrew. He had taught for fifty years "as if he
were born to it," as Betsy Hearne, who met him at the University
of Chicago, asserts in a eulogy that serves as her foreword to this
posthumous volume. Rescued from the pit through the dedication
of Chava Schwarcz, his widow, and ALA editor Tina MacAyeal, *The
Picture Book Comes of Age* is a work destined to exemplify for years
to come the possibilities of picture book analysis, exceeded only
by Jean Perrot's *Du jeu, des enfants and des livres* (Paris: Editions du
Cercle de la Librairie, 1987).

As originally planned, Schwarcz's book was intended to address
first the representations of the physical world, particularly of body
and gesture, then those of such psychological elements as identity
formation, and, finally, those of the social sphere. Clearly, in many
ways the book exceeds the promise of its original plan, while in a
few, less important ways, it falls short. When the book soars, as it
does especially in the treatment of the work of Anthony Browne,
it goes well beyond the boundaries of psychological reference and

*Children's Literature* 21, ed. Francelia Butler, Christine Doyle Francis, Anne K.
Phillips, and Julie K. Pfeiffer (Yale University Press, © 1993 The Children's Literature Foundation, Inc.).

other "matter" toward a consideration of the aesthetic principles that make Browne's work so successful. Schwarcz's writing reaches its heights when it acknowledges and develops levels of interpretation and response rarely accorded picture book art, an art too often treated in vacuo and not as an integral part of the history of images. Schwarcz's knowledge of art history is reflected both in his excellent handling of design and compositional issues and in his alertness to pictorial allusion. He gains credibility and persuasiveness by emphasizing the immediacy of a particular picture book reading experience without denying the relevance of extensive study elsewhere. With such timely disclaimers as "the philosophical and psychological implications are too complex and far-reaching to be sorted out in the present context" (103), Schwarcz gives us the room and, implicitly, the encouragement we need to test our own observations and answers.

Among the "areas" of representation he explores, Schwarcz writes with unparalleled sensitivity and acuity when he examines the psychological dimension of the story and its images. The second chapter, "A Close Look at a Picture Book," in which he follows a "diagram of emotional states" to visualize what goes on in the mind of Peter, the protagonist in Ezra Jack Keats's *Whistle for Willie*, is a masterpiece of picture book interpretation. The next four chapters (on "Stress and the Picture Book," "Love and Anxiety in the Supportive Family," "Grandparents and Grandchildren," and "Longing for Love, Contending for Love") sustain the quality of writing and insight, despite chapter titles that some may find awkward or sentimental. It may be that after reading his rich analyses of two works by Anthony Browne in chapter 6, we meet the accelerated treatment of a greater variety of texts in chapter 7 ("The Emergence of Identity") with regret. The slight disappointment we may feel with this chapter may also lie in the initial prominence accorded Bettelheim's *Uses of Enchantment*, even as "different psychological persuasions" are mentioned but not named (84); it is a measure of Schwarcz's own higher expectations for criticism that by the end of this chapter he, too, offers regrets: "The present discussion is an uneven one for several reasons. The most significant among these is, as was already stated at the beginning, [that] the theme of identity is a complex one, owing to the inspiring and at times confusing richness of concepts and definitions and their application in interpreting the way in which the personality grows and matures" (110). Nevertheless,

even in this less favored chapter, Schwarcz reclaims our attention
with a seven-page exposition and analysis of Browne's illustrations
for Annalena McAfee's *Kirsty Knows Best* and soon after, in "Digression: Focus on Ugliness," offers, as it were, a brilliant cadenza on
recent picture books that feature "nonbeautiful" protagonists. This
digression, effortless, improvisatory, reminds us of another facet of
Schwarcz's scholarship: its international scope. For his brief turn
on the plain and the homely, he chooses several picture books in
Swedish and German and but two in English. Elsewhere we find
him describing and analyzing picture books from Australia as well
as England, Canada, and the United States along with many not
yet translated into English from Scandinavia, Czechoslovakia, the
formerly divided Germanies, Italy, Japan, Venezuela, and Israel.

With the treatment of the social world in the picture book,
Schwarcz's writing, as he acknowledges, loses its edge. Either because the picture books themselves do not inspire as much careful
exposition and analysis or because the themes and issues regarding
the environment ("A Sense of Place," "Social Action for the Socially
Disadvantaged," and "The Threat of War and the Quest for Peace")
do not admit as much "play" in the interpretative process, or for
some other reasons, these chapters are, with a few significant exceptions, less compelling. Important exceptions include his discussions
of Kurusa's *La Calle es libre* [The street is free], illustrated by Monica
Doppert (1981); Tomi Ungerer's *Allumette* (1974); Toshi Maruki's
*Hiroshima No Pika* [The flash of Hiroshima, 1980]; and Roberto
Innocenti's and Christophe Gallaz's *Rose blanche* (1985). Schwarcz's
comments on picture books related to social and cultural diversity,
to ethnic conflict and ethnic heritage, are surprisingly muted here,
especially for one who lived so long in the Middle East and worked
on behalf of the Center for Research and Development of Arab
Education in Israel.

Before turning to the final chapter, I would mention other aspects and qualities of the book that, for some, may lessen its appeal.
Although Schwarcz writes about the work of eighty-four illustrators, he does not (cannot) include everyone who might, indeed,
deserve a place. From Austria, his birthplace, no recognition of
the work of either Mira Lobe or Lisbeth Zwerger; in his treatment
of a sense of place, no mention of Mitsumasa Anno; in discussing
issues of anxiety and identity, no word of Arnold Lobel or Bernard
Waber. The Hobans, Dr. Seuss, Remy Charlip, Michel Tournier,

Janosch, Klaus Ensikat: their absence here is puzzling if one imagines the book to be a testament to the coming of age of the picture book. But in spite of its title, Schwarcz's last work is neither a
compendium nor a historical treatise; it is a highly selective herme-
neutical adventure, a largely intensive *re*reading of picture books
he has keenly experienced. Thus, while it makes pioneering dis-
coveries of particular picture books unknown or overlooked in the
anglophone world (for example, the illustrations of Margherita Sac-
caro, Christina Oppermann-Dimow, and Nicholas Heidelbach), it
reflects somewhat idiosyncratic (but nonetheless laudable) choices
and pays little attention to previous critical responses to specific
picture books unless those responses help him unlock a secret of
a particular book. The volume contains a wealth of illustrations,
thanks to the untiring efforts of Chava Schwarcz, but, alas, all are
in black and white, and one could wish for better quality of reproduction. And few (I found only two) typos mar what is otherwise a
remarkably well-written and well-edited book.

As a gift to the reader, the editor and Mrs. Schwarcz have
provided as the final chapter a translation from the German of
Schwarcz's previously published essay on Sendak's "trilogy." Although this essay offers provocative responses to other critics of the
trilogy and again demonstrates Schwarcz's prowess as a reader of
images, it also reminds us of our great loss in not having a grand
finale from the master himself. By turning our attention once again
to the world of Sendak, the book indeed sends a message about the
many levels and dimensions of communication in the picture book,
and that alone may be enough to take us into the next century.

# Obvious Subversions

## Lois R. Kuznets

*Don't Tell the Grown-Ups: Subversive Children's Literature,* by Alison
Lurie. Boston: Little, Brown, 1990.

I always enjoy reading Alison Lurie's prose, fiction or nonfiction.
The pieces collected in this volume, most of which I had read in
the seventies in *Children's Literature,* the *New York Review of Books,*
and the *New York Times Book Review,* reveal her usual self-confident
erudition, wit, and determination to treat the writers and writing
of children's literature seriously while taking her role as critic and
scholar with the proverbial grain of salt. These qualities are not
always found in the rather ponderous American critics and scholars (among whom I include myself) of children's literature. The
British are better practitioners of belle-lettres, and Lurie reveals
her transatlantic affinities admirably.

Ties with the British literary tradition can be seen not only in
Lurie's style but also in her subject matter and theoretical approach.
With few exceptions, the authors and works Lurie considers are
British of the late nineteenth and twentieth centuries. Like many
British critics who write about children's literature (Humphrey Car-
penter, for instance), Lurie likes to link authors and works through
telling biographical detail while generally shunning Freudian analy-
sis of the texts.

As Lurie notes in her foreword, in her childhood she discovered
that there were:

> two sorts of books on [the library] shelves. . . . The first kind,
> the great majority, told me what grown-ups had decided I
> ought to know or believe about the world. . . . But there was
> another sort of children's literature. . . . These books . . . recom-
> mended—even celebrated—daydreaming, disobedience, an-
> swering back, running away from home, and concealing one's
> private thoughts and feelings from unsympathetic grown-ups.
> They overturned adult pretensions and made fun of adult

*Children's Literature* 21, ed. Francelia Butler, Christine Doyle Francis, Anne K.
Phillips, and Julie K. Pfeiffer (Yale University Press, © 1993 The Children's Litera
ture Foundation, Inc.).

institutions, including school and family. In a word, they were
subversive, just like many of the rhymes and jokes and games
I learned on the school playground. [ix–x]

And in her first chapter, Lurie attempts to tie together the wide-
ranging subjects in the volume under the rubric of "subversive
literature," dubbing as subversive all those works that seem to challenge the didactic mode of many children's books from the eighteenth through the twentieth centuries. As she loosely defines it,
the subversive may be discovered in the scatological sexuality of
skiprope rhymes as well as in texts that portray relatively powerless characters—like the children and the protagonists of fairy
tales—who subtly challenge or evade prevailing adult authority.
She also includes in her idea of subversion a somewhat stronger
anti-establishment stance, rarer in children's literature: such politically challenging tendencies as T. H. White's pacifism in the face of
World War II or E. Nesbit's late nineteenth-century Fabianism.

Only the foreword—in which Lurie expresses her own childhood
preference for such subversive literature—seems to have been written especially for this volume, which is made up of diverse works,
including book reviews. The subsequent chapters seem not to have
undergone much change from their original presentation, although
she has occasionally combined two pieces. The short studies that
follow Lurie's initial thematic linking chapter meander into many
areas and consider the following: folktales as liberating for female
and male protagonists; American novelists of the twentieth century ("Fitzgerald to Updike") who employ fairytale motifs; books
about elves that have become "Fashionable Folklore for Adults";
the literary and personal effects of Kate Greenaway's relationship
with John Ruskin; Lucy Clifford's "Tales of Terror"; the fairy
tales of Ford Madox Ford; Beatrix Potter's struggle, expressed
in her animal stories, to emerge from her suffocating family; the
"Modern Magic" of E. Nesbit; J. M. Barrie's Peter Panism; Frances
Hodgson Burnett's need for happy endings; A. A. Milne's retreat
to "Pooh Corner"; J. R. R. Tolkien and T. H. White as producing "Heroes for Our Time"; the godlike bear in Richard Adams's
*Shardik;* William Mayne's *Games of Dark;* and finally, the rhymes,
games, jokes, riddles, and superstitions that belong to the "Folklore
of Childhood."

*Don't Tell the Grown-Ups* also includes an extensive bibliography of primary texts, classic biographies of writers, and a scattering of well-known secondary works of a more general scholarly or critical nature, like structuralist analyses of fairy tales. Noticeably in short supply are articles from periodical literature. Just two are noted, both from *Children's Literature.*

In the original process of discussing these topics or reviewing new books about them, Lurie brought to the attention of a general reading public many interesting and intriguing figures and texts—often those remembered vaguely from childhood and frequently those that are unfamiliar to even well-read Americans. Some of the essays provocatively dispute popular opinions; one such is "The Boy Who Wouldn't Grow Up," which first appeared in the *New York Review of Books* in 1975 and, in its complex analysis of J. M. Barrie, as embodied in *both* Captain Hook and Peter Pan, is especially good in offering insight into the attractions and limitations of the original *Peter Pan* (and its many subsequent versions). Lurie writes: "In fact, Peter Pan and Captain Hook are not so much opposites as two sides of the same coin. After Peter has defeated Hook in their final duel there is a tableau; Barrie writes in the stage directions, 'The curtain rises to show Peter a very Napoleon on his ship. It must not rise again lest we see him on the poop in Hook's hat and cigars, and with a small iron claw'" (131).

Publication of Lurie's pieces in prestigious periodicals was a real service to the field of children's literature in that they made known to those outside the field what it is that attracts us to it. Widely marketed with its catchy title, the book itself should do the same thing, and it will certainly provide excellent introductory material for undergraduate students of children's literature.

I do not think, however, that the intended audience of this book is the children's literature professional who, in any given chapter, may find provocative statements but relatively little that is new in the way of scholarly material or engagement in dialogue with other scholars or critics who have considered the same texts. Since the formation of the Children's Literature Association some twenty years ago and the subsequent establishment of Children's Literature as a division of the Modern Language Association, several journals devoted to scholarly and critical approaches to such texts as Lurie considers have become well established. In addition to *Children's Literature,* there are the *Lion and the Unicorn,* the *Children's Literature Association*

*Quarterly, Children's Literature in Education,* and the British *Signal,*
to name the most prominent. Linnea Hendrickson's *Children's Literature: A Guide to Criticism* (G. K. Hall, 1987) admirably surveys the
literature of these and other journals (and one looks forward to an
updated bibliography soon).

Lurie might not have wished to involve herself with this periodical literature in writing her occasional pieces, but had she intended this book for a scholarly audience, she would certainly have
engaged in the usual search of periodical literature to see what
others were saying. As a professor of English at Cornell University,
she knows the ropes. However, the original *New York Times* and *New
York Review of Books* audiences for the majority of these pieces were
not deeply engaged in the study of children's literature; the pieces
are reprinted here as chapters with little attempt to change their
basic focus or to update Lurie's initial insights.

Criticism and scholarship have snowballed in recent years; thus,
since 1975, when Lurie first published her study of Barrie and *Peter
Pan,* a myriad of articles have appeared about the book. In considering that text and others from the same period, William Blackburn
(1977) and Charles Frey (1978) have both established a wider context for the subversion that concerned Lurie a few years earlier.
In another case of the growth of interest in the field, Lurie is not
concerned with answering feminists, like Karen Rowe (in *Women's
Studies,* 1979), who seem to challenge some of Lurie's initial propositions about the "feminism" of traditional fairy tales. In her bibliography and a footnote, Lurie mentions Ruth Bottigheimer's *Bad
Girls and Bold Boys* and Jack Zipes's *Trials and Tribulations of Little
Red Riding Hood* (although not Zipes's *Don't Bet on the Prince*), both
written later than her original piece and from a more radical feminist stance, but she does not examine, or even allude to, either of
these texts in her essay.

Lurie's presentation of Lucy Clifford's tales of terror (in an
article that appeared in 1975) provides important biographical
background and makes provocative comparisons between Clifford
and Henry James, but only flirts with the deeper psychic possibilities of Clifford's extraordinary tale, "The New Mother" (possibilities, as Lurie duly notes, suggested in private communication by
Sanjay Sircar of the Humanities Research Center of the Australian
National University). I wonder how Lurie might have reacted to
Anita Moss's feminist analysis of Clifford's "New Mother" in an

article in the *Lion and the Unicorn* (December 1988), possibly after Lurie's volume went to press, in which Moss finds a far more radical subversion of the patriarchal stance on motherhood than Lurie ever, here or elsewhere, contemplates.

Indeed, even Lurie's overarching idea of subversion, which is supposed to pull these studies together, will seem relatively old hat to many in the field, though it is still valid and attractive on one level. And for a children's literature professional intrigued by the notion of subversion, much more examination of the concept is needed, going considerably beyond Romantic notions of the child as the clear-eyed discerner of the emperor's nudity, or as rebel against the Olympians.

Lurie's text is largely a collection of loosely connected pieces that might have been more openly acknowledged as such. But all too often reviewers want the author of the text they are reviewing to have written a different book from the work that has appeared— that is, a book the reviewer would have wanted to write. Had Lurie gone as deep and wide as I might have liked, she perhaps would have sacrificed the virtues of *Don't Tell the Grown-Ups*—its easy, flowing style, the eclectic nature of its concerns, and the frequent provocative insights it can provide. For Lurie does offer an interesting introduction to the field of children's literature for a general audience, and in the process she challenges other children's literature professionals to write as clearly and appealingly as she does. That is no mean challenge.

# Link in a Missing Chain

## Elizabeth Lennox Keyser

*Breaking the Angelic Image: Woman Power in Victorian Children's Fantasy,* by Edith Lazaros Honig. Contributions in Women's Studies, 97. Westport: Greenwood Press, 1988.

In this brief book Edith Lazaros Honig argues that women and girls in Victorian children's fantasy constitute "the missing link" between the submissive heroines of Victorian adult fiction and modern liberated heroines. Missing from Honig's argument, however, is evidence for the uniform docility of Victorian heroines or for the uniform independence of their modern counterparts. Further, Honig excludes from her examination both Victorian adult fantasy and realistic fiction for children. The chain she purports to complete is thus left for the reader to construct.

Honig focuses on "book-length works of fantasy intended for the older child" (4), especially on the works of Lewis Carroll and George MacDonald. She devotes each of her four chapters to a different female character type: mothers, spinsters, girls, and magical women. Her book, then, falls into the now familiar—and in its simplest form outmoded—genre of the "images of women" study. The introduction anticipates the findings of each chapter: mothers are often absent or distant to avoid having to create stereotypical "true women" and to allow the child protagonist more freedom for adventure; spinsters are often portrayed positively and serve as admirable role models; girls are strong and self-assertive; and magical women combine power with maternal qualities. The text that follows provides numerous examples of these character types but fails to move beyond basic formulations. Honig's tone is often that of a children's book narrator, a friendly guide taking her young charge by the hand. For example, the first chapter concludes with a series of questions: "Are mothers absent or do they play a minor role to indicate that women are unimportant? . . . Are mothers absent or distant in order to do away with a boring character? . . . Are mothers absent or distant so that the book can focus on the child

*Children's Literature* 21, ed. Francelia Butler, Christine Doyle Francis, Anne K. Phillips, and Julie K. Pfeiffer (Yale University Press, © 1993 The Children's Literature Foundation, Inc.).

alone?" (37–38). The predictable answers are no, to some extent, and yes, "This is our strongest explanation" (38). Undergraduates will perhaps appreciate this pedagogical technique, but children's and Victorian literature specialists, to whom the book seems addressed, will probably weary of rhetorical questions that the author stands ready to answer. Even undergraduates and general readers may feel, as children do in response to some books designed for them, that they are being treated with condescension.

Of Honig's four chapters "Spinsters" is the weakest, "Girls" the strongest. Many of the "spinsters" described are simply older girls who, however independent initially, surrender their freedom upon marriage. For example, the heroine of Ford Madox Ford's *Queen That Flew* learns to fly and travels extensively but then marries a "ploughman," grounds herself in order to cure his blindness, and surrenders her throne, advising her country to choose a king in her stead. Honig's conclusion—that Ford "gives us a positive model of how a woman can grow and achieve success and independence in a single state" (52)—hardly seems warranted. Other examples offered of nonstereotypical spinsters are hard to take seriously. Does one really perceive the cook in *Alice's Adventures* as "independent and effectual . . . a successful working woman" (61)? In this and other instances, Honig seems to be doing what the spinsters themselves are doing—making the best of a hard lot. As Honig writes of one character, "Not having had the wits to catch a husband, she yet seems wise and important . . . an independent, happy, and successful middle-aged spinster" (53). Finally, the chapter on spinsters, like the chapter on mothers, leads one to conclude that while the older female characters in Victorian children's fantasy did not adhere to the true woman stereotype, neither were they very consequential. They may not have upheld the angelic image, but they certainly did not break it. In fact, one begins to suspect that the angelic image is a kind of straw woman. Honig refers to her presence in the "romantic girls' novels, the magazine fiction, and the instructive manuals for girls" (69), but she seldom cites this material, leaving her reader to take the assertion on faith.

In the chapter "Girls," Honig provides sound and useful, if not wholly original, readings of *Alice's Adventures, The Golden Key,* and *Peter and Wendy,* as well as Mrs. Molesworth's *Cuckoo Clock* and E. Nesbit's *Enchanted Castle.* But even in this chapter Honig occasionally belabors the obvious, as when she reminds the reader that "any time we read about a character who journeys, we expect that the journey will involve changes in the selfhood of that character" (76). Perhaps beginning students of literature need such reminders, but not literary scholars. However, scholars do expect to see references to their work beyond complaints that "Poor Alice" has been "subjected to every tortured form of analysis modern literary criticism can devise" (75). Honig's own analysis of Alice's uneven development, how she vacillates between self-assertion and self-abnegation, represented in part by changes in size, is sensible. But one must question whether Carroll "often makes us feel that Alice's horizons are boundless" (88). After all, she is at the bottom of a rabbit hole! And one also questions whether Alice shows "full promise" of remaining "heroic and independent" (108). Significantly, Honig neglects to deal with the story's frame. True, Alice's adventures end with her defiance of the pack of cards, but the book ends with Alice's more conventional sister projecting a future in which Alice, "a grown woman" with "the simple and loving heart of her childhood," conforms to the angelic image, rather than challenging it. Nor does Honig deal with *Through the Looking-Glass,* in which the crown representing Alice's maturity weighs heavily upon her head.

Honig's reading of *Peter and Wendy* as a "feminist statement condemning the position of nineteenth-century woman" (102) is more convincing than her claim that Barrie's "brief portrayal of the brave girl Wendy links *Peter and Wendy* to the golden chain of great fantasy that dares to break the submissive, domesticated images of girls" (107), for Honig's few explicit comparisons of children's fantasy and adult realism suggest that the image had already been broken. For example, Honig writes that Molesworth "is akin not only to Austen, but also to another author for adults, Charlotte Brontë. Molesworth's heroines seem to be modeled after the child Jane Eyre. They are plain, spirited, sensitive, and rebellious" (93). MacDonald's Lillith and Nesbit's Mabel are both described as "reminiscent of" Catherine Earnshaw in *Wuthering Heights* (48, 98). Honig "cannot deny that *Peter and Wendy* is more closely allied to the Victorian adult fiction, written primarily by women, that makes a statement about the plight of the female precisely by presenting bold, independent, somewhat androgynous girls who grow into women imprisoned by a patriarchal society" (107). Had she converted this concession to a claim and extended it to the other works she analyzes, Honig would perhaps have a more compelling thesis, a genuine link between realistic fiction for adults and fantasy for children.

# Dramatic Victorians

Jan Susina

*Private Theatricals: The Lives of the Victorians,* by Nina Auerbach. Cambridge: Harvard University Press, 1990.

*Alice on Stage: A History of the Earlier Theatrical Productions of* Alice in Wonderland, by Charles C. Lovett. Westport: Meckler, 1990.

In different ways, these two books focus on the importance of theatricality and performance in nineteenth-century British culture. Referring to theater as "that alluring pariah," Nina Auerbach suggests that, to the anti-theatrical Victorians, it became a subversive anticulture. But as Auerbach argues in this wide ranging yet slender volume, "the Victorian theater shared—and eventually, self-consciously aped—the paradoxes of Victorian culture as a whole." Instead of brushing theater aside as the least successful literary form of the period, as is often done, Auerbach embraces theatricality in its many manifestations as a central aspect of the age.

Auerbach interprets the meaning of theatricality in the broadest possible terms; she discusses melodrama, pantomime, the dramatizations of such popular novels as Ellen Wood's *East Lynne* and Mary Braddon's *Aurora Floyd,* and the theatrical passages in Charles Dickens's *Great Expectations* and Charlotte Brontë's *Jane Eyre,* as well as the presentation of character in Elizabeth Gaskell's *Life of Charlotte Brontë* and John Forster's *Life of Charles Dickens.* Charles Lovett, in contrast, limits his study to the role that theater played in the life and work of Lewis Carroll, culminating in the successful collaboration with Henry Savile Clarke for the stage adaptation in 1886 of the *Alice* books, which Carroll had called a "dream-play."

In sweeping assertions and generalizations, Auerbach convinces in her plea to restore theater to its central and pervasive place in the Victorian imagination; she notes that it has often been arbitrarily isolated from the period's literary culture. These essays explore the importance of performance in childhood, conversion, and death in the Victorian imagination. Stimulating in its approach and analysis

*Children's Literature* 21, ed. Francelia Butler, Christine Doyle Francis, Anne K. Phillips, and Julie K. Pfeiffer (Yale University Press, © 1993 The Children's Literature Foundation, Inc.).

of a broad range of Victorian culture, *Private Theatricals* is at times frustrating in its lack of details. Yet Auerbach presents a theoretical outline for reading Victorian theatricality that future studies can build upon.

To those interested in children's literature and the image of the child in popular culture, Auerbach's most useful chapter is "Little Actors," which carefully examines the dramatic presentation of childhood in children's and adult texts. The dying Willie Carlyle, from the immensely popular dramatization of Ellen Wood's *East Lynne,* is offered as the period's paradigm of the dying child who reappears in countless other Victorian novels. Pip and Jane Eyre are viewed as representative child figures of conventional theatrical pathos who become the visual realizations that structured Victorian pictorial theater. Theatricality even permeates Victorian biography, with Gaskell and Forster structuring lives of Brontë and Dickens around primary scenes rooted in scarred childhood that reveal the child as "soul and source of the adult's authentic perceptions" (39). Auerbach argues that by the end of the century children's fantasy— having been heavily influenced by pantomime, melodrama, and extravaganza—owes more to the theater than to nature.

Lovett's *Alice on Stage* is more single-minded in its examination of Victorian theatricality. A successful children's bookdealer specializing in Carroll, Lovett approaches the history of dramatic presentations of the *Alice* books with a bibliographer's intensity and attention to detail. Yet in his concern for detail he fails to place the dramatic presentations of Carroll's texts into the larger social and cultural context of Victorian theater.

The volume's appendixes, which include the 1886 script of Savile Clarke's "Alice in Wonderland" and a selection of Carroll's writing on the theater, make this a valuable book for Carroll scholars. Still, the great strength of Lovett's volume is that it is the first to quote extensively from the Charles Dodgson–Savile Clarke correspondence in the Berol Collection of New York University. Only a small representative sampling of this correspondence appeared in Morton Cohen's *Letters of Lewis Carroll,* and the projected volume of this eighty-letter collection has yet to be published.

But this book is more than the sum of its appendixes, no matter how useful they are. Lovett shows how theatricality and performance lie at the heart of Lewis Carroll–Charles Dodgson, who assiduously attempted to keep his public and private personae separate. Beginning with Carroll's boyhood marionette theater and the scripts he wrote and performed for his family, Lovett documents Carroll's lifelong relationship with the theater. In 1855, Carroll recorded in his diary his ambition to compose marionette plays for children. He never completed the project, and the only extant script is "La Guida di Bragia," his parody of *Bradshaw's Railway Guide.* While such other critics as Jean Gattegno have discussed the importance of theater in Carroll's life, Lovett shows how Carroll participated in the theater as an ardent, although amateur, performer in family theatricals, despite his father's strong opposition. Carroll's love of theater ran counter to his religious training and undoubtedly was partially responsible for ending his religious education at the level of deacon; beyond that he would have been forbidden from attending theater altogether.

One can only speculate on the direction Carroll's writing might have taken if Edmund Yates, the man who provided him with his famous pseudonym, had used Carroll's "Miss Jones," a comic medley based on many popular tunes of the day, in his "Invitations" of 1862, or if Tom Taylor had encouraged Carroll to complete the outline of the melodrama "Morning Clouds," which Carroll had submitted to the playwright in 1863.

In spite of attempts to join the theater world as a writer, Carroll was most involved as a member of the audience. Significantly, theater provided him a way of interacting with children, who often accompanied him to plays. Lovett points out that Carroll's ear for dialogue found its way into his children's books as well as his *Euclid and His Modern Rivals,* a geometry text that is structured as a four-act drama and contains more than 250 pages of dramatic dialogue.

A compulsive theatergoer, Carroll was keenly aware of the dramatic possibilities of *Alice in Wonderland* and its debut to the pantomime tradition. Less than two years after its publication, Carroll expressed interest in staging *Wonderland,* and in 1872 he requested that his publisher register *Wonderland* and *Through the Looking-Glass* as drama under the erroneous assumption that doing so would prevent anyone from producing them on stage without his approval. Carroll carried out a protracted correspondence with Arthur Sullivan in the vain hope that the Victorian composer of operettas might set his work to music. While there had been limited productions of the *Alice* books, including one at the Royal Polytechnic Institute in London involving magic lantern slides, it was not until Henry Savile Clarke contacted Carroll in 1886 with the possibility of making an operetta that the works were to receive a full-scale production.

Unlike his contentious relationships with his illustrators, Carroll's relationship with Savile Clarke was remarkably amenable. This did not prevent Carroll from making numerous suggestions to Savile Clarke, but he tended to defer to the dramatist's expertise.

Carroll outlined his ideal children's theater as one in which the performances would be such "that any lady could take her Daughters to without the slightest fear that anything would be introduced that she could possibly object to their seeing or hearing" (17). Carroll's objection to coarse language and sexual topics was so intense that in "The Stage and the Spirit of Reverence," published in *Theatre,* he criticized a production of Gilbert and Sullivan's "*H. M. S. Pinafore*" for having girls sing the chorus, "He said 'Damn me!' He said 'Damn me!'" Another of Carroll's uncompleted projects was an edition of Shakespeare's plays for girls, since he felt that Bowdler's was not sufficiently expurgated.

Lovett is meticulous in his study of Carroll's relationship to the theater, but he is less successful in placing the dramatic productions of the *Alice* books into a theatrical context, particularly children's pantomime that frequently based productions on fairy tales. Lovett's conclusion that the *Alice* books are not essentially dramatic seems to contradict much of the point of his book. His suggestion that the *Alice* books are a series of loosely related episodes, each charming but lacking in dramatic coherence, seems to overlook the structure of popular theatrical forms of pantomime, harlequinade, extravaganza, and spectacular that were such a large part of the Victorian stage. Lovett's assertion that it was the undramatic aspects of the *Alice* books that were their chief attraction to dramatists is curious.

The opposite point can be made, of course, and much of Lovett's research supports the contention that Savile Clarke and others were drawn to these famous children's texts because they were, as Alice suggests, full of "pictures or conversation." Tenniel's pictures transfer easily to the stage as costumed actors and the text becomes dialogue. Leonard Marcus has noted that Tenniel's illustrations consistently use the convention of illustration as theatrical tableau. Carroll provided many of the songs, and in some cases even the melodies, in the original texts. The *Alice* books could almost be considered closet dramas simply waiting to be adapted to the stage.

Nevertheless, despite these relatively minor shortcomings, both volumes will introduce readers, especially those interested in chil-

dren's literature, to the frequently forgotten world of Victorian theater. Auerbach reminds the reader, as Philippe Ariès has observed,
that for every period of history there is a corresponding privileged
age, and childhood became the privileged age for the nineteenth
century. In celebrating the Victorian period as one of the zeniths
of children's literature, literary critics have tended to value fiction
more highly than poetry, drama, and nonfiction. In doing so, they
have inadvertently overlooked the debt many classic nineteenth-
century children's texts owe to popular theater. But Auerbach and
Lovett remind us that the theater and theatricality were instrumental in shaping a dramatic facet of the Victorian image of the child.

# Dissertations of Note

## Compiled by Rachel Fordyce

Becker-Slaton, Nelle Frances. "The Role of Oral Tradition in Influencing Reading and Reading Comprehension." Ph.D. diss. Claremont Graduate School, 1988. 248 pp. DAI 49:3290A.

Becker-Slaton explores how oral tradition shapes parent-child interaction. "Results showed that low-income parents of gifted children consistently had informal narrative communication with their children, while parents of at-risk students did not."

Belgrade, Kathleen Ann. "Teachers' Use and Perceived Value of Fairy Tales in California and British Elementary Schools." Ed.D. diss. University of San Francisco, 1988. 267 pp. DAI 50:1284A.

Belgrade discusses cultural differences as well as "psycho-social, historical, and educational factors" as they influence teachers' use of fairy tales. She found no significant difference between the two cultural groups, although British teachers had greater knowledge of fairy tales. Each teacher used fairy tales primarily as a "reading skill builder" rather than as literature.

Bleecker, Timothy Jonathon. "The Christian Romanticism of George MacDonald: A Study of His Thought and Fiction." Ph.D. diss. Tufts University, 1990. 280 pp. DAI 51:3750A.

Although this study focuses on MacDonald's theological romances, Bleecker discusses MacDonald's fantasies as "subversive myths" that "form a mythological core underlying the rest of his work." He gives particular attention to *The Princess and the Goblin, The Princess and Curdie, The Wise Woman,* and *At the Back of the North Wind.*

Born, Daniel Keith. "The Late Victorian and Edwardian Novel and the Birth of Liberal Guilt." Ph.D. diss. City University of New York, 1990. 309 pp. DAI 51:3750A.

Born shows how Kipling becomes "a lightning rod for liberal antipathy" when compared with such writers as Dickens, Eliot, Gissing, Conrad, Forster, and Wells.

Branch, Piyada Vajaranant. "The Development of Theatre for Children in Thailand." Ph.D. diss. University of Kansas, 1990. 201 pp. DAI 51:3562A.

Branch traces the history of theater for children in Thailand from the inception of Western children's theater in the early twentieth century through the infusion of television in the later 1950s and the founding of the first theater designed exclusively for children in 1975—although drama for children is still found mainly in universities in Thailand. Branch notes recent attempts "to move away from Western playscripts and to turn to traditional sources" for plays.

Bremser, Martha. "The Poetry of Walter de la Mare." Ph.D. diss. Oxford University, 1986. 333 pp. DAI 50:3598A.

Bremser demonstrates "the profound concerns of a poet whose imagination runs deeper, and darker, than a deceptively charming verse style may suggest," and for this reason her work should have an impact on those who view de la Mare as a poet primarily for children. In the second part of the dissertation she examines his critical writings and alliances and finds him "both isolated in his own unique pursuit and yet of a haunting relevance to our modern age."

*Children's Literature* 21, ed. Francelia Butler, Christine Doyle Francis, Anne K. Phillips, and Julie K. Pfeiffer (Yale University Press, © 1993 The Children's Literature Foundation, Inc.).

Cerra, Kathie Krieger. "Intellectual Freedom and the Use of Books in the Elementary School: Perceptions of Teachers." Ph.D. diss. University of Minnesota, 1990. 135 pp. DAI 51:1905A.

Cerra gives attention to elementary teachers' perceptions of intellectual freedom and censorship. She shows that most support the First Amendment but also alter texts when reading them aloud if they think language or subject matter offensive or inappropriate. Almost all teachers said they had had a course in children's literature, but only 37 percent reported having a class devoted to intellectual freedom.

Chartrand, Claudine Denise. "Fairyland Revisited: A Gynocentric Reading of Selected English, French, and German Folk and Fairy Tales." Ph.D. diss. Pennsylvania State University, 1990. 357 pp. DAI 51:3063A.

Chartrand considers the works of Joseph Jacob, Mme d'Aulnoy, Mme de Murat, Mme Leprince de Beaumont, and the Brothers Grimm in light of how they treat women in fairy tales of the eighteenth and nineteenth centuries. She questions the feminist condemnation of the roles of women in fairy tales and finds that older women and stepmothers are generally portrayed as evil. But she locates "inspiring and dynamic heroines who are not as helpless as commercialized heroines" such as Cinderella, Snow White, and Sleeping Beauty. She also finds that French and English heroines have greater control over their fate than the German heroine, whom authors never permitted "to transgress the social order in which she lives."

Conlon, Alice C. "A Survey of the Kinds of Books and Book-Related Experiences Teachers Provide to Students in Church-Related Preschools." Ed.D. diss. University of Houston, 1990. 258 pp. DAI 51:1902A.

Conlon finds that teachers in church-related schools tend to use a wide variety of traditional books, such as alphabet and counting books, picture books, easy readers, and folk and fairy tales. They also tend to rely on their own judgment for choices in literature, and they rarely use "filmstrips, VCR or movie tapes, or book-related television programs at school."

Eastman, Jacqueline Fisher. "A Study of the 'Madeline' Books of Ludwig Bemelmans." Ph.D. diss. University of Alabama, 1989. 200 pp. DAI 51:846A.

Eastman shows the relation between the five Madeline books and Bemelmans' other works, as well as the many "spin-offs" of the books. She concludes that "nature's dependably recurrent cycles establish a sense of time much like that which Bemelmans conveys" and that "the depiction of time as space, generic to any picturebook, and the use of the cartooned, conceptual image, further establish within the books a sense of the eternal present, and with it, a dominant mood of hope."

Entwistle, Dorothy M. "Children's Reward Books in Nonconformist Sunday Schools, 1870–1914: Occurrence, Nature, and Purpose." Ph.D. diss. University of Lancaster, 1990. 449 pp. DAI 51:3522A.

In her history of the Sunday school reward, Entwistle predictably concludes that the choice of rewards reflected contemporary social influences on children and that they were an "attempt by the Sunday schools to influence the attitudes and moral standards of their pupils under social conditions perceived to be threatening to them."

Fasick, Laura. "Women's Moral Role in Selected Victorian Religious Novels." Ph.D. diss. Indiana University, 1990. 422 pp. DAI 51:3751A.

Fasick believes that such authors as Charlotte Yonge, Dinah Craik, and Elizabeth Sewell "show independent female selfhood within the seemingly repressive gender roles that harden into genuine repressiveness in the works of such writers as Charles Kingsley and George MacDonald." She finds that the male writers "exalt a woman's eroticized submission," "stigmatize or ignore" the spinster, and make women "disciples, rather than moral agents."

Fillingham, Lydia Alix. "Counting People, Accounting Books, and Recounting Crime: The Collection and Display of Information in Victorian Texts." Ph.D. diss. Stanford University, 1989. 284 pp. DAI 50:3961A.

Fillingham, in the final chapters of her study, analyses Conan Doyle's Sherlock Holmes, who "supplements the bureaucracy, corrects the readings of the bureaucratic police, and protects the private sphere from invasion by mediating between public and private spheres."

Gilbertson, Irvyn Gayle. "Alphabet Books in the United States from 1875–1975." Ph.D. diss. University of Minnesota, 1990. 147 pp. DAI 51:3685–86A.

Gilbertson discusses both continuity and change in alphabet books over the past hundred years, noting among other things a marked decrease in rhymed texts and didacticism, little attempt to teach children phonetics, and a tendency toward more realistic images of animals and inanimate objects.

Harris, Ruby M. "A Survey and Content Analysis of the Black Experience as Depicted in Contemporary Fiction for Children." Ph.D. diss. Boston College, 1989. 231 pp. DAI 50:1937A.

According to Harris, between 1978 and 1988 the number of black characters in children's books has declined, although books that did include black characters were either good or excellent: 60 percent of the books were culturally conscious, and "the portrayal of Black characters was generally positive." She also finds more stories with girls as heroines, more stories set in ghettos and raising serious social issues, particularly about families in strife, and "more negative racial images," uses of dialect, sexual situations, and derogatory terms.

Jarvis, Shawn Cecilia. "Literary Legerdemain and the *Märchen* Tradition of Nineteenth-Century German Women Writers." Ph.D. diss. University of Minnesota, 1990. 214 pp. DAI 51:2031A.

Jarvis shows that Jacob and Wilhelm Grimm are famous for their retelling of fairy tales but that German women writers of the same caliber are virtually ignored. She analyzes the works of Benedikte Naubert, Amalie von Helwig, Amalia Schoppe, and Gisela von Arnim and speculates why critical literature has neglected these writers.

Johnson, Dianne Anita. "For the Children of the Sun: What We Say to Afro-American Youth through Story and Image." Ph.D. diss. Yale University, 1988. 255 pp. DAI 50:1345A.

"This study is a history of Afro-American children's literature—that literature written largely by Black authors, especially, though not exclusively for Black youth." Johnson explores "Black psychology" and shows the relations among black literature for children, black literature for adults, and mainstream literature in an attempt to point out the significance of black children's literature to Afro-American culture.

Kantar, Maythee Jensen. "Children's Responses to Televised Adaptations of Literature." Ph.D. diss. University of Minnesota, 1990. 194 pp. DAI 51:2666A.

Kantar evaluates the reactions of children in grades three through six to televised versions of *Anne of Green Gables, The Lion, the Witch, and the Wardrobe* and *Taking Care of Terrific.* Data suggest that these adaptations encouraged students to read books "in genres they would not normally read" and that this age group was capable of making critical judgments about the quality of the adaptation.

Lake, Wendy M. "Aspects of Ireland in Children's Fiction: An Historical Outline and Analysis of Children's Fiction Set in Ireland (1850–1986)." D.Phil. diss. University of Ulster, 1989. 319 pp. DAI 51:3754A.

Lake analyzes the treatment of Ireland in terms of "landscape, character-ization and the expression of ideas and beliefs," and she gives specific attention to books set in Northern Ireland and "the effect of 'The Troubles' on fiction for young people." She finds that the works consistently reflect the ideas, beliefs, and literary trends of the periods in which they were written and that only re-cently have stories depicted images of Ireland that do not rely on nostalgia or stereotype.

Lastinger, Valérie Cretaux. "Littérature feminine et écriture enfantine: Quelques implications de la critique féministe." (French Text) Ph.D. diss. University of Geor-gia, 1989. 245 pp. DAI 50:2919A.

Lastinger attempts "to redefine children's literature as a genre" and to ex-amine the stereotypes associated with the genre and its writers while observing the many parallels between women's writing and writing for children. She gives special attention to Sophie de Ségur and the value of using feminist criticism to evaluate children's literature because "feminist critics too often overlook the artistic values of so-called 'sexist' images and merely practice a new form of moralism."

Lundqvist, Aina Theres. "Linguistic Adjustment—A Syntactic Analysis of Material from Children's Books." Fil.Dr. diss. Göteborgs Universitet (Sweden), 1988. 288 pp. DAI 50:416C.

Lundqvist uses a quantitative method to describe the syntactic structure of books for young readers, for readers age twelve through fourteen, and for those fifteen and older to determine how popular Swedish authors adapt lan-guage and style to these age groups. She notes that adaptation is more marked in works for young children and that recent texts employ more "direct speech" than earlier ones.

Maguire, Gregory. "Themes in English Language: Fantastic Literature for Children, 1938–1988." Ph.D. diss. Tufts University, 1990. 374 pp. DAI 51:2013A.

According to Maguire, fantasy literature experienced a resurgence in this century "less [as] a result of stable Western governments and societies than [as] a reaction to the energetic anxiety which preceded World War II. . . . Significantly more mythopoeic than whimsical, fantasies of the second golden age answer the desires of children for adventure, security at home, and identity at large." He also writes that current worldwide political and social uncertainties and tensions are responsible for the contemporary themes in fantasy for children: "desires for heroism, adventure, and otherness; for domestic safety, friends and family, and a sense of belonging in the cycle of nature; for awareness of one's place in metaphysical or religious reality [and] the reaches of incomprehensible time."

Michalson, Karen Ann. "Victorian Fantasy Literature and the Politics of Canon-Making." Ph.D. diss. University of Massachusetts, 1990. 300 pp. DAI 51:2755A.

In a study devoted to Ruskin, MacDonald, Kingsley, Haggard, and Kipling, Michalson "examines the non-literary and non-aesthetic reasons underlying the bias in favor of realism in the formation of the traditional literary canon of nineteenth-century British fiction" to the obvious exclusion of fantasy writers. She attributes this fact to the influence of the Anglican church and "Non-Conformist or Dissenting evangelical sects in the educational institutions of nineteenth-century Britain in the first half of the century" since both church and empire required realism to promote "conservative ideology."

Miller, Carolyn Pishny. "Biographies about Abraham Lincoln for Children (1865–1969): Portrayals of His Parents." Ph.D. diss. University of Illinois at Urbana-Champaign, 1990. 547 pp. DAI 51:4046A.

Miller examines the literary style and historical perspectives of seventeen popular children's works about Lincoln written between 1865 and 1969 to determine what effect they have on "public image." She finds the texts characterized by adulation rather than accuracy and by intimacy of author with subject. According to Miller, they are more often used as sources for emulation, inspiration, and instruction than for factual information.

Moreno, Barbara Dubé. "Empowering Young Children to Think and Act Critically through Folktales: An Experience in Critical Pedagogy." Ed.D. diss. University of San Francisco, 1990. 295 pp. DAI 51:4046A.

Moreno investigates how children think critically and concludes that they "are both capable of and responsive to the dialogic process." By analyzing their reactions to fairy and folk tales she substantiates "the belief that young children can think critically about their own lives and that they can become active protagonists, applying the lessons from folk/fairy tales to everyday situations."

Mothersole, Brenda. "Female Philanthropy and Women Novelists of 1840–1870." Ph.D. diss. Brunel University (United Kingdom), 1989. 622 pp. DAI 51:1807A.

Mothersole looks at female philanthropists in the social protest novels of Elizabeth Gaskell, Charlotte Yonge, Charlotte Brontë, and George Eliot and contrasts them with those in novels by Charles Dickens, Benjamin Disraeli, and Charles Kingsley, noting that male novelists tend to stereotype these female characters, creating "ministering angels" rather than "revolutionary women."

Myatt, Rosalind. "The Child and the Story: The Search for Identity." Ph.D. diss. University of California, Los Angeles, 1990. 733 pp. DAI 51:466A.

Myatt's dual purpose is to explain "the personal meanings children constructed from their favorite stories throughout childhood and to describe the individual child's response as an active reader." She concludes that differences in response between girls and boys become more marked as each matures, that separation is a major issue for young children, that girls are more concerned with success, heroines as rescuers, "separation from parent figures, peer and sibling rivalry, and interpersonal issues," whereas boys are more concerned with achievement, power, associations with a father figure, and "heroism, including magic posers and animal companions."

Nelson, Claudia B. "From Androgyne to Androgen? Ideals of Gender and the Gender of Ideals in Novels for Boys, 1857–1917." Ph.D. diss. Indiana University, 1989. 289 pp. DAI 51:867A.

Nelson believes that real Victorian women were stronger and more admired than modern stereotypes admit and that Victorian novels for boys "typically seek to inculcate many of the same values and virtues as novels for girls." But as Darwinian "sexology" redefined "manliness," exalted machoism "to discourage the effeminate," and created "homoemotionalism," literature for boys changed, emphasizing an "evangelical creed" and rejecting feminine behavior.

Peacock, Jeffrey W. "The Unreconstructed Man: The Fiction of Philip K. Dick." Ph.D. diss. University of Liverpool, 1988. 324 pp. DAI 51:854A.

In the opening chapter, Peacock links the American science fiction writer Philip K. Dick's novel *Ubik* with the "literary tradition established by Lewis Carroll."

Pena, Sally J. "Images of Heroism: A Cross-Generational Comparison of Two Children's Television Programs." Ph.D. diss. University of Idaho, 1989. 120 pp. DAI 50:3149A.

Pena investigates the psychological and social behaviors of heroes and villains, "the dimensions and magnitude of the heroes' struggles," and the audiovisual difference between the 1950s children's series starring Roy Rogers and the 1980s series featuring Brave Starr. She notes significant differences and concludes that aggression in the earlier show is more characteristic of the acts of young children and that "the Brave Starr program was more often related to the type of aggression characteristic of older children and adults."

Seifert, Lewis Carl. "The Time That (N)ever Was: Women's Fairy Tales in Seventeenth-Century France." Ph.D. diss. University of Michigan, 1989. 198 pp. DAI 51:178A.

Seifert writes that "close readings of the tales of the *conteuses* (Aulnoy, Auneuil, Bernard, Durand, La Force, Lhéritier, and Murat) reveal deep-seated ambivalences about gender roles in their treatment of the narrative structures that uphold a patriarchal 'time that ever was.'" He analyzes the tension between "resistance and conservativism" in the works of these authors and concludes that the tone of tales by women writers in seventeenth-century France is characterized by ambivalence toward power, authority, and the difficulty they had revising images of gender.

Smart, Karl Lyman. "A Man for All Ages: The Changing Image of Benjamin Franklin in Nineteenth-Century American Popular Literature." Ph.D. diss. University of Florida, 1989. 261 pp. DAI 51:855A.

Drawing heavily on the extensive collection of children's books in the Baldwin Library of the University of Florida, Smart discusses Franklin's carefully created autobiographical image and the selective images created by his biographers, particularly those who wrote for children. He suggests that this biographical selectivity became "the means of inculcating the rising generation with values and attitudes deemed most important" and that the person "D. H. Lawrence [and other critics of Franklin] reacted against and the image which still remains popular are largely a creation of the nineteenth century."

Smith, Donald Milton. "English Religious and Moral Verse for Children, 1686–1770." Ph.D. diss. New York University, 1989. 461 pp. DAI 50:2913A.

Smith analyzes the religious children's verse of John Bunyan, Isaac Watts, John Wright, Thomas Foxton, Philip Doddridge, Nathaniel Cotton, John Marchant, Charles Wesley, and Christopher Smart and concludes that the limited critical reception to this body of work has produced faulty generalizations and observations that are either "misleading or untrue." He suggests that more recognition and closer study will reveal more about religious and secular attitudes toward children during this period.

Stone, James Clement. "The Evolution of Civil War Novels for Children." Ph.D. diss. Ohio State University, 1990. 190 pp. DAI 51:2299A.

Stone looks at seventy books for children about the Civil War written between 1863 and 1987 to show evolving attitudes toward characterization and history. Notable are a progressive shift toward realism and a finer realization of setting, though no decrease in stereotyping of black characters and black culture.

Swan, Ann M. "An Analysis of Selected Pseudoscientific Phenomena in Children's Literature." Ph.D. diss. University of Akron, 1991. 224 pp. DAI 51:3656A.

Swan surveys the use of ghosts and poltergeists in children's fiction to determine whether they depict "fantasy elements or serious representations of reality." She looks at forty books written for children between the ages of nine and fourteen, concluding that psychic phenomena are usually employed in a fantasy setting, that children can recognize the treatment of ghosts as fantasy, and that the works do not encourage children to believe in ghosts.

Troyano, Thomas Vincent. "Conceptions of Childhood in American Juvenile Fiction between 1865 and 1915." Ed.D. diss. Rutgers University, 1989. 236 pp. DAI 50:3594A.

Troyano is concerned primarily with changing social attitudes toward growth and maturity of children between 1865 and 1915 and the effect of the Darwinian notion that "the changes in society were moving it slowly toward a higher and better plane." He concludes that this attitude is upheld in the books he examined and that adult expectations of childhood behavior have changed considerably between 1915 and the present.

Vallone, Lynne Marie. "Happiness and Virtue: The History and Ideology of the Novel for Girls." Ph.D. diss. State University of New York at Buffalo, 1990. 271 pp. DAI 51:2759A.

"This study traces the history and ideology of fiction for girls from the birth of the novel in eighteenth-century England to the serial girl heroine of nineteenth-century America." Vallone focuses on both canonical and non-canonical works, such as *Pamela, Mansfield Park, Little Women,* Sarah Fielding's *Governess; or, Little Female Academy,* Mary Sherwood's *History of the Fairchild Family,* and Hannah More's *Coelebs in Search of a Wife,* and how they helped create a feminine literary history. She argues that "as these texts establish a feminine/maternal discourse between author and reader, teacher and student, metaphoric mother and daughter, they are not only didactic enactments of [the ideology of obedience, innocence, and purity] but also empowering appropriations of it."

Walker, Michael Joseph. "Some Versions of Violence: Writing Civilization in Victorian Literature." Ph.D. diss. University of Oregon, 1990. 343 pp. DAI 51:3759A.

Though he does not focus strictly on children's literature, Walker deals with the work of Charles Dickens, Emily Brontë, and Lewis Carroll, among others, and focuses on instructional, institutional, and occasional violence.

White, Elinor Maureen. "Translated Children's Books: A Study of Successful Translations and a Comprehensive Listing of Books Available in the United States, 1989–1990." Ph.D. diss. Texas Woman's University, 1990. 207 pp. DAI 51:3264A.

White identifies 131 "successful" translations drawn from a list of 550 translated works in print in 1989–1990, predominantly from French and German, representing fantasy, folklore, and realistic fiction, with books about fairy tales, animal tales, folklore specific to one country, and World War II dominating the list. She notes an increase in interest in translating works for children but continued caution by publishers in what they publish, drawing primarily from the classics, popular authors, and works in public domain.

Woods, Robert Michael. "Imagination, Religion, and Morality in the Shorter Imaginative Fiction of George MacDonald." Ph.D. diss. Florida State University, 1990. 166 pp. DAI 51:3070A.

Woods focuses on MacDonald's childhood, his strict Scottish Calvinistic background, and how he reveals his religious values and develops a theory of imagination in his fiction. He also analyzes the considerable effect MacDonald had on the writing of Lewis Carroll, C. S. Lewis, J. R. R. Tolkien, G. K. Chesterton, and T. S. Eliot.

Wright, Marjorie Evelyn. "The Cosmic Kingdom of Myth: A Study in the Myth-Philosophy of Charles Williams, C. S. Lewis, and J. R. R. Tolkien." Ph.D. diss. University of Illinois at Urbana-Champaign, 1960. 196 pp. DAI 21:3464A.

According to Wright, the reaction of Williams, Lewis, and Tolkien to the "utter, unfocused disillusionment" and denial that were a response to the 1920s and early 1930s was an attempt to define basic truths using "psychological realism, neo-orthodox Christianity, and myth-philosophy." Although each insists on "hierarchy as a principle or social order," each uses a different set of archetypes, cosmologies, and types of characters to explore the theme of evil and to create "living myth."

210                                                    RACHEL FORDYCE

Yandell, Carol Evangeline Trew. "Spiritual Values Identified by Children's Librarians and Elementary School Children in Newbery Medal and Honor Books." Ed.D. diss. University of Arkansas, 1990. 100 pp. DAI 51:3632A.

Yandell studies eight librarians to identify and create a list of spiritual values in Newbery Medal and Honor books. She concludes that children and librarians identify similar values in books: those most often cited by librarians concern "family unity, kindness/caring, acceptance of [self] and others, reference to God and biblical truths," and those cited by children are "kindness/caring, love, bravery, growth, and determination."


*Also of Note*

Anderson, Mary Janelle. "Toward a Christian Approach to Literature: The Critical Theories of C. S. Lewis as a Model for Christian Literary Criticism." Ph.D. diss. University of South Florida, 1988. 117 pp. DAI 50:131A.

Ashdown, Jane Elizabeth. "Nursery Storytime as Social Drama." Ph.D. diss. University of Pennsylvania, 1990. 174 pp. DAI 51:1499–1500A.

Bassett, William Clyde. "The Formulation of a Basis for Counseling from a Christian Theory of Personality as Represented by C. S. Lewis and Watchman Nee." Ed. D. diss. University of Arkansas, 1976. 221 pp. DAI 37:2625A.

Bat-Ami, Miriam Beatrice. "'Allye, allye oxen free!': Play, Game, and the Search for Completion in Shakespeare's Tragedies." Ph.D. diss. University of Pittsburgh, 1989. 344 pp. DAI 51:509A.

Beattie, Mary Josephine, R.S.M. "The Humane Medievalist: A Study of C. S. Lewis' Criticism of Medieval Literature." Ph.D. diss. University of Pittsburgh, 1967. 210 pp. DAI 28:3136A.

Bown, Roger. "Children and Popular Television." Ph.D. diss. University of Wales College of Cardiff, 1988. 262 pp. DAI 51:1583A.

Bradbard, Paula. "Improving Problem-Solving through Writing Based on Children's Literature." Ed.D. diss. University of Lowell, 1990. 110 pp. DAI 51:1935A.

Britsch, Barbara Martin. "Walking around Inside Stories: How Children Make Meaning from Narrative Discourse." Ph.D. diss. University of Toledo, 1990. 183 pp. DAI 51:1935A.

Brown, Victoria Leigh. "Integrating Drama and Sign Language: A Multisensory Approach to Language Acquisition and Its Effects on Disadvantaged Preschool Children." Ph.D. diss. New York University, 1990. 212 pp. DAI 51:1108A.

Carnell, Corbin Scott. "The Dialectic of Desire: C. S. Lewis' Interpretation of 'Sehnsucht.'" Ph.D. diss. University of Florida, 1960. 219 pp. DAI 20:4653A.

Corbin, Denee Joyce. "Using Literature to Teach Historical Concepts in Fifth-Grade Social Studies." Ph.D. diss. University of Iowa, 1990. 177 pp. DAI 51:4082A.

Dupont, Sherry Ann. "The Effectiveness of Creative Drama as an Instructional Strategy to Enhance the Reading Comprehension Skills of Fifth-Grade Remedial Readers." Ph.D. diss. Pennsylvania State University, 1989. 228 pp. DAI 51:3026A.

Frost, Anne Duval. "Mnemonic Strategies and Parent Recall of Principles of Early Childhood Development." Ph.D. diss. New York University, 1988. 139 pp. DAI 49:3103B.

Futch, Ken. "The Syntax of C. S. Lewis's Style: A Statistical Look at Some Syntactic Features." Ph.D. diss. University of Southern California, 1969. 472 pp. DAI 30:2002A.

Ginnetti, Philip E. "An Analysis of Intermediate Grade Gifted Students and Their Book Experiences as Preschool Children." Ph.D. diss. University of Akron, 1989. 162 pp. DAI 50:1614A.

Green, Jeanette Evelyn. "Literary Revisions of Traditional Folktales: Bowen, Carter,

Hong Kingston, Morrison, Oates, Sexton, Welty, and Capote." Ph.D. diss. University of Texas at Austin, 1989. 295 pp. DAI 51:511A.

Hade, Daniel Dean. "Stances and Events as Foundations of Children's Responses to Literature: An Ethnographic Study of a Second and Third Grade Literature-Based Reading Classroom." Ph.D. diss. Ohio State University, 1989. 338 pp. DAI 50:3874A.

Harms, Paul W. F. "C. S. Lewis as Translator." Ph.D. diss. Northwestern University, 1973. 306 pp. DAI 34:3592A.

Harper, Cheryl M. "Role of Causal Relationships in the Story Comprehension of Children." Ph.D. diss. University of Illinois at Urbana-Champaign, 1990. 122 pp. DAI 51:3017A.

Haut, Judith Ellen. "Children's Belief: A Folkloristic Study of Conceptualization, Experimentation and Communication." Ph.D. diss. University of California, Los Angeles, 1989. 282 pp. DAI 50:1400A.

Hoey, Mary Amy. "An Applied Linguistic Analysis of the Prose Style of C. S. Lewis." Ph.D. diss. University of Connecticut, 1966. 160 pp. DAI 27:3441A.

Imdieke, Sandra Jean. "A Study of Adult Responses to Remembered Children's Books." Ph.D. diss. University of Minnesota, 1989. 167 pp. DAI 50:2412A.

Jagusch, Sybille Anna. "First among Equals: Caroline M. Hewins and Anne C. Moore, Foundations of Library Work with Children." Ph.D. diss. University of Maryland, College Park, 1990. 407 pp. DAI 51:1428A.

Jordan, Peggy Ann. "The Effects of Fairy Tales on the Self-Esteem and Reading Achievement of Children." Ph.D. diss. Oklahoma State University, 1990. 110 pp. DAI 51:3372A.

Kilany, Mohamed Ahmed Elsadek. "A Critical Study of Rousseau's Philosophy of Education." Ph.D. diss. University of Exeter, 1982. 321 pp. DAI 51:1544A.

Lee, Hsiao-Hung. "Narrative Transgression in Selected Novels of Charlotte Brontë and Charles Dickens." Ph.D. diss. Drew University, 1990. 321 pp. DAI 51:2026A.

Matthews, Gail Vigeant-Sangster. "Looking at Life Funny: Reflexivity in American Ventriloquism." Ph.D. diss. Indiana University, 1989. 366 pp. DAI 50:2195A.

Moorman, Charles W. "Myth and Modern Literature: A Study of the Arthurian Myth in Charles Williams, C. S. Lewis, and T. S. Eliot." Ph.D. diss. Tulane University, 1953. 345 pp. DAI W1953.

Neuleib, Janice Witherspoon. "The Concept of Evil in the Fiction of C. S. Lewis." Ph.D. diss. University of Illinois at Urbana-Champaign, 1974. 196 pp. DAI 35:4539A.

Rappoport, Karen Simon. "The Effects of Creative Dramatics on Reading Comprehension and Language/Thought of Second-Grade Children." Ph.D. diss. University of Kansas, 1989. 145 pp. DAI 51:1103A.

Riddell, Cecilia. "Traditional Singing Games of Elementary School Children in Los Angeles." Ph.D. diss. University of California, Los Angeles, 1990. 527 pp. DAI 51:1543A.

Ruppel, Richard Jeffrey. "Kipling, Conrad, and the Popular Exotic Short Fiction of the 1890s." Ph.D. diss. University of North Carolina at Chapel Hill, 1987. 215 pp. DAI 49:2234A.

Saint Paul, Thérèse. "The Magical Mantle, the Drinking Horn and the Chastity Test: A Study of a 'Tale' in Arthurian Celtic Literature." Ph.D. diss. University of Edinburgh, 1987. 474 pp. DAI 50:440A.

Schaafsma, Karen. "Beyond the Between: The Paradoxical Journey of Fantasy Literature." Ph.D. diss. University of California, Davis, 1990. 254 pp. DAI 51:3739A.

Underwood, Roy Madison, Jr. "'Dark and Bloody Mystery': Mark Twain's Relationship with Detective Fiction." Ph.D. diss. University of Alabama, 1990. 253 pp. DAI 51:1615A.

Wimmer, Astrid. "Victim—Saint—Rebel: Voices of Children in German and American Literature of the Nineteenth Century." Ph.D. diss. State University of New York at Stony Brook, 1989. 207 pp. DAI 50:2482A.

Workman, Nancy Victoria. "A Victorian 'Arabian Nights' Adventure: A Study in Intertextuality." Ph.D. diss. Loyola University of Chicago, 1989. 293 pp. DAI 50:958A.

Young, Michael Andrew. "The Structure and Ideology of Romance Fiction." Ph.D. diss. University of Minnesota, 1988. 147 pp. DAI 50:151A. [On Kingsley, Kipling, and Haggard]

Ziegler, Mervin Lee. "Imagination as a Rhetorical Factor in the Works of C. S. Lewis." Ph.D. diss. University of Florida, 1973. 158 pp. DAI 35:1277–78A.

# Contributors and Editors

RUTH B. BOTTIGHEIMER is currently completing a study of European and American children's Bibles entitled *The Bible for Children from the Age of Gutenberg to the Present*. Adjunct associate professor in comparative studies at SUNY Stony Brook, she specializes in teaching the minimal narrative, which includes the international fairy tale.

MARTHA BREMSER wrote her doctoral thesis on Walter de la Mare and childhood at Oxford University.

FRANCELIA BUTLER, founding editor of *Children's Literature*, has published many books on children's literature, including *Skipping Around the World: The Ritual Nature of Folk Rhymes*.

JOHN CECH, book review editor of *Children's Literature*, teaches in the English Department at the University of Florida. He is the author of a book for children, *My Grandfather's Journey* (1991), and recently completed a book on the works of Maurice Sendak.

YU CHAI FANG received her B. A. from the Central Chinese Teachers' University in 1964 and works as a chief editor in Hubei Children's Publishing House. Her story *A Hard Night* was published in her collection *Growing Up Together*.

RACHEL FORDYCE, former executive secretary of the Children's Literature Association, has written four books, most recently *Lewis Carroll: A Reference Guide*. She is dean of humanities and social sciences at Montclair State College.

CHRISTINE DOYLE FRANCIS, at the University of Connecticut, has recently completed curriculum guides on Gerald McDermott's and E. L. Konigsburg's books. Her research interests include the application of feminist and myth criticism to children's literature and the work of Louisa May Alcott.

LEN HATFIELD writes about speculative fiction, postmodernism, and literary theory from the English Department at Virginia Tech, where he is associate professor. He will soon finish work on *Compelling Speculations*, in which he explores patterns of textual authority and social criticism in contemporary speculative fiction.

SYLVIA PATTERSON ISKANDER, professor of English at the University of Southwestern Louisiana, recently edited the *1991 Proceedings of the ChLA Conference* and received a grant to teach a summer seminar on censorship in young adult literature.

ELIZABETH LENNOX KEYSER, associate professor of English at Hollins College, is the author of *Whispers in the Dark: The Fiction of Louisa May Alcott*, forthcoming from the University of Tennessee Press, and the editor for volume 22 of *Children's Literature*.

VALERIE KRIPS teaches English at the University of Pittsburgh. She has published on children's literature and literary theory and is writing a book about contemporary children's literature.

LOIS R. KUZNETS is a professor in the Department of English and Comparative Literature at San Diego State University. She has written a Twayne volume on Kenneth Grahame and published numerous articles on children's literature. At present she is writing a book on toys as characters in literature for Yale University Press.

VALÉRIE C. LASTINGER teaches French Literature at West Virginia University. She publishes regularly on Sophie de Ségur, as well as on Denis Diderot.

WANG LIN holds degrees from Southwestern Teachers' University (B.A., 1982) and

213

Sichuan Institute of Foreign Languages (M.A., English literature, 1987). He currently teaches courses on English-Chinese translation and selected readings in English literature and American culture at Sichuan Institute.

ANNE SCOTT MACLEOD is professor and acting dean in the College of Library and Information Services, University of Maryland at College Park. She is the author of *A Moral Tale: Children's Fiction and American Culture, 1820–1860* (Archon, 1990) and of numerous articles on the connections between children's literature and culture.

MICHAEL W. MENARD teaches at the University of Connecticut. His research interests include the influence of Renaissance poetry on such Modernist poets as Eliot and Pound.

WILLIAM MOEBIUS has taught in the Department of Comparative Literature at the University of Massachusetts since 1967. His "Room with a View: Bedroom Scenes in Picture Books" appeared in volume 19 of *Children's Literature*.

PETER F. NEUMEYER, professor of English and comparative literature at San Diego State University, served as a scholar-in-residence at International Youth Libe (Munich) in October–November 1992. A visiting professor at the University of Rhode Island in the spring of 1993, he is the resident director of the California State University systems in Germany, 1993–94. His *Annotated Charlotte's Web* (HarperCollins) is scheduled to appear at Christmas 1993.

JULIE K. PFEIFFER teaches at the University of Connecticut and is writing a dissertation on Milton's influence on Charlotte Brontë. Her work focuses on nineteenth-century novels and children's books.

ANNE K. PHILLIPS, at the University of Connecticut, has contributed to a festschrift in honor of Charleton Laird and was coauthor of the instructor's manual for *The Bedford Introduction to Literature*. Her research interests include the influence of Transcendentalism on late nineteenth- and early twentieth-century American popular fiction.

ALAN RICHARDSON, associate professor of English at Boston College, teaches mainly in Romantic literature and nineteenth-century children's literature. He is the author of *A Mental Theatre: Poetic Drama and Consciousness in the Romantic Age* and is completing a book on education, the social construction of childhood, and literature in the Romantic era.

GARY D. SCHMIDT, professor of English at Calvin College, is the author of *Robert McCloskey* (1990) and *Hugh Lofting* (1992). He has also co-edited *The Voice of the Narrator in Children's Literature* (1989) and *Sitting at the Feet of the Past: The Retelling of the North American Folktale* (1992).

SHERYL A. SPITZ has taught in the Departments of Slavic Languages and Literatures and of the Humanities at Stanford University, and has published on psychosocial themes in Slavic folk songs.

JOHN STEPHENS teaches mainly children's literature and early English literature at Macquarie University, in Sydney, Australia. He is author of numerous articles about children's, medieval and contemporary literatures, and of three books, including *Language and Ideology in Children's Fiction*.

JAN SUSINA teaches children's literature at Illinois State University. He is working on a study of nineteenth-century fairy tales for children.

SAMANTHA WILCOX, a graduate of the University of Connecticut, served as an intern for *Children's Literature* in the spring of 1991. She is currently working as a lobbyist for the food industry in Washington, D.C.

IAN WOJCIK-ANDREWS, assistant professor at Eastern Michigan University, teaches children's literature and literary theory. He chaired a panel at the 1992 MLA meeting in New York on "Theories of Class" and guest edited a special issue of

*The Lion and the Unicorn,* also on the relationship between children's literature and class.

FEENIE ZINER, professor of English at the University of Connecticut, has published many books, including *Squanto* and *Full House.* She teaches graduate seminars in children's literature and, with her undergraduate publishing course students, produced *The Small Press in Connecticut* in the fall ot 1991. An account of her trip to Lithuania appeared in *Northeast* magazine in August 1992.

# Index to Volumes 16–20

## Compiled by Samantha Wilcox

# Award Applications

The article award committee of the Children's Literature Association publishes a bibliography of the year's work in children's literature in the *Children's Literature Association Quarterly* and selects the year's best critical articles. For pertinent articles that have appeared in a collection of essays or journal other than one devoted to children's literature, please send a photocopy or offprint with the correct citation and your address written on the first page to Dr. Gillian Adams, 5906 Fairlane Dr., Austin, TX 78731. Papers will be acknowledged and returned if return postage is enclosed. Annual deadline is May 1.

The Phoenix Award is given for a book first published twenty years earlier that did not win a major award but has passed the test of time and is deemed to be of high literary quality. Send nominations to Alethea Helbig, 3640 Eli Rd., Ann Arbor, MI 48104.

The Children's Literature Association offers three annual research grants. The Margaret P. Esmonde Memorial Scholarship offers $500 for criticism and original works in the areas of fantasy or science fiction for children or adolescents by beginning scholars, including graduate students, instructors, and assistant professors. Research Fellowships are awards ranging from $250 to $1000 (number and amount of awards based on number and needs of winning applicants) for criticism or original scholarship leading to a significant publication. Recipients must have postdoctoral or equivalent professional standing. Awards may be used for transportation, living expenses, materials, and supplies, but not for obtaining advanced degrees, for creative writing, textbook writing, or pedagogical purposes. The Weston Woods Media Scholarship awards $1000 and free use of the Weston Woods studios to encourage investigation of the elements and techniques that contribute to successful adaptation of children's literature to film or recording, or to developing materials for television and video. For full application guidelines on all three grants, write the Children's Literature Association, c/o Marianne Gessner, 22 Harvest Lane, Battle Creek, MI 49015. Annual deadline for these awards is February 1.

**Order Form**    Yale University Press, 92A Yale Station, New Haven, CT 06520

Customers in the United States and Canada may photocopy this form and use it for ordering all volumes of **Children's Literature** available from Yale University Press. Individuals are asked to pay in advance. We honor both MasterCard and VISA. Checks should be made payable to Yale University Press.

The prices given are 1993 list prices for the United States and are subject to change. A shipping charge of $2.75 is to be added to each order, and Connecticut residents must pay a sales tax of 6 percent.

| Qty. | Volume | Price | Total amount | Qty. | Volume | Price | Total amount |
|------|--------|-------|--------------|------|--------|-------|--------------|
| ___ | 8 (cloth) | $45.00 | _____ | ___ | 15 (cloth) | $45.00 | _____ |
| ___ | 8 (paper) | $16.00 | _____ | ___ | 15 (paper) | $16.00 | _____ |
| ___ | 9 (cloth) | $45.00 | _____ | ___ | 16 (paper) | $16.00 | _____ |
| ___ | 9 (paper) | $16.00 | _____ | ___ | 17 (cloth) | $45.00 | _____ |
| ___ | 10 (cloth) | $45.00 | _____ | ___ | 17 (paper) | $16.00 | _____ |
| ___ | 10 (paper) | $16.00 | _____ | ___ | 18 (cloth) | $45.00 | _____ |
| ___ | 11 (cloth) | $45.00 | _____ | ___ | 18 (paper) | $16.00 | _____ |
| ___ | 11 (paper) | $16.00 | _____ | ___ | 19 (cloth) | $45.00 | _____ |
| ___ | 12 (cloth) | $45.00 | _____ | ___ | 19 (paper) | $16.00 | _____ |
| ___ | 12 (paper) | $16.00 | _____ | ___ | 20 (cloth) | $45.00 | _____ |
| ___ | 13 (cloth) | $45.00 | _____ | ___ | 20 (paper) | $16.00 | _____ |
| ___ | 13 (paper) | $16.00 | _____ | ___ | 21 (cloth) | $45.00 | _____ |
| ___ | 14 (cloth) | $45.00 | _____ | ___ | 21 (paper) | $16.00 | _____ |
| ___ | 14 (paper) | $16.00 | _____ | | | | |

Payment of $_____ is enclosed (including sales tax if applicable).

MasterCard no. _____

4-digit bank no. _____ Expiration date _____

VISA no. _____ Expiration date _____

Signature _____

SHIP TO: _____

See the next page for ordering issues from Yale University Press, London.

Volumes 1–7 of **Children's Literature** can be obtained directly from John C. Wandell, The Children's Literature Foundation, Box 370, Windham Center, Connecticut 06280.

**Order Form**     Yale University Press, 23 Pond Street, Hampstead, London NW3, 2 PN, England

Customers in the United Kingdom, Europe, and the British Commonwealth may photocopy this form and use it for ordering all volumes of **Children's Literature** available from Yale University Press. Individuals are asked to pay in advance. We honour Access, Visa, and American Express accounts. Cheques should be made payable to Yale University Press.

The prices given are 1993 list prices for the United Kingdom and are subject to change. A post and packing charge of £1.75 is to be added to each order.

| Qty. | Volume | Price | Total amount | Qty. | Volume | Price | Total amount |
|---|---|---|---|---|---|---|---|
| — | 8 (cloth) | £40.00 | ———— | — | 15 (cloth) | £40.00 | ———— |
| — | 8 (paper) | £13.95 | ———— | — | 15 (paper) | £13.95 | ———— |
| — | 9 (cloth) | £40.00 | ———— | — | 16 (paper) | £13.95 | ———— |
| — | 9 (paper) | £13.95 | ———— | — | 17 (cloth) | £40.00 | ———— |
| — | 10 (cloth) | £40.00 | ———— | — | 17 (paper) | £13.95 | ———— |
| — | 11 (cloth) | £40.00 | ———— | — | 18 (cloth) | £40.00 | ———— |
| — | 11 (paper) | £13.95 | ———— | — | 18 (paper) | £13.95 | ———— |
| — | 12 (cloth) | £40.00 | ———— | — | 19 (cloth) | £40.00 | ———— |
| — | 12 (paper) | £13.95 | ———— | — | 19 (paper) | £13.95 | ———— |
| — | 13 (cloth) | £40.00 | ———— | — | 20 (cloth) | £40.00 | ———— |
| — | 13 (paper) | £13.95 | ———— | — | 20 (paper) | £13.95 | ———— |
| — | 14 (cloth) | £40.00 | ———— | — | 21 (cloth) | £40.00 | ———— |
| — | 14 (paper) | £13.95 | ———— | — | 21 (paper) | £13.95 | ———— |

Payment of £_____ is enclosed.

Please debit my Access/Visa/American Express account no. _____

Expiry date_____

Signature_____ Name_____

Address_____

Volumes 1–7 of **Children's Literature** can be obtained directly from John C. Wandell, The Children's Literature Foundation, Box 370, Windham Center, Connecticut 06280.